Lecture Notes in Computer Science **9402**

Commenced Publication in 1973
Founding and Former Series Editors:
Gerhard Goos, Juris Hartmanis, and Jan van Leeuwen

More information about this series at http://www.springer.com/series/7412

Tomaž Vrtovec · Jianhua Yao
Ben Glocker · Tobias Klinder
Alejandro Frangi · Guoyan Zheng
Shuo Li (Eds.)

Computational Methods and Clinical Applications for Spine Imaging

Third International Workshop and Challenge, CSI 2015
Held in Conjunction with MICCAI 2015
Munich, Germany, October 5, 2015
Revised Selected Papers

 Springer

Editors
Tomaž Vrtovec
University of Ljubljana
Ljubljana
Slovenia

Jianhua Yao
National Institutes of Health
Bethesda, MD
USA

Ben Glocker
Imperial College London
London
UK

Tobias Klinder
Philips GmbH Innovative Technologies
Hamburg
Germany

Alejandro Frangi
University of Sheffield
Sheffield
UK

Guoyan Zheng
University of Bern
Bern
Switzerland

Shuo Li
University of Western Ontario
London, ON
Canada

ISSN 0302-9743   ISSN 1611-3349 (electronic)
Lecture Notes in Computer Science
ISBN 978-3-319-41826-1   ISBN 978-3-319-41827-8   (eBook)
DOI 10.1007/978-3-319-41827-8

Library of Congress Control Number: 2016943824

LNCS Sublibrary: SL6 – Image Processing, Computer Vision, Pattern Recognition, and Graphics

Printed on acid-free paper

This Springer imprint is published by Springer Nature
The registered company is Springer International Publishing AG Switzerland

Preface

The spine represents both a vital central axis for the musculoskeletal system and a flexible protective shell surrounding the most important neural pathway in the body, the spinal cord. Spine-related diseases and conditions, such as degenerative disc disease, spinal stenosis, scoliosis, osteoporosis, herniated discs, fracture/ligamentous injury, infection, tumor, and spondyloarthropathy, are common and cause a huge burden of morbidity as well as cost to society. Treatments vary with the disease, and the clinical scenario can be nonspecific. As a result, imaging is often required to help make the diagnosis, and studies include plain radiographs, dual-energy X-ray absorptiometry (DXA), bone scans, computed tomography (CT), magnetic resonance (MR), ultrasound (US), and nuclear medicine. Computational methods play a steadily increasing role in improving speed, confidence, and accuracy in reaching a final diagnosis. Although there has been great progress in the development of computational methods for spine imaging over the recent years, there are still a number of challenges in both methodology and clinical applications.

The goal of the workshop series on "Computational Methods and Clinical Applications for Spine Imaging (CSI)" is to bring together scientists, clinicians, and industrial vendors in the field of spine imaging, for presenting and reviewing the state-of-art techniques, sharing the novel and emerging analysis and visualization approaches, and discussing the clinical challenges and open problems in this rapidly growing field. Contributions are welcome on all major aspects related to spine imaging, including clinical applications of spine imaging, computer-aided diagnosis of spine conditions, computer-aided detection and emerging computational imaging techniques for spine-related diseases, fast three-dimensional (3D) reconstruction of the spine, feature extraction, multiscale analysis, pattern recognition and image enhancement of spine imaging, image-guided spine intervention and treatment, multimodal image registration and fusion for spine imaging, novel visualization and segmentation techniques, statistical and geometrical modeling of spinal structures, and localization of the spine and vertebrae.

The Third Workshop and Challenge on Computational Methods and Clinical Applications for Spine Imaging, MICCAI–CSI2015[1], was held on October 5, 2015, in Munich, Germany, as a satellite event of the 18th International Conference on Medical Image Computing and Computer-Assisted Intervention — MICCAI 2015. After the success of the first workshop, and the second workshop and challenge, this was the third consecutive MICCAI event on this particular topic, inviting general "workshop" papers as well as contributions for the "Automatic Intervertebral Disc Localization and Segmentation from 3D T2 MRI Data" computational challenge. Each submission underwent a double-blind review by three members of the Scientific Review Committee consisting of researchers who actively contributed to the field of spine imaging

---

[1] http://csi2015.weebly.com

in the past. Overall, 15 papers were accepted that are grouped in these final proceedings into "workshop" contributions (9) and "challenge" contributions (6), while one paper was rejected. In order to give a deeper insight into the field of spine imaging and stimulate further ideas, three invited talks were held during the workshop: "Osteoporosis Imaging at the Spine: Clinical Needs and Technical Challenges" by Dr. Thomas Baum from Technische Universität München, Germany, "Spinal Imaging in Surgical Planning and Navigation" by Dr. Martin Haimerl from Brainlab AG, Germany, and "Vertebral Fracture Identification Using Dual Energy X-Ray Absorptiometry" by Dr. Margaret Paggiosi from University of Sheffield, UK.

Finally, we would like to thank everyone who contributed to this joint workshop and challenge: the authors for their contributions, the members of the Program and Scientific Review Committee for their review work, promotion of the workshop, and general support, the invited speakers for sharing their expertise and knowledge, and the MICCAI society for the general support. The event was supported by the SpineWeb[2] initiative, a collaborative platform for research on spine imaging and image analysis, and sincere gratitude goes to Brainlab AG, Germany,[3] for the financial support.

May 2016

Tomaž Vrtovec
Jianhua Yao
Ben Glocker
Tobias Klinder
Alejandro Frangi
Guoyan Zheng
Shuo Li

[2] http://spineweb.digitalimaginggroup.ca
[3] http://www.brainlab.com

Organization

Workshop Organizing Committee

Jianhua Yao	National Institutes of Health, USA
Ben Glocker	Imperial College London, UK
Tobias Klinder	Philips Research, Germany
Tomaž Vrtovec	University of Ljubljana, Slovenia
Alejandro Frangi	University of Sheffield, UK
Guoyan Zheng	University of Bern, Switzerland
Shuo Li	GE Healthcare and University of Western Ontario, Canada

Challenge Organizing Committee

Guoyan Zheng	University of Bern, Switzerland
Dimitris Damopoulos	University of Bern, Switzerland
Shuo Li	GE Healthcare and University of Western Ontario, Canada

Program Committee

Michel A. Audette	Old Dominion University, USA
Ulas Bagci	University of Central Florida, USA
Jonathan Boisvert	National Research Council, Canada
Ananda Chowdhury	Jadavpur University, India
Vipin Chaudhary	SUNY Buffalo, USA
Daniel Forsberg	Sectra and Linköping University, Sweden
Bulat Ibragimov	University of Ljubljana, Slovenia
Jianfei Liu	Duke University, USA
Xiaofeng Liu	Google, USA
Yixun Liu	Broncus Medical, USA
Cristian Lorenz	Philips Research, Germany
Alberto Santamaria-Pang	GE Global Research, USA
Alexander Seitel	University of British Columbia, Canada
Greg Slabaugh	City University London, UK
Sovira Tan	National Institutes of Health, USA
Tamas Ungi	Queen's University, Canada

Scientific Review Committee

Michel A. Audette	Old Dominion University, USA
Ulas Bagci	University of Central Florida, USA

Program Chairs

Contents

Workshop (Computational Methods and Clinical Applications for Spine Imaging)

Automated Pedicle Screw Size and Trajectory Planning by Maximization of Fastening Strength.   3
   Dejan Knez, Boštjan Likar, Franjo Pernuš, and Tomaž Vrtovec

Automatic Modic Changes Classification in Spinal MRI   14
   Amir Jamaludin, Timor Kadir, and Andrew Zisserman

Patient Registration via Topologically Encoded Depth Projection Images in Spine Surgery.   27
   Songbai Ji, Xiaoyao Fan, Jonathan D. Olson, Linton T. Evans,
   Keith D. Paulsen, David W. Roberts, Sohail K. Mirza, and S. Scott Lollis

Automatic Localisation of Vertebrae in DXA Images Using Random Forest Regression Voting.   38
   Paul A. Bromiley, Judith E. Adams, and Timothy F. Cootes

Robust CT to US 3D-3D Registration by Using Principal Component Analysis and Kalman Filtering   52
   Rebeca Echeverría, Camilo Cortes, Alvaro Bertelsen, Ivan Macia,
   Óscar E. Ruiz, and Julián Flórez

Cortical Bone Thickness Estimation in CT Images: A Model-Based Approach Without Profile Fitting   64
   Oleg Museyko, Bastian Gerner, and Klaus Engelke

Multi-atlas Segmentation with Joint Label Fusion of Osteoporotic Vertebral Compression Fractures on CT.   74
   Yinong Wang, Jianhua Yao, Holger R. Roth, Joseph E. Burns,
   and Ronald M. Summers

Statistical Shape Model Construction of Lumbar Vertebrae and Intervertebral Discs in Segmentation for Discectomy Surgery Simulation   85
   Rabia Haq, Joshua Cates, David A. Besachio, Roderick C. Borgie,
   and Michel A. Audette

Automatic Intervertebral Discs Localization and Segmentation: A Vertebral Approach   97
   Amir Jamaludin, Meelis Lootus, Timor Kadir, and Andrew Zisserman

Challenge (Automatic Intervertebral Disc Localization and Segmentation from 3D T2 MRI Data)

Segmentation of Intervertebral Discs in 3D MRI Data Using Multi-atlas
Based Registration 107
  Chunliang Wang and Daniel Forsberg

Deformable Model-Based Segmentation of Intervertebral Discs from MR
Spine Images by Using the SSC Descriptor 117
  *Robert Korez, Bulat Ibragimov, Boštjan Likar, Franjo Pernuš,
  and Tomaž Vrtovec*

3D Intervertebral Disc Segmentation from MRI Using
Supervoxel-Based CRFs.. 125
  Hugo Hutt, Richard Everson, and Judith Meakin

Automatic Intervertebral Disc Localization and Segmentation in 3D MR
Images Based on Regression Forests and Active Contours 130
  Martin Urschler, Kerstin Hammernik, Thomas Ebner, and Darko Štern

Localization and Segmentation of 3D Intervertebral Discs from MR Images
via a Learning Based Method: A Validation Framework 141
  Chengwen Chu, Weimin Yu, Shuo Li, and Guoyan Zheng

Automated Intervertebral Disc Segmentation Using Probabilistic Shape
Estimation and Active Shape Models............................. 150
  *Aleš Neubert, Jurgen Fripp, Shekhar S. Chandra, Craig Engstrom,
  and Stuart Crozier*

Author Index 159

Workshop (Computational Methods and Clinical Applications for Spine Imaging)

Automated Pedicle Screw Size and Trajectory Planning by Maximization of Fastening Strength

Dejan Knez$^{(\boxtimes)}$, Boštjan Likar, Franjo Pernuš, and Tomaž Vrtovec

Faculty of Electrical Engineering, University of Ljubljana, Ljubljana, Slovenia
{dejan.knez,bostjan.likar,franjo.pernus,tomaz.vrtovec}@fe.uni-lj.si

Abstract. Spinal fusion combined with vertebral fixation through pedicle screw placement is the preferred surgical treatment for several spinal deformities. The accuracy of pedicle screw placement is directly related to the surgical outcome, however, manual planning of screw size and trajectory is time-consuming, while automated approaches do not take into account the screw fastening strength. We propose a novel automated method for optimal planning of pedicle screw size and trajectory that takes into account both geometric (i.e. morphometry) and anatomical (i.e. bone mineral density) properties of vertebrae to maximize the screw fastening strength. The size and trajectory of 61 pedicle screws, determined by the automated method in computed tomography images of nine patients, were in high agreement with preoperative manual plans defined by a spine surgeon (mean difference of 0.6 mm in diameter, 4.0 mm in length, 1.7 mm in pedicle crossing, and (6.1°) in screw insertion angles), and an increased fastening strength was observed for 50 cases (82 %).

1 Introduction

Spinal fusion combined with vertebral fixation is the preferred surgical treatment for several spinal deformities, such as scoliosis, kyphosis or vertebral fractures [1]. Vertebral fixation is commonly achieved by placement of pedicle screws (Fig. 1(a)), which consists of screws being inserted through vertebral pedicles representing fasteners onto which stabilizing rods are attached, resulting in a limited compression of affected vertebrae. The accuracy of pedicle screw placement is directly related to the surgical outcome and is therefore of significant importance, as inaccurate placement can lead to serious nerve or viscus injuries [1]. Therefore, preoperative surgery planning has become essential for safe pedicle screw placement [2,3]. During planning the surgeon studies in detail the spinal anatomy of the treated patient by relying on preoperative images, nowadays usually in the form of three-dimensional (3D) computed tomography (CT) scans.

However, manual planning of pedicle screw size and insertion trajectory is time-consuming, besides it is practically impossible to take into account all important parameters, such as the screw fastening strength. Especially for subjects with low bone mass, such as patients with osteoporosis [4], the screw fastening strength should be as high as possible, and was in fact proved to be directly related to the underlying vertebral bone mineral density (BMD) [2,5].

© Springer International Publishing Switzerland 2016
T. Vrtovec et al. (Eds.): CSI 2015, LNCS 9402, pp. 3–13, 2016.
DOI: 10.1007/978-3-319-41827-8_1

Manual (visual) determination of BMD is also a demanding and time-consuming task, as it requires accurate analysis of a larger number of 3D image cross-sections in different planes of view. Moreover, such analysis has to be repeated for each change in size and/or insertion trajectory of each pedicle screw. As a result, guiding and navigation techniques for computer-assisted orthopedic surgery were developed [1,6,7]. A few studies also focused on automated pedicle screw planning based on preoperative image analysis [3,8], although without taking into account the screw fastening strength. By applying computer-assisted quantitative analysis of 3D images, the screw fastening strength can be estimated through BMD for each observed screw size and insertion trajectory, and a combination that maximizes the screw fastening strength can be determined through an optimization procedure. If the subjective interpretation of the surgeon is reduced, the reliability of preoperative planning can be increased.

In this paper, we describe a novel automated method for optimal preoperative planning of pedicle screw size and insertion trajectory. The proposed method aims to maximize the screw fastening strength by taking into account both geometric (i.e. morphometry) and anatomical (i.e. BMD) properties of vertebrae, extracted from non-segmented 3D CT spine images that were acquired preoperatively for the purpose of manual planning of surgical treatments involving pedicle screw placement and spinal fusion.

2   Methodology

For an adequate pedicle screw planning, the knowledge of the 3D anatomy of vertebral bodies and pedicles is indispensable, as the size (i.e. diameter and length) and insertion trajectory (i.e. pedicle crossing point and inclination angles) of each pedicle screw have to be defined so that it is positioned strictly within the vertebral body and the corresponding pedicle (i.e. does not leave the bone structures), does not perforate the anterior wall of the vertebral body, and does not intersect with the screw through the opposite pedicle (Fig. 1(a)). Pedicle screw planning can be therefore achieved by appropriate modeling of vertebral structures and pedicle screws in 3D through quantitative analysis of 3D images.

2.1   Modeling of Vertebral Structures in 3D

Modeling of vertebral structures is limited to vertebral bodies and pedicles, and achieved using the superquadric approach [9]. The parametric form of a superquadric (i.e. a generalized quadric surface in 3D) directly indicates whether an arbitrary point is located inside, lying on, or located outside the superquadric surface, which is advantageous for positioning pedicle screws strictly within vertebral bodies and pedicles. Moreover, the parameters of a superquadric are directly related to the morphometry of the underlying anatomical structure, which proved to be related to clinically meaningful anatomical deformations [10].

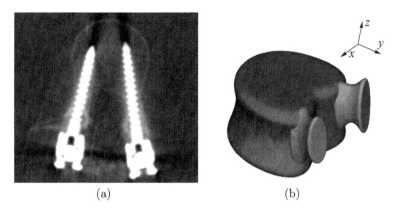

(a)   (b)

Fig. 1. (a) An example of successful pedicle screw placement, shown in a postoperative computed tomography axial image cross-section. (b) An illustrative example of three-dimensional parametric modeling of the vertebral body and pedicles.

Parametric Modeling of Vertebral Bodies. The superquadric for the initial 3D vertebral body shape $V_i(\boldsymbol{x})$ is represented by an elliptical cylinder [9]:

$$V_i(\boldsymbol{x}) = \left(\frac{x^2 + y^2}{r(\theta)^2}\right)^{10} + \left(\frac{z}{h}\right)^{20}; \qquad r(\theta) = \frac{ab}{\sqrt{(a\sin\theta)^2 + (b\cos\theta)^2}}, \qquad (1)$$

where $\boldsymbol{x} = (x, y, z)$ is a point in 3D space, $r(\theta)$ represents the trace of an ellipse with semi-major axis a and semi-minor axis b, $\theta = \arctan(y/x)$ is the radial angle, and h is the cylinder half-height. A more detailed 3D vertebral body shape $V_d(\boldsymbol{x}) = T_V(V_i(\boldsymbol{x}))$ is obtained by introducing 22 additional parameters, which define transformation T_V and represent specific 3D anatomical deformations of the vertebral body [9], i.e. (1) the shape of the elliptical cylinder at the location of the left pedicle, right pedicle, vertebral foramen and anterior part of the vertebral body, (2) the concavity of the vertebral body wall at its anterior part and at the vertebral foramen, (3) concavities and sagittal inclinations of vertebral endplates, and (4) the increasing size and torsion of the vertebral body. The final 3D model of the vertebral body $V(\boldsymbol{x}) = R_V(V_d(\boldsymbol{x}))$ is obtained after its rigid alignment R_V to the 3D image (Fig. 1(b)). The similarity criterion used to determine T_V and R_V is composed of two components that take into account the properties of CT images [9]. The intensity component $C_{\mathcal{I}}$ is based on 3D image intensities and maximizes the amount of the bone structures inside the 3D model and the amount of the soft tissues outside the 3D model:

$$C_{\mathcal{I}} = \sqrt{1 - \sum_s \sqrt{p_{in}(s)\, p_{out}(s)}}, \qquad (2)$$

where p_{in} and p_{out} are probability distributions of image intensities s within the 3D model and a volume surrounding the 3D model, respectively. The shape component $C_{\mathcal{G}}$ is based on 3D image intensity gradients and maximizes their agreement against 3D model surface normals:

$$C_{\mathcal{G}} = \sum_{\boldsymbol{x} \in \mathcal{V}_{in}} \left(\left\langle \boldsymbol{g}(\boldsymbol{x}), \boldsymbol{n}_{in}(\boldsymbol{x}) \right\rangle \frac{e^{\frac{-d(\boldsymbol{x})^2}{2}}}{\sqrt{2\pi}} \right) \sum_{\boldsymbol{x} \in \mathcal{V}_{out}} \left(\left\langle \boldsymbol{g}(\boldsymbol{x}), \boldsymbol{n}_{out}(\boldsymbol{x}) \right\rangle \frac{e^{\frac{-d(\boldsymbol{x})^2}{2}}}{\sqrt{2\pi}} \right), \quad (3)$$

where $d(\boldsymbol{x})$ is the Euclidean distance between point $\boldsymbol{x}$ and the 3D model surface, and $\langle \boldsymbol{g}(\boldsymbol{x}), \cdot \rangle$ is the dot product of normalized 3D image intensity gradients $\boldsymbol{g}(\boldsymbol{x})$ and inward-pointing $\boldsymbol{n}_{in}(\boldsymbol{x})$ or outward-pointing $\boldsymbol{n}_{out}(\boldsymbol{x})$ 3D model unit surface normals within, respectively, volume $\mathcal{V}_{in}$ spanned inwards or volume $\mathcal{V}_{out}$ spanned outwards of the 3D model surface. Optimal transformations T_V and R_V, respectively representing anatomical deformations and rigid alignment, are obtained by maximizing the joint intensity and shape similarity criterion:

$$\{T_V, R_V\} = \arg\max_{\{T, R\}} \left((C_{\mathcal{I}} C_{\mathcal{G}}) \big|_{\{T,R\} \to V(\boldsymbol{x})} \right). \quad (4)$$

Parametric Modeling of Pedicles. The superquadric for the initial 3D pedicle shape $P_i(\boldsymbol{x})$ is represented by an elliptical cylinder (1), and is automatically initialized from parameters of the final 3D model of the vertebral body $V(\boldsymbol{x})$ that define the initial location and orientation of the left (or right) pedicle. The elliptical cylinder is then deformed into a detailed 3D pedicle shape by introducing additional parameters that represent specific 3D anatomical deformations of the pedicle. Although the same modeling approach is used as for the vertebral body, the parameters corresponding to 3D anatomical deformations of the pedicle are defined independently by observing its anatomy in 3D, therefore representing a novel approach to parametric modeling of pedicles. As a result, a more detailed 3D pedicle shape $P_d(\boldsymbol{x}) = T_P(P_i(\boldsymbol{x}))$ is obtained by 22 parameters of transformation T_P representing (1)the offset of the inner pedicle shape, (2)the concavity of the pedicle at its anterior, posterior, right and left parts, (3)the pedicle axis concavity in the coronal and sagittal plane, and (4) the tear drop deformation of the pedicle in the axial plane. The final 3D model of the pedicle $P(\boldsymbol{x}) = R_P(P_d(\boldsymbol{x}))$ is obtained after its rigid alignment R_P to the 3D image (Fig. 1(b)). Optimal transformations T_P and R_P are obtained by maximizing the joint intensity and shape similarity criterion $(C_{\mathcal{I}} C_{\mathcal{G}}) \big|_{\{T,R\} \to P(\boldsymbol{x})}$ (2)–(4).

2.2   Modeling of Pedicle Screws in 3D

The superquadric for the 3D pedicle screw model $S_i(\boldsymbol{x})$ is represented by a circular cylinder, which defines its size, i.e. the diameter and length. The final 3D pedicle screw model $S(\boldsymbol{x}) = R_S(S_i(\boldsymbol{x}))$ is obtained after its rigid alignment R_S to the 3D image, which defines its insertion trajectory, i.e. the crossing point through the mid-coronal plane of the pedicle and inclination angles.

Pedicle Screw Size and Insertion Trajectory. The 3D pedicle screw model is defined by parameters $s = \{D, L, p, \omega_x, \omega_z\}$ representing the pedicle screw size by its diameter D (i.e. $D = 2a = 2b$ in (1)) and length L (i.e. $L = 2h$ in (1), measured as the length of the screw within the vertebra), and the pedicle screw insertion trajectory by its pedicle crossing point $p = (x_p, y_p, z_p)$, and sagittal ω_x and axial ω_z inclination angle in the reference coordinate system (Fig. 2).

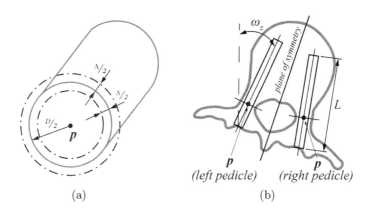

(a)   (b)

Fig. 2. The pedicle screw model with labeled diameter D, offset Δ around the diameter, length L, pedicle crossing point p and axial inclination angle ω_z, shown (a) in a three-dimensional view and (b) in the axial view.

Pedicle Screw Planning. The screw fastening strength is a predictor for the screw pullout strength, which should be as high as possible due to fragile characteristics of the bone structures. Lehman et al. [5] performed a biomechanical analysis of the thoracic pedicle screw trajectory on cadaveric specimens and concluded that the screw pullout strength, and therefore the screw fastening strength, correlates with BMD. As BMD is also linearly correlated with underlying CT image intensities [2,5,11], the screw fastening strength can be estimated as [2]:

$$F = \int_0^L \int_0^{2\pi} \int_0^{D/2} r\, I\,(r, \varphi, z) \, \mathrm{d}r\, \mathrm{d}\varphi\, \mathrm{d}z, \tag{5}$$

where L is the screw length, $D/2$ is the screw radius, and $I(r, \varphi, z)$ is the 3D image intensity under cylindrical coordinates (r, φ, z). However, such definition of the screw fastening strength takes into account the whole screw volume, which is, in our opinion, not optimal as intensities close to the screw centerline do not contribute to its fastening strength. We therefore define the screw fastening strength as:

$$F = \int_0^L \int_0^{2\pi} \int_{(D-\Delta)/2}^{(D+\Delta)/2} r\, I\,(r, \varphi, z) \, \mathrm{d}r\, \mathrm{d}\varphi\, \mathrm{d}z; \qquad F_n = \frac{F}{\pi D \Delta L}, \tag{6}$$

where Δ is the offset around the screw radius, and F_n is the normalized screw fastening strength, computed as F per unit of volume $\pi D \Delta L$ spanned between $(D - \Delta)/2$ and $(D + \Delta)/2$ (Fig. 2(a)). Besides the fact that, in contrast to the definition of Linte et al. [2], the intensities close to the screw centerline are not taken into account, we also introduce F_n, which is maximized to determine the optimal 3D pedicle screw model, as maximization of F would favor larger screw diameters and lengths. Maximization is additionally limited by vertebral anatomy obtained from the 3D vertebral body model $V(\boldsymbol{x})$ and 3D pedicle model $P(\boldsymbol{x})$, i.e. the 3D pedicle screw model $S(\boldsymbol{x})$ must be located within both $V(\boldsymbol{x})$ and $P(\boldsymbol{x})$, and must not cross the vertebral plane of symmetry obtained from $V(\boldsymbol{x})$ to prevent intersection with the opposite pedicle screw (Fig. 2(b)). Parameters $\boldsymbol{s}^* = \{D^*, L^*, \boldsymbol{p}^*, \omega_x^*, \omega_z^*\}$ of $S(\boldsymbol{x})$ that define its optimal size and insertion trajectory are therefore obtained as:

$$\boldsymbol{s}^* = \arg\max_{\boldsymbol{s}} \left(F_n \Big|_{\boldsymbol{s} \to S(\boldsymbol{x}), V(\boldsymbol{x}), P(\boldsymbol{x})} \right). \tag{7}$$

3   Experiments and Results

3.1   Patients

Experiments were performed for nine patients (7 males and 2 females; mean age 18.7 years; range $14 - 34$ years) with adolescent idiopathic scoliosis (7 patients) and degenerative disc disease (2 patients) in the thoracic spinal region, who were referred for pedicle screw placement surgery and preoperatively undertook CT scanning (pixel size $0.26 - 0.46$ mm; slice thickness 0.6 mm). Manual planning of the size and insertion trajectory for 61 pedicle screws in the acquired CT scans was performed by a spine surgeon, who was experienced with the dedicated software for navigating through 3D images and manipulating with 3D screw models, and required at least 10 min to plan each pedicle screw. From these preoperative plans, patient-specific drill guides were manufactured and physically laid over the visible part of the spine during surgery, which was performed by the same spine surgeon, and then pedicle screws with predefined size were placed along these guides defining their insertion trajectory [12].

3.2   Implementation Details

The proposed automated method was implemented in C++ without code optimization and executed on a personal computer (Intel Core i7 at 3.2 GHz and 32 GB memory) with graphics processing unit acceleration (Nvidia GeForce GTX 760). For each observed vertebra, a 3D vertebral body model $V(\boldsymbol{x})$ (initialized as an elliptical cylinder by a single manually defined point within the vertebral body) and corresponding left and right 3D pedicle models $P(\boldsymbol{x})$ (automatically initialized as elliptical cylinders using parameters of $V(\boldsymbol{x})$) were obtained by applying the Nelder-Mead optimization method [13] to (4). The proposed 3D vertebral body model was used for both thoracic and lumbar vertebrae, and similarly the proposed 3D pedicle model was used for both thoracic and lumbar pedicles. Automated pedicle screw planning was obtained by initializing each 3D pedicle screw model using parameters of both $V(\boldsymbol{x})$ and $P(\boldsymbol{x})$, and then finding the optimal 3D pedicle screw model $S(\boldsymbol{x})$ by maximization of the normalized screw fastening strength F_n (6), (7); $\Delta = 0.1D$), again by using the Nelder-Mead optimization method [13].

Table 1. Comparison between manual and automated pedicle screw planning in terms of mean absolute difference (MAD) and corresponding standard deviation (SD).

Vertebral level	T2	T3	T4	T5	T6	T7	T8	T9	T10	T11	T12	All
No. of screws	2	3	1	2	6	10	8	10	10	5	4	**61**
Screw size: diameter D (mm)												
MAD	0.7	0.8	0.6	0.3	0.7	0.6	0.8	0.5	0.6	0.1	0.4	**0.6**
SD	0.5	0.2	0.0	0.4	0.4	0.5	0.6	0.3	0.5	0.2	0.5	**0.4**
Screw size: length L (mm)												
MAD	1.1	5.5	0.8	7.2	2.8	3.9	3.8	5.4	4.5	2.3	7.3	**4.0**
SD	0.1	2.9	0.0	9.4	1.5	3.3	2.1	3.1	4.2	1.4	6.0	**3.5**
Screw insertion trajectory: pedicle crossing point p(mm)												
MAD	1.6	1.8	1.2	1.8	2.0	1.5	1.3	1.5	2.0	2.2	1.4	**1.7**
SD	0.6	1.1	0.0	1.2	1.2	1.1	1.0	1.5	1.3	1.1	0.9	**1.2**
Screw insertion trajectory: sagittal inclination angle $\omega_x(°)$												
MAD	9.5	5.8	7.7	8.1	7.2	6.0	5.5	5.6	6.6	4.8	5.4	**6.5**
SD	8.6	4.7	0.0	8.9	8.0	3.6	4.2	3.0	4.1	2.7	7.2	**4.8**
Screw insertion trajectory: axial inclination angle $\omega_z(°)$												
MAD	3.8	5.0	10.4	10.7	4.6	4.7	2.5	6.7	3.9	4.3	5.9	**5.7**
SD	2.7	4.8	0.0	9.9	4.4	4.5	2.9	3.1	3.1	2.5	4.8	**3.9**
Screw planning: normalized fastening strength $F_n(\text{mm}^3)$												
MAD	44	67	42	191	69	92	65	111	97	68	57	**82**
SD	63	42	0	211	61	60	59	87	131	50	72	**87**

3.3   Results

For the 73 vertebral bodies and 146 pedicles, the mean absolute difference (MAD) $\pm$ standard deviation (SD) of corresponding modeling by 3D vertebral body models $V(\boldsymbol{x})$ and 3D pedicle models $P(\boldsymbol{x})$ was estimated to 1.2 ± 0.3 mm and 0.7 ± 0.5 mm, respectively, in terms of the radial Euclidean distance to manually placed ground truth points. The obtained automated plans for placement of 61 pedicle screws were compared to corresponding manual plans (Table 1),

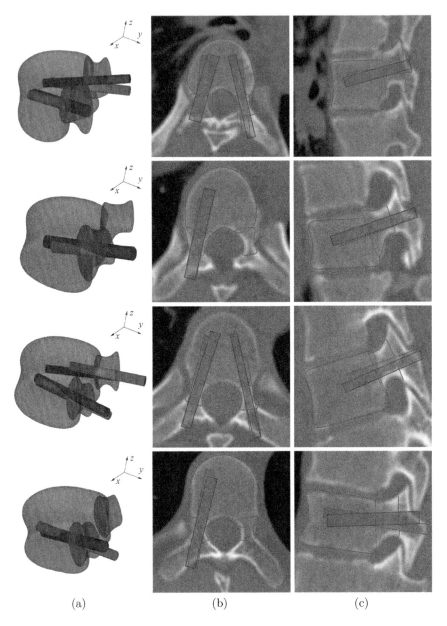

(a)   (b)   (c)

Fig. 3. Visual comparison between the proposed automated (in red color) and manual (in blue color) pedicle screw planning for a selected vertebra of two patients with adolescent idiopathic scoliosis (first and second row) and two patients with degenerative disc disease (third and fourth row), shown in (a) a three-dimensional view, (b) in a selected axial view, and (c) in a selected sagittal view (left pedicle only). (Color figure online)

resulting in a high agreement with an overall MAD $\pm$ SD of 0.6 ± 0.4 mm for diameter D and 4.0 ± 3.5 mm for length L related to the pedicle screw size, and 1.7 ± 1.2 mm for pedicle crossing point $\boldsymbol{p}$, $6.5 \pm 4.8°$ for sagittal inclination angle ω_x and $5.7 \pm 3.9°$ for axial inclination angle ω_z related to the pedicle screw insertion trajectory.

On average, automated planning of each pedicle screw took around 6 min (i.e. 3.7 min for 3D vertebral body modeling, 2.2 min for 3D pedicle modeling and 3 s for pedicle screw planning). When applying automated planning, an increased fastening strength in comparison to manual planning was observed for 50 pedicle screws (82 %), with an overall increase of 96 ± 87 /mm^3 in terms of F_n (agreement to manual plans of 0.6 ± 0.4 mm for diameter D and 4.4 ± 3.7 mm for length L related to the pedicle screw size, and 1.6 ± 1.0 mm for pedicle crossing point $\boldsymbol{p}$, $6.2 \pm 4.3°$ for sagittal inclination angle ω_x and $5.0 \pm 4.1°$ for axial inclination angle ω_z related to the pedicle screw insertion trajectory). On the other hand, a smaller drop of 38 ± 41 /mm^3 in terms of F_n was observed for the remaining 11 screws (agreement to manual plans of 0.5 ± 0.5 mm for diameter D and 3.0 ± 3.1 mm for length L related to the pedicle screw size, and 2.1 ± 1.7 mm for pedicle crossing point $\boldsymbol{p}$, $5.5 \pm 6.3°$ for sagittal inclination angle ω_x and $4.7 \pm 4.1°$ for axial inclination angle ω_z related to the pedicle screw insertion trajectory). A statistically significant difference ($p < 0.01$) was observed between the obtained automated and manual pedicle screw planning. Examples of automated and manual screw planning are also shown in Fig. 3. The proposed automated methods failed in one case because there was no proper pedicle shape due to its narrow width (Fig. 4), however, in practice surgeons avoid pedicles where screws cannot be placed.

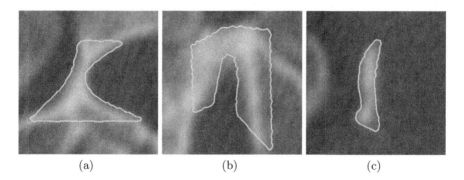

(a)   (b)   (c)

Fig. 4. The case where the proposed automated methods for parametric modeling of the pedicle and pedicle screw planning failed because there was no proper pedicle shape due to its narrow width. The figure shows the resulting parametric 3D pedicle model (in yellow color) in a selected (a) axial, (b) sagittal, and (c) coronal view. (Color figure online)

4   Discussion and Conclusion

We described a novel automated method for preoperative pedicle screw planning that is based on maximization of the screw fastening strength. We proposed a modified screw fastening strength (6), which takes into account only the region around the screw surface, as only this region is actually in contact with its thread and only the corresponding BMD therefore contributes to its fastening. Moreover, we proposed to maximize the normalized screw fastening strength (7) in order to equally treat and be able to compare screws of different sizes. The performed experiments and obtained results revealed that the proposed automated pedicle screw planning is highly in agreement with manual plans defined by an experienced spine surgeon. However, a higher normalized screw fastening strength was obtained for 82 % of the observed pedicle screws, indicating the main potential of the proposed automated method in the field of computer-assisted orthopedic surgery. Moreover, although computation times are comparable to those required for manual planning, automated pedicle screw planning can be performed offline, and the surgeon would then only have to verify and eventually adjust the proposed plans, which would result in a considerably faster preoperative planning. Future research will be focused on increasing the size of the patient database by considering also the diversity in patient age and pathology, evaluating the intra- and inter-observer variabilities of preoperative manual planning, and comparing the results to actual postoperative pedicle screw insertion trajectories.

Acknowledgements. This work was supported by the Slovenian Research Agency under grants P2-0232, J2-5473, J7-6781 and J2-7118. The authors thank Ekliptik d.o.o., Slovenia, for providing images and manual preoperative pedicle screw placement plans.

References

1. Manbachi, A., Cobbold, R., Ginsberg, H.: Guided pedicle screw insertion: techniques and training. Spine J. **14**(1), 165–179 (2014)
2. Linte, C., Augustine, K., Camp, J., Robb, R., Holmes III, D.: Toward virtual modeling and templating for enhanced spine surgery planning. In: Li, S., Yao, J. (eds.) Spinal Imaging and Image Analysis. LNCVB, vol. 18, pp. 441–467. Springer, Heidelberg (2015)
3. Lee, J., Kim, S., Kim, Y., Chung, W.: Optimal surgical planning guidance for lumbar spinal fusion considering operational safety and vertebra-screw interface strength. Int. J. Med. Robot. **8**(3), 261–272 (2012)
4. van Dijk, J., van den Ende, R., Stramigioli, S., Köchling, M., Höss, N.: Clinical pedicle screw accuracy and deviation from planning in robot-guided spine surgery. Spine **40**(17), E986–E991 (2015)
5. Lehman Jr., R., Polly Jr., D., Kuklo, T., Cunningham, B., Kirk, K., Belmont Jr., P.: Straight-forward versus anatomic trajectory technique of thoracic pedicle screw fixation: a biomechanical analysis. Spine **28**(18), 2058–2065 (2003)

6. Tian, N., Huang, Q., Zhou, P., Zhou, Y., Wu, R., Lou, Y., Xu, H.: Pedicle screw insertion accuracy with different assisted methods: a systematic review and meta-analysis of comparative studies. Eur. Spine J. **20**(6), 846–859 (2011)

7. Helm, P., Teichman, R., Hartmann, S., Simon, D.: Spinal navigation and imaging: history, trends and future. IEEE Trans. Med. Imaging **34**(8), 1738–1746 (2015)

8. Lee, J., Kim, S., Kim, Y., Chung, W.: Automated segmentation of the lumbar pedicle in CT images for spinal fusion surgery. IEEE Trans. Biomed. Eng. **58**(7), 2051–2063 (2011)

9. Štern, D., Likar, B., Pernuš, F., Vrtovec, T.: Parametric modelling and segmentation of vertebral bodies in 3D CT and MR spine images. Phys. Med. Biol. **56**(23), 7505–7522 (2011)

10. Štern, D., Njagulj, V., Likar, B., Pernuš, F., Vrtovec, T.: Quantitative vertebral morphometry based on parametric modeling of vertebral bodies in 3D. Osteoporos. Int. **24**(4), 1357–1368 (2013)

11. Homolka, P., Beer, A., Birkfellner, W., Nowotny, R., Gahleitner, A., Tschabitscher, M., Bergmann, H.: Bone mineral density measurement with dental quantitative CT prior to dental implant placement in cadaver mandibles: pilot study. Radiology **224**(1), 247–252 (2002)

12. Tominc, U., Vesel, M., Al Mawed, S., Dobravec, M., Jug, M., Herman, S., Kreuh, D.: Personalized guiding templates for pedicle screw placement. In: Proceedings of 37th International Convention on Information and Communication Technology, Electronics and Microelectronics - MIPRO 2014, pp. 249–251. IEEE (2014)

13. Press, W., Teukolsky, S., Vetterling, W., Flannery, B.: Numerical Recipes: The Art of Scientific Computing, 3rd edn. Cambridge University Press, Cambridge (2007)

Automatic Modic Changes Classification in Spinal MRI

Amir Jamaludin[1(✉)], Timor Kadir[2], and Andrew Zisserman[1]

[1] University of Oxford, Oxford, UK
{amirj,az}@robots.ox.ac.uk
[2] Mirada Medical, Oxford, UK
timor.kadir@mirada-medical.com

Abstract. This paper describes a novel automatic system for Modic changes classification of vertebral endplates. Modic changes are classes of vertebral degenerations visible as intensity variations in magnetic resonance images (MRI). The system operates on T1 and T2 MRI. We introduce three main novelties: 1. a vertebrae alignment scheme via precise bounding boxes obtained through corner localisation, 2. vertebral endplate classification in three dimensions, and 3. Modic changes classification. The system was trained and validated using a large dataset of 785 patients, containing MRIs sourced from a wide range of acquisition protocols. The proposed system achieved 87.8 % classification accuracy on our dataset.

1 Introduction

The objective of this work is the automated classification of Modic changes in magnetic resonance imaging (MRI) sagittal lumbar scans. Modic changes are classes of vertebral degenerations visible as intensity variations in MRI. There are three types of Modic changes and each type possesses varying correlation with the degradation of the vertebral bodies (VBs) with Modic type 1 having the highest correlation with clinical pain scores [1]. Classification of these changes in vertebral endplates is highly beneficial as it gives a measure of health of a vertebra which would help in the diagnosis of lower back pain. To our knowledge, this is the first system to automatically classify Modic changes and vertebral endplates degeneration in general. An example of the vertebral regions associated with the task is shown in Fig. 1.

The system is trained and its performance validated using a clinical dataset which is heterogeneous, i.e. the scans are sourced from different clinical centres using different machines and protocols. The scans in the dataset possess a variation of field-of-view, field strength, resolution, and are susceptible to bias field corruption. Since it is a necessity for Modic changes classification to use both T1 and T2 scans, we also have to localize the vertebrae of the spine in the two scans. The advantages of such an automated system are improvement of radiological score consistency, which varies from one radiologist to another, and ease of pathological detection of Modic changes.

© Springer International Publishing Switzerland 2016
T. Vrtovec et al. (Eds.): CSI 2015, LNCS 9402, pp. 14–26, 2016.
DOI: 10.1007/978-3-319-41827-8_2

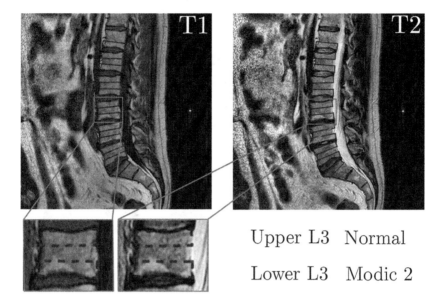

Upper L3   Normal

Lower L3   Modic 2

Fig. 1. The task: Given T1 and T2 weighted lumbar sagittal MRI volumes, detect, localise, label, and predict the states of the endplates of the vertebrae from the lower endplate of T12 to the upper endplate of S1. In the example, only single slices of T1 and T2 are shown but in practice, the system operates on every slice in the scans. Bounding boxes, shown in red, represent the regions used in the classification of the endplates. (Color figure online)

1.1   Modic Changes

The variation of voxel intensities in an MRI scan can be said to be caused by the variation of proton densities of different organs. One good assumption is that a specific organ would roughly consist of the same material hence possess a narrower range of proton densities unique to that organ. By extension, a healthy or normal vertebra would exhibit homogeneous intensity distributions in its T1 and T2 scans. The opposite is true for some abnormal vertebrae where visible discolourations can be seen in both their T1 and T2 scans, as first discovered by Modic et al. [2], aptly named Modic changes and at times might also be referred to as marrow or vertebral body changes.

Modic postulated that such discolourations in the form of visible intensity changes of the vertebrae might be caused by the evolution of marrow of the vertebral endplate in response to the degeneration of the corresponding inter-vertebral disc [2,3]. This response is hypothesised to be either mechanical or bacterial in cause but which or both has yet to be determined [1].

There are three different types of Modic changes, each characterized by a change in intensity of the vertebral endplates in both the T1 and T2 scans. See Fig. 2 and Table 1.

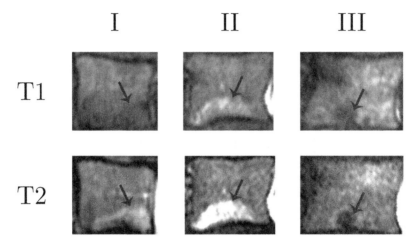

Fig. 2. Each column pair of images is from an individual vertebra scanned with T1 and T2 weightings and each pair represents an example of the type of Modic changes they belong to. These discolourations only appear on the endplates of the vertebrae adhering to the definition set forth by Modic et al. [2].

Several studies have been conducted to find the relationship between Modic changes and lower back pain. Modic type 1 has the strongest correlation with lower back pain and type 1 endplates may stabilise into Modic type 2 over time, which has a lower correlation with lower back pain [4–6]. This suggests that patients with lower back pain might possibly be monitored by observing just the state of their endplates.

1.2   Related Work

This work is the first fully automated system to classify Modic changes but there exists another system proposed by Vivas et al. [7] that is semi-automatic, requiring inputs for disc detections, and only does binary classification i.e. a simple Modic/non-Modic classification instead of a multi-class classification scheme into the three types or normal.

Table 1. An overview of the definition of the 3 types of Modic changes where we follow a standard radiological intensity terminology where a hyperintense area refers to an area with higher intensity in comparison to its surrounding and vice versa.

Modic type	T1 endplate intensity	T2 endplate intensity
I	*Hypo*intense	*Hyper*intense
II	*Hyper*intense	*Iso*intense/*Hyper*intense
III	*Hypo*intense	*Hypo*intense

Most research in analysis of spine imaging has focused on the interverte-bral discs rather than the VB. Typically, disc classifications methods use both intensity and shape information of the discs [8,9]. Existing work on VB analyses mainly focused on vertebral fractures [10] and sclerotic metastases [11]. Verte-bral fracture analysis classification requires a highly accurate per vertebra region of interest (ROI) fit because fractures are correlated with the height of the ver-tebra [10]. This is unlike Modic changes which are independent of the shape of the vertebra, focusing only on intensity. In this paper, we compare our feature with the normalised intensity histogram, Hist+, by Lootus et al. [9]. Our pro-posed features are also comparable to the spatial binned ROI intensity features by Ghosh et al. [8].

2   Approach Overview

Our method has five stages: 1. two-dimensional (2D) vertebrae detection and labelling in all slices of a given scan, 2. corner localisation, 3. vertebrae align-ment, 4. three-dimensional (3D) vertebrae extent detection, and 5. classification. See Fig. 3.

2.1   2D Vertebrae Detection and Labelling – Stage 1

To detect and label the vertebrae, we follow and adapted the detection and labelling scheme proposed by Lootus et al. [12] which uses a combination of a deformable part model (DPM) detector [13] and labelling via graphical model. The input to this stage is a 3D MRI volume and the output is a series of approximate bounding boxes with the vertebrae labels from T12 to the combined sacrum (S1 and S2). The detector and graphical model is trained using scans with annotated ground truth bounding boxes with labels as described in the work of Lootus et al. [12].

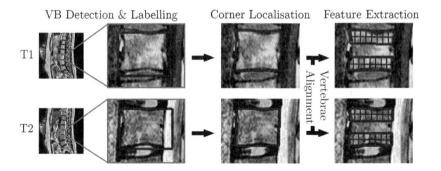

Fig. 3. An overview of our approach. The arrows indicate the processes while the images show a close up view of the vertebra in both scans. This is repeated in all of the slices of the volume.

2.2   Corner Localisation – Stage 2

There is an issue with using the loose bounding boxes as our classification features which is: the variation of fit of the bounding boxes, both intra-scan and inter-scan, which can be seen in Fig. 4.

We propose a finer localisation post-processing of these bounding boxes such that the resulting bounding boxes are more consistent and tightly aligned with the vertebrae. Tighter alignment leads to improvements in localizing the regions used to extract the features, and also helps in the alignment of the vertebrae in the T1 and T2 scans (Sect. 2.3).

We adapt the supervised descent method (SDM) by Xiong et al. [14] originally developed for the detection of facial landmarks to improve the localisation accuracy of the bounding boxes. The input to this stage is the image together with its bounding box from the vertebrae detection and labelling stage and the output is an irregular quadrilateral, with a tighter fit around the vertebra.

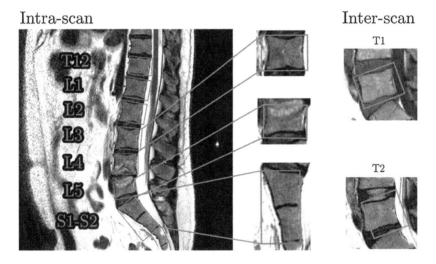

Fig. 4. An example output using the detection and labelling system described in the work of Lootus et al. [12]. The enlarged set of images of the vertebrae show the variation of fit of the bounding boxes to the vertebrae. Intra-scan variability: Note the sacrum bounding box contains both S1 and S2. The L3 bounding box contains all of the vertebra but is slightly loose while the L5 bounding box is missing the upper endplate of the vertebra. Inter-scan variability: Both images show the same L5 vertebra at the different contrasts and their respective bounding boxes.

At test time, the algorithm works by first regressing the corner points of the loose bounding boxes to a learned mean vertebrae corner points. Then, these intermediate corner points are iteratively updated via regression based on scale-invariant feature transform (SIFT) features around the points. The regression can be solved iteratively and can be represented as:

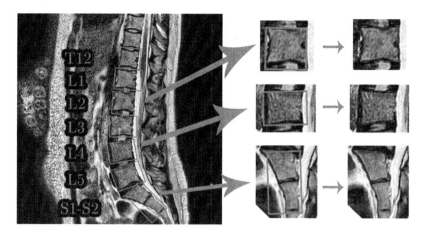

Fig. 5. Examples of inputs, shown in red, and outputs, shown in green, of the corner localisation. Note the sacrum bounding box is now more specific, containing only S1 instead of both S1 and S2, and the variation of bounding boxes fit is reduced. (Color figure online)

$$x_{k+1} = x_k + \Delta x_k, \tag{1}$$

where $\lim_{k\to\infty} x_k = x_*$. x_0 are the four points of the loose bounding boxes and x_* are the vertebral corner points. After several iterations, $k = 10$ works well in our dataset, the regression is stopped and the final points become the new corner points describing the best quadrilateral fit for the vertebra.

Training the regressor is posed as a minimisation task of Δx:

$$\operatorname*{argmin}_{\Delta x} f(x_0 + \Delta x) = \|\mathbf{h}(\mathbf{d}(x_0 + \Delta x)) - \phi_*\|_2^2, \tag{2}$$

where $\mathbf{h}$ is the feature transformation, which in this case is SIFT, of that point and $\phi_* = \mathbf{h}(\mathbf{d}(x_*))$ represents the SIFT features at the ground truth. To overcome overfitting, ridge regression was used. The regularizer, λ, is a general singular value penalty imposed per iteration.

Since the size of the vertebrae in the dataset vary, a normalisation step has to be conducted prior to regression. An individual vertebra is resized according to the height, V_h, of its bounding box and the image is translated such that the centre of the bounding box is the point of origin. Examples of corner localised vertebrae given its raw bounding boxes can be seen in Fig. 5.

2.3   Vertebrae Alignment – Stage 3

This section describes the vertebrae alignment stage which is necessary because there is no guarantee of a good alignment between the T1 and T2 scans. The inputs to this stage are two tight bounding boxes, one each from the T1 and

T2 scans, that contain one vertebra and the outputs are rigid transforms that describe the motion between the two scans specifically for that single vertebra.

A good alignment of the vertebra in both T1 and T2 scans is important since features extracted from both scans are jointly used for classification. The two main reasons for misalignments of the vertebrae are: 1. the movements of the patients in between scans and 2. the inter-scan difference in bounding boxes, both in terms of position and shape, detected in the T1 and T2 scans as shown in Fig. 4.

For the alignment, the vertebrae are assumed to be rigid bodies and any motion related to them is assumed to be only in-slice pitch and translation i.e. slice correspondence is assumed to be valid. As such, any extreme movement especially any yaw and roll would result in failure in alignment. These assumptions work well since scanning procedures dictate that patients should lie in the same orientation for both the T1 and T2 scans. Thus, the solution for the motion or transformation between the scans of the same vertebra can be expressed as:

$$\mathbf{V}_{T1} = \mathbf{R}(\theta)\mathbf{V}_{T2} + \mathbf{T}, \tag{3}$$

which describes both rotational, $\mathbf{R}$ (2×2 matrix), and translational, $\mathbf{T}$ (2×1 vector), motions between T1 and T2. Both, $\mathbf{V}_{T1}$ and $\mathbf{V}_{T2}$ are 2D coordinate feature points which are detected in both images.

We use the four corner points obtained in the previous stages in both T1 and T2 to be the feature points for alignment. However, the regressed corner points are not without mistakes. This is because vertebral corners tend to be smooth making it hard to pinpoint the exact locations of the corner points. Thus, a mechanism for identifying these mistakes and being tolerant to them is needed. We use a random sample consensus (RANSAC)-like approach to estimate the transformation and identify inliers/outliers simultaneously [15]. Detected outliers are removed from $\mathbf{V}_{T1}$ and $\mathbf{V}_{T2}$. After the rigid transformation of each vertebra has been obtained, we transform one scan to the other, aligning them, and use these as the inputs for Modic classification.

2.4   3D Vertebrae Extent Detection – Stage 4

Our aim in this stage is to determine the 3D extent of the vertebrae from the 2D quadrilaterals in each sagittal slice; this requires determining where the original detections should start and end slice-wise. This is important since the positions of the vertebrae in a scan are initially unknown and there exist slices which contain only partial volumes of the vertebrae, mostly containing tissue. These partial vertebrae are problematic if they are selected as ROIs for feature extraction. To this end we utilise a classifier to distinguish non-vertebrae and vertebrae quadrilaterals.

We follow a standard image classification scheme, discussed by Chatfield et al. [16], where the sequential steps are: 1. dense SIFT feature extraction over the quadrilaterals, 2. Fisher vector (FV) encoding of the features, 3. spatial tiling of the features in the image and 4. classification via linear support vector machines (SVM). This is done on a per slice basis on every slice. Quadrilaterals classified as vertebrae are passed through to the Modic classification stage.

3   Classification

The classification of the vertebral endplates starts with feature extractions of the endplate regions which then are fed into the classifier. There are four different types of classes an endplate might be classified as, namely: normal and the three different types of Modic changes.

3.1   Feature Extraction

Prior to classification, the right features have to be extracted such that they best separate the different classes which in this case are the different types of Modic changes. Since the very definition of the different Modic types is dependent on the joint intensity of the images, we propose a feature that captures this information between T1 and T2: a spatially-binned joint histogram of intensities (SJT). As a baseline measure, our feature is compared with a histogram based scheme by Lootus et al. [9] tested on radiological disc grading (Hist+).

The ROIs for feature extractions are the upper and lower thirds of the vertebra-aligned corner-localised tight quadrilaterals of T1 and T2. These ROIs are essentially shorter quadrilaterals, one each for upper and lower endplates shown in Figs. 1 and 6, which cover the vertebral endplates. We have also experimented on using vertebrae segmentation proposed in the work of Lootus et al. [9] but since the nature of the problem itself is dependent on intensity, segmentation of the vertebrae proved to be unhelpful due to the intensity variation of endplate with Modic changes. The intensity of each endplate ROI is median normalised using both the intensity distributions of the vertebra and its neighbouring vertebra. This reduces the effect of bias field and protocol intensity variation while preserving actual per vertebra variation which is crucial for Modic classification.

SJT. Each ROI is spatially-binned, 2×8 bins, so that there is a measure of spatial statistics of the Modic changes and from each corresponding T1-T2 pair of spatial cells we construct a 16×16 joint intensity histogram. The joint histogram is constructed by binning every pixel pair (T1 and T2 in the ROI) according to its joint-intensity; see Fig. 6. The overall dimension of the feature vector is 4096. Since the histogram is quite sparse, images are upsampled three times with respect to their original sizes prior to feature extraction [17].

Hist+: For each ROI, an intensity histogram, 16 bins, with its moments (mean, standard deviation, kurtosis, skewness, and entropy) is constructed. This forms a feature vector with 21 dimensions (16 intensity bins + 5 moments) for each ROI. The T1 and T2 features are concatenated forming the final feature vector.

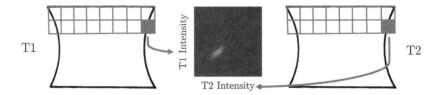

Fig. 6. An example of a joint histogram of one cell in the whole region. By introducing spatial bins, we capture the localisation of the intensity changes of the vertebral endplates.

3.2   Learning

For the classification task, a linear SVM is used. The classification is assessed with a 50:50 split of the dataset described in Sect. 4.1. To obtain the statistical variation of the classifier, the assessment is done 20 times, each time with a randomly selected 50:50 split according to patients. The optimal value for the parameter C is found via a 5-fold cross validation of the training set. A uni-slice classifier is trained using vertebral endplate labels marked by a radiologist where the best slice is used per endplate. The best slice is manually selected using the endplate labels from the radiologist as reference i.e. if the endplate is labelled to show Modic 1 change, the slice which best represent type 1 change is used. We use the one-versus-rest approach for the multi-class classification task e.g. for a Modic 1 classifier, the positive examples are Modic 1 endplates while the negative examples are the opposite and vice versa. To handle classification in multiple slices (3D extent of the endplates), the detection of which is discussed in Sect. 2.4, we use mean pooling of the classifier scores.

3.3   Data Augmentation

To further enhance the accuracy of our classification task, we applied several different augmentation transforms, five in total, to the data. To automatically choose the five best transforms i.e. five extra augmented samples in both train and test sets that help capture the invariances of the vertebrae in our dataset the image transformation pursuit (ITP) algorithm by Paulin et al. [18] was used. The transforms, 43 overall, we experimented on are as follows:

- 1 flip/mirror,
- 20 rotations: $\theta = -10°$ to $10°$ at $1°$ increment,
- 16 shifts: $\uparrow, \downarrow, \leftarrow, \rightarrow, \searrow, \nearrow, \searrow, \nearrow$ with two pixel distances (5 and 10 pixels),
- 6 bounding box scales: 85 % to 115 % in 5 % increment.

The five chosen augmentations samples are used as extra samples in training and we pool (mean) the classifier scores from the unaugmented samples with its corresponding five augmentations at test time.

4   Results and Discussion

4.1   Dataset

The dataset used to train and validate our system came from a range of different MRI machines and protocols. In all, the dataset consists of 785 patients of which 683 possess radiological scores (graded by a single radiologist) e.g. Modic changes, Pfirrmann grading etc. These patients are scanned on the basis that they are already diagnosed with back pain and no patient can be classified as healthy.

Of the 785 patients, 341 were used to train stages 1 to 4 described in Sect. 2 while 444 were used for stage 5, classification. There is no overlap of patients in training stages 1 to 4 and the patients in the classification. Only 388 patients out of the 444 possess labels for Modic changes, see Table 2.

4.2   Corner Localisation

Two sets of models are trained for corner localisation, each set having a single regressor for the standard VB from the T12 to the L5 vertebrae, and a more specific S1 regressor. The first set, termed the 1st stage, is for more coarse localisation, and the second set, termed the 2nd stage is for a precise corner regression. Both sets of models are trained with the same ground truth used in training the detection and labelling system. Overall, 4274 T12-L5 and 720 S1 vertebrae were used in training the VB and S1 models respectively. The results of the trained models on an unseen validation set is shown in Fig. 7.

There are only four parameters that have to be optimised; they are: the normalised height of the VB, V_h, the size of the SIFT patch, the regularizer of the ridge regression, λ, and the number of iterations, k. They are optimized such that they minimize the error on a hold-out validation set. In general, 91.1 % of the S1 vertebrae and 95.3 % of the VB have errors less than 2 mm which is a considerable improvement over the original bounding box detections with none of the S1 vertebrae and 41.6 % of the VB at the same error threshold.

Table 2. There is a total of 388 patients and 4656 endplates where 194 patients are used for training and 194 for testing i.e. 50:50 random splits with no overlap of patients in training and testing. Most patients with Modic changes possess more than one Modic endplates and some of the patients possess more than one Modic types resulting in the total of the numbers shown in the table to be different than the actual total.

Endplate class	Patients	Endplates
Normal	144	3921
Modic 1	111	249
Modic 2	195	551
Modic 3	18	42

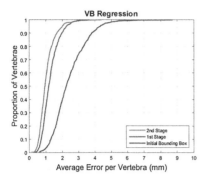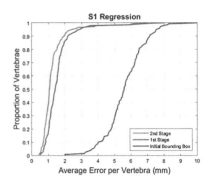

Fig. 7. (Left) Error per vertebra of the VB regression. (Right) Error per vertebra of the S1 regression. The red, blue, and yellow plots represent the errors of the raw bounding boxes, 1st stage and 2nd stage respectively. Both stages outperform the initial bounding box considerably. This is especially true for S1 which has a larger fit variance of the bounding boxes compared to VB. (Color figure online)

4.3   3D Vertebrae Extent Detection

For classification of vertebrae and non-vertebrae, the same patients that trained the corner regressors were used; a total of 66556 VB quadrilaterals (39309 vertebrae and 27247 non-vertebrae) with 50:50 train and test split. In general, this stage of the system performs well with an accuracy of 95.6 %.

4.4   Classification

For the classification task, the results can be separated into two parts: area under curve (AUC) of the receiver operating characteristic (ROC) curve of the one-versus-rest classifiers and overall accuracy of the multi slice classification task. Results are shown in Table 3.

Table 3. Automatic endplate classification: (Left) Area under curve (AUC) of the receiver operating characteristic (ROC) curve of the one-versus-rest classifiers. (Right) Accuracy of the classification.

	AUC of ROC				
Features	Normal	Modic 1	Modic 2	Modic 3	Accuracy
Hist+	83.8 ± 1.4	81.6 ± 2.7	81.2 ± 1.4	89.3 ± 8.7	85.8 ± 0.7
SJT	88.8 ± 0.9	85.5 ± 2.6	86.1 ± 1.0	90.1 ± 6.5	$\mathbf{87.8 \pm 0.6}$

It can be seen that the suggested SJT features outperform the Hist+ features by a considerable margin with a 2.0 % difference in accuracy and roughly between $4-5\%$ difference in AUC of ROC. Furthermore, the standard deviation of the

SJT features is consistently slightly less than that of Hist+ which suggests SJT to be more robust in learning. Note that the vertebral endplate as a whole is classified but this does not localise the slices that the Modic changes occur in. The result of the classification, 87.8 % in accuracy, is better than the accuracy without augmentation at 87.4 % and the chance accuracy at 69.4 %.

Up to this point we have assessed a fully automatic classification of the endplates by pooling the uni-slice classifications across the vertebra. In comparison, if only a single hand-picked best slice for each vertebra was used at test time i.e. manually select the slice that most clearly show the Modic change, we see a slightly better performance of 88.3 %, a minor difference of 0.5 %.

5   Conclusion

This paper has presented the first system to classify Modic changes automatically and validated using a large dataset. Since the ROIs extracted by the system are highly accurate and consistent, they can be used in other vertebral tissue classification problems which we hope to explore, alongside segmentation and localisation of Modic changes, in the near future.

Acknowledgements. We are grateful for discussions with Prof. Jeremy Fairbank, Dr. Meelis Lootus, and Dr. Jill Urban. This work was supported by the RCUK CDT in Healthcare Innovation (EP/G036861/1). The data used in this research was obtained during the EC FP7 project HEALTH-F2-2008-201626

References

1. Albert, H., Kjaer, P., Jensen, T., Sorensen, J., Bendix, T., Manniche, C.: Modic changes, possible causes and relation to low back pain. Med. Hypotheses **70**(2), 361–368 (2008)
2. Modic, M., Steinberg, P., Ross, J., Masaryk, T., Carter, J.: Degenerative disk disease: assessment of changes in vertebral body marrow with MR imaging. Radiology **166**(1), 193–199 (1988)
3. Emch, T., Modic, M.: Imaging of lumbar degenerative disk disease: history and current state. Skeletal Radiol. **40**(9), 1175–1189 (2011)
4. Mitra, D., Cassar-Pullicino, V., McCall, I.: Longitudinal study of vertebral type-1 end-plate changes on MR of the lumbar spine. Eur. Radiol. **14**(9), 1574–1581 (2004)
5. Rahme, R., Moussa, R.: The Modic vertebral endplate and marrow changes: pathologic significance and relation to low back pain and segmental instability of the lumbar spine. AJNR Am. J. Neuroradiol. **29**(5), 838–842 (2008)
6. Toyone, T., Takahashi, K., Kitahara, H., Yamagata, M., Murakami, M., Moriya, H.: Vertebral bone-marrow changes in degenerative lumbar disc disease: an MRI study of 74 patients with low back pain. J. Bone Joint Surg. Br. **76**(5), 757–764 (1994)
7. Vivas, E., Oliva, F., Aguilar, R., González, A., Cruz, J., Ávila, J.: Application of a semiautomatic classifier for Modic and disk hernia changes in magnetic resonance. Coluna/Columna **14**(1), 18–22 (2015)

8. Ghosh, S., Alomari, R., Chaudhary, V., Dhillon, G.: Computer-aided diagnosis for lumbar MRI using heterogeneous classifiers. In: Proceedings of 8th IEEE International Symposium on Biomedical Imaging - ISBI 2011, pp. 1179–1182. IEEE (2011)

9. Lootus, M., Kadir, T., Zisserman, A.: Automated radiological grading of spinal MRI. In: Yao, J., Glocker, B., Klinder, T., Li, S. (eds.) Recent Advances in Computational Methods and Clinical Applications for Spine Imaging. LNCVB, vol. 20, pp. 119–130. Springer, Heidelberg (2015)

10. Roberts, M., Pacheco, E., Mohankumar, R., Cootes, T., Adams, J.: Detection of vertebral fractures in DXA VFA images using statistical models of appearance and a semi-automatic segmentation. Osteoporos. Int. **21**(12), 2037–2046 (2010)

11. Burns, J., Yao, J., Wiese, T., Munoz, H., Jones, E., Summers, R.: Automated detection of sclerotic metastases in the thoracolumbar spine at CT. Radiology **268**(1), 69–78 (2013)

12. Lootus, M., Kadir, T., Zisserman, A.: Vertebrae detection and labelling in lumbar MR images. In: Yao, J., Klinder, T., Li, S., et al. (eds.) Computational Methods and Clinical Applications for Spine Imaging. LNCVB, vol. 17, pp. 219–230. Springer, Heidelberg (2014)

13. Felzenszwalb, P., Girshick, R., McAllester, D.: Cascade object detection with deformable part models. In: Proceedings of 2010 IEEE Conference on Computer Vision and Pattern Recognition - CVpPR 2010, pp. 2241–2248. IEEE (2010)

14. Xiong, X., de la Torre, F.: Supervised descent method and its applications to face alignment. In: Proceedings of 2013 IEEE Conference on Computer Vision and Pattern Recognition - CVPR 2013, pp. 532–539. IEEE (2013)

15. Fischler, M., Bolles, R.: Random sample consensus: a paradigm for model fitting with applications to image analysis and automated cartography. Comm. ACM **24**(6), 381–395 (1981)

16. Chatfield, K., Lempitsky, V., Vedaldi, A., Zisserman, A.: The devil is in the details: an evaluation of recent feature encoding methods. In: Proceedings of 2011 British Machine Vision Conference - BMVC 2011, pp. 76.1–76.12. BMVA Press (2011)

17. Kadir, T., Brady, M.: Estimating statistics in arbitrary regions of interest. In: Proceedings of 2005 British Machine Vision Conference - BMVC 2005. BMVA Press (2005)

18. Paulin, M., Revaud, J., Harchaoui, Z., Perronnin, F., Schmid, C.: Transformation pursuit for image classification. In: Proceedings of 2014 IEEE Conference on Computer Vision and Pattern Recognition - CVPR 2014, pp. 3646–3653. IEEE (2014)

Patient Registration via Topologically Encoded Depth Projection Images in Spine Surgery

Songbai Ji[1,2]([✉]), Xiaoyao Fan[1], Jonathan D. Olson[1], Linton T. Evans[2],
Keith D. Paulsen[1,2,3], David W. Roberts[2,3], Sohail K. Mirza[2,3],
and S. Scott Lollis[2,3]

[1] Thayer School of Engineering, Dartmouth College, Hanover, USA
{songbai.ji,xiaoyao.fan,jonathan.d.olson}@dartmouth.edu
[2] Geisel School of Medicine, Dartmouth College, Hanover, USA
linton.t.evans@dartmouth.edu
[3] Dartmouth Hitchcock Medical Center, Lebanon, USA
{keith.d.paulsen,david.w.roberts,sohail.k.mirza,
s.scott.lollis}@dartmouth.edu

Abstract. Accurate and efficient patient registration is essential for surgical image-guidance. Here, we present a registration pipeline to establish spatial correspondence between tracked intraoperative stereovision (iSV) and preoperative computed tomography (pCT) for spine surgery. First, depth projection images encoding the common vertebral dorsal surface "height" were generated from pCT and iSV. For pCT, vertebral pose was adjusted when necessary based on anatomic landmarks. For iSV, multiple reconstructed surfaces were combined to generate a unified projection image with accounting of overlapped regions to maximize the sampling of the surgical scene. Rigid registration between the resulting projection images produced an initial alignment for refined registration using an improved iterative closest point algorithm. The technique was applied to four explanted porcine spines in a total of eight poses. Registration accuracy was assessed using bone-implanted mini screws. The average fiducial registration error and target registration error (TRE) for ground-truth probe registration was 0.50 ± 0.08 and 0.63 ± 0.08, respectively. The accuracy for iSV registration was 1.77 ± 0.31 mm in TRE and was 2.01 ± 0.44 mm for surface reconstruction. The entire registration completed within 2 min. These results suggest potential for application of the method in human patients.

1 Introduction

Accurate and efficient patient registration is the cornerstone of surgical image-guidance. While image-guidance has become ubiquitous in open skull neuro-surgery, its application in open spinal procedures is largely limited to screw insertion for fusion surgeries [1]. Resistance to wider acceptance in spine appears to be the result of inefficient and often ineffective patient registration. In spinal operations, skin-affixed fiducials do not provide sufficient accuracy, and instead, spinal registration involves exposure and identification of anatomic landmarks

© Springer International Publishing Switzerland 2016
T. Vrtovec et al. (Eds.): CSI 2015, LNCS 9402, pp. 27–37, 2016.
DOI: 10.1007/978-3-319-41827-8_3

within the surgical field which is tedious and time-consuming [1]. Additionally, the one-time registration prior to surgery does not account for the intervertebral motion that occurs after surgery begins. Although intraoperative image-guidance using computed tomography (CT) or fluoroscopy overcomes some of these shortcomings, the added radiation exposure presents health risks to the patient, and possibly, the surgical team. Substantial capital costs of the imaging equipment also limit their wider deployment.

Radiation-free intraoperative images from ultrasound [2] and stereovision (iSV) [3] have recently been employed to facilitate patient registration in spine surgery. Both feature- and intensity-based techniques can be used for registration with preoperative CT (pCT). The previous iSV approach, while promising, presents certain challenges. First, iterative closest point (ICP) algorithms [4] to register iSV and pCT point-clouds strongly depend on a favorable three-dimensional (3D) initial alignment. Second, multiple tracked iSV acquisitions are usually necessary to maximize the sampling of the surgical field. However, combining them to generate a unified reconstructed surface would require non-standard processing and an accounting of the overlapping regions. As a practical consideration, therefore, only one iSV image was utilized in the previous method. Third, registration of bony features may require their segmentation from iSV; at a practical level, broader clinical adoption of iSV-based registration requires that this process be automated [3].

In this study, we present a registration pipeline to transform iSV-to-pCT 3D point-cloud geometrical registration first into a two-dimensional (2D) rigid image registration by exploiting common vertebral topological features in iSV and pCT. The resulting 2D registration provides a global initial starting point for the subsequent 3D registration. Although a manual, approximate initial registration is still needed in 2D, a full 3D initialization is avoided, and the technique could become more automated once a shape model [5] becomes available for patient cases in the future. Further, the technique efficiently and conveniently combines multiple iSV reconstructed surfaces into uniformly sampled areas without the need for bony feature segmentation in iSV, which is an important improvement over the previous technique [3].

Conceptually, our registration technique is analogous to solving the well-studied shape correspondence problem [6], which has been extensively explored in medical imaging (e.g., using surface features computed in the frequency domain [7] or employing a marker-less global surface matching to initiate a subsequent fine registration [8]). However, the use of 2D projection images for patient registration appears not to have been reported in the spine, although we note similar applications in the brain [9,10]. Their difference is that topological or shape information was used to generate projection images for the spine, whereas vessels from the exposed cortical surface were used for the brain.

The iSV-to-pCT registration technique was applied to four porcine spines (eight poses/imaging sessions in total). We evaluated its accuracy using bone-implanted mini screws as the gold standard. The current study focuses on assessing whether the iSV-based registration is able to achieve sufficient accuracy relative to that obtained from bone-implanted fiducials when no spinal intervertebral motion occurs, as both images were acquired at the same surgical stage. Results from this study may provide the foundation for future investigations to compensate for spinal intervertebral motion with the iSV technique and/or for clinical applications in human patients.

2   Materials and Methods

Following Institutional Animal Care and Use Committee (IACUC) approval, four explanted porcine spines were obtained from purpose-bred swine weighing between 35–70 kg. Muscular tissues were cleared from the dorsal aspect of each spine, exposing the spinous processes, lamina, facets, and transverse processes, similarly to that in human patients. Four Leibinger titanium mini screws (1.5 mm diameter, 3 mm depth) were implanted into each exposed vertebra. Each spine underwent two independent imaging sessions at two arbitrary postures (in an attempt to capture potential intervertebral motion). During a session, preoperative CT (pCT) images were acquired with a pixel resolution of 0.27 mm × 0.27 mm × 0.60 mm. To reduce computational cost, in-plane pCT images were down-sampled (selecting one every two pixels). Immediately after pCT acquisition, iSV images were obtained with a custom stereovision system (consisting of two C-mount cameras; Flea2 model FL2G-50S5C-C, Point Grey Research Inc., Richmond, BC, Canada) was rigidly mounted to a Zeiss surgical microscope (OPMI® Pentero™, Carl Zeiss, Inc., Oberkochen, Germany) through a binocular port. Exposed vertebrae were sampled along the dorsal surface, rostrally to caudally, with the microscope focused at the corresponding spinous process and the optical axis approximately perpendicular to the spine's dorsal surface. Additional iSV images were captured with the microscope optical axis obliquely aligned to maximize the sampling of the surgical field. Typically, $6 - 10$ iSV images were acquired during a given imaging session.

The position and orientation of the microscope, and hence, the reconstructed iSV geometrical surface, were available from a StealthStation® navigation system (Medtronic, Inc., Louisville, CO, USA). Tips of the bone-implanted screws were localized with a digitization stylus for independent fiducial-based patient registration as well as for assessing the accuracy of the iSV registration in this study.

2.1   Patient Registration Pipeline

Establishing a spatial transformation between the patient in the operating room (OR) and the individual's preoperative scans by registering tracked intraoperative images is well established [2,3,9,10]. For the spine, when the spatial transformation between iSV and pCT image volumes (i.e., $^{pCT}T_{iSV}$) is directly available, patient registration ($^{pCT}T_{patient}$) can be readily computed from

$$^{pCT}T_{patient} = {}^{pCT}T_{iSV} \times {}^{iSV}T_{world} \times \text{inv}\left({}^{patient}T_{world}\right), \qquad (1)$$

where $^{patient}T_{world}$ and $^{iSV}T_{world}$ are the spatial positions and orientations of two trackers rigidly fixed to the porcine sample (to an adjacent spinous process near the surgical field) and the surgical microscope-stereovision camera assembly, respectively.

The coordinate systems and transformations involved in patient registration are visually illustrated in Fig. 1. Essentially, establishing correspondence between the patient in the OR and pCT becomes an iSV-to-pCT registration.

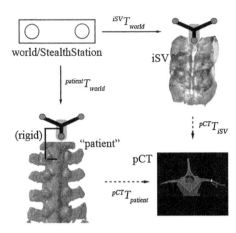

Fig. 1. Coordinate systems involved in patient registration. Solid/dashed arrows indicate transformations determined from calibration/registration. A transformation reversing the arrow direction is obtained by matrix inversion.

Here, direct intensity-based image registration may not be possible because the texture information captured in iSV does not correspond to the same intensity features in pCT. Therefore, feature-based registration of 3D point clouds generated from the two imaging data streams is a logical option, e.g., via an improved ICP algorithm [4]. Unfortunately, ICP-based methods are sensitive to initial alignment and data noise. Further, multiple reconstructed iSV surfaces were available from which to represent the surgical field, but they typically overlapped and did not sample the surgical scene uniformly. Therefore, specialized programs are likely necessary to process them.

To overcome these challenges, we designed a preprocessing pipeline (Fig. 2) to facilitate registration by topologically encoding depth in 2D projection images generated from pCT and iSV. An image intensity-based rigid registration was then performed by maximizing mutual information (MI). This result provided an initial starting position for a second, refined registration achieved with an improved ICP [4].

2.2   pCT Depth Projection Image and Vertebral Pose Adjustment

The pCT images were preprocessed (standard thresholding, erosion, identification of the largest connected region, and dilation (kernel size of 5 pixels for both erosion and dilation)) in order to create a binary volume representing the spine. A 2D image was created with its dimensions determined by the number of column and slice indices, j and k, of the pCT volume, respectively. For each non-zero voxel, its row index, i, in the image volume (corresponding to its distance relative to a local xz-plane, or "height" along the ventral-dorsal direction) was recorded at the corresponding (j, k) position in the 2D image (illustrated in Fig. 1). The intensity of each (j, k) location in the 2D image was determined as the largest recorded i-index scaled by the appropriate voxel dimension along this direction (i.e., to convert to millimeters). This 3D-to-2D projection was invertible because each 2D pixel can be uniquely traced back to its 3D correspondence on the vertebral dorsal surface.

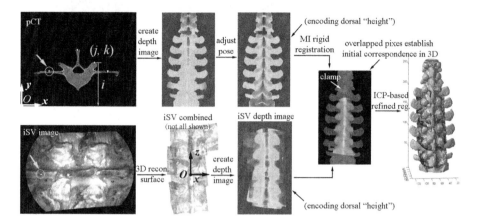

Fig. 2. The iSV-to-pCT registration pipeline. The pose-adjusted pCT depth projection image is rigidly registered with that from iSV (both encoding vertebral dorsal "height"). The resulting registration provides an initial starting position for a second refined registration. Texture information in iSV allows unambiguous identification of bone-implanted screws, permitting reliable assessment of accuracy in registration and iSV surface reconstruction.

Essentially, the resulting depth projection image was determined by the spinal posture in pCT. However, the vertebrae may be aligned in pCT in a way that could produce a depth projection image having intensities which did not necessarily correspond to a "neutral" posture as in iSV (see Sect. 2.3; Fig. 3(a) and (b)), and could degrade the MI registration performance. To avoid this possibility, the pCT was rigidly transformed and re-sampled with a template-based segmentation to identify individual lumbar vertebra and the corresponding anatomical tips of the transverse processes. The template vertebra was defined as the volume bound by two axial planes passing through two adjacent intervertebral discs. The tips of the transverse processes of the template were also identified. Both the vertebra template and tips were manually determined here, although a shape model could automate the process in the future [5]. The template vertebral volume was then registered with the L1 vertebra in pCT by locating it in an appropriate starting position. Upon convergence, the newly identified vertebra served as a template with which to identify and register its neighboring segment. The initial starting position for the next registration was assigned by using a typical inter-vertebral distance of $\sim$25–40 mm. The tips of the transverse processes in the new template were similarly used to identify their correspondences in the targeted vertebra (e.g., by localizing their closest points on an iso-surface). The procedure was repeated until all lumbar vertebrae were registered and anatomic features identified.

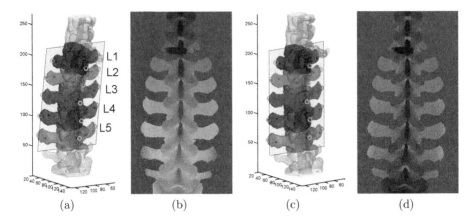

Fig. 3. Vertebral pose adjustment via rigid transformation and resampling based on vertebral feature points (circles) obtained through a template-based segmentation and identification (vertebrae color-coded in (a) and (c)). The resulting depth projection images are shown in (b) and (d). Automatically identified bone-implanted screws appear as black dots in (a) and (c). (Color figure online)

The identified tips of the transverse processes defined a plane which represented the relative spinal pose within the coordinate system (Fig. 3(a)). Subsequently, a rigid-body transformation was determined from the angles of the fitted plane relative to the major axes, and was used to transform and re-sample the pCT (Fig. 3(c)). An updated, pose-adjusted depth projection image was created following the algorithm described above (Fig. 3(d)).

2.3   iSV Projection Image and Combining Multiple iSV Acquisitions

For each porcine spine imaging session, the iSV acquisitions were individually recon-structed into 3D geometrical surfaces using an optical-flow correspondence matching technique [10]. Because all iSV acquisitions were tracked, the reconstructed surfaces were transformed into the common coordinate system of the patient tracker rigidly attached to the spine. To generate a composite depth projection image from this data, a local coordinate system was created with its origin located at the centroid of the reconstructed surface nodal positions (Fig. 2). Because the iSV images were acquired first with the microscope focused on the tips of the spinous processes and the optical axis perpendicular to the spine dorsal surface, the z-axis of a local coordinate system was established along the spinal inferior-to-superior direction. The x- and y-axes were subsequently determined along the lateral and ventral-to-dorsal directions, similarly to the pCT coordinate system.

Next, a 2D mesh was created in the xz-plane with a nodal density of 0.5 mm per pixel in both directions (to match the resolution of the re-sampled pCT). The mesh physical dimensions, and hence, the image size, were determined from the combined iSV sampling area. For each reconstructed iSV surface, nodal positions were projected into the xz-plane with their y-coordinates assigned to the closest mesh nodes. For each mesh node, multiple assignments were possible due to sampling overlap, and they were averaged to produce a unique value representing the dorsal surface "height" in the ventral-dorsal direction. The algorithm was repeated for all iSV reconstructed surfaces. Because the topological intensity values were averaged at a pre-determined set of mesh nodes, multiple iSV acquisitions were easily combined. Similarly to pCT, the iSV 3D-to-2D projection remained numerically invertible because the corresponding 3D coordinate for each 2D image pixel (and vice versa) was uniquely determined as long as the surfaces were free of "image folding" (average coordinate in the overlapping region). Additional thresholding and Gaussian smoothing (e.g., kernel size of 4 pixels) were performed on the resulting depth projection image prior to intensity-based MI rigid registration using Insight Segmentation and Registration Toolkit (ITK).

2.4 iSV-to-pCT Refined Registration

Before iSV-to-pCT MI registration of their 2D projection images, an initial alignment was manually produced to ensure proper correspondence occurred between vertebral segments (e.g., by clicking on the same vertebral segments in iSV and pCT projection images to inform their correspondence). This initial alignment was only intended to be approximate to allow the same vertebral segments in iSV and pCT corresponded to each other. In future clinical patient cases, this initial alignment may be obviated, e.g., by imaging and localizing in iSV the spinous process adjacent to the one on which the patient tracker was affixed. By matching the localized spinous process with that automatically extracted segment from a spine shape model [5], a direct global initialization could be attained. On the other hand, it is important to recognize that some user input may be unavoidable, due to the largely repetitive pattern of the vertebral segment geometry and the limited imaging region in iSV (i.e., the exposed surgical area only). This is justified, however, because the surgeon will most likely manually verify and confirm the registration, regardless, given the potential catastrophic consequences should mis-alignment or mis-registration occur in this surgical specialty [3].

Nevertheless, upon convergence of the 2D MI registration, an initial pixel-wise correspondence between pCT and iSV was obtained in the overlapping region (Fig. 2). Independently, these 2D pixels were mapped back to their respective 3D coordinates in pCT and iSV through the inverse of the projection transformations. For pCT, an additional rigid-body transformation was necessary to account for spinal pose adjustment. The resulting one-to-one correspondences of the 3D point pairs between pCT and iSV allowed a rigid-body transformation to be directly computed via singular value decomposition. Subsequently, all of the combined iSV surface nodes were back-projected from the depth projection image into the 3D coordinate system, and were further transformed into the pCT image space. As a final step to refine the registration, an improved ICP algorithm [4] was performed on the transformed iSV surface points (serving as "stationary") and the same pCT point clouds corresponding to the overlapping region. Because the pCT point cloud corresponded to a subset of the iSV data, the registration avoided the need for iSV segmentation, which was required in the previous method [3].

Finally, because pCT and iSV image acquisitions of the porcine spines occurred at the same surgical stage with an identical spinal posture, no intervertebral motion compensation was necessary for their registration in this study. In clinical patients, obviously their image acquisitions may be performed at different stages (e.g., when patient is in supine vs. prone for pCT and iSV, respectively), in which case intervertebral motion compensation becomes important. In these cases, the iSV-to-pCT registration technique developed here that treats the combined imaging area as a single unit will provide an initial starting position for a subsequent, refined registration performed at each individual vertebral level. The performance of the iSV-based vertebral motion compensation will be reported in the future.

2.5   Data Analysis

The iSV-to-pCT registration was conducted on four explanted spine samples each with two independent image sessions/poses (i.e., total of eight). The high-resolution iSV texture images (pixel size of ~0.2 mm) allowed accurate and unambiguous localization of bone-implanted screws (albeit, the projection 2D image was effectively down-sampled to match with the pCT resolution and also to reduce the computational cost). To evaluate the performance of the iSV-based registration, the spine samples were also independently registered with the pCT using ten ($N = 10$) ordered bone-implanted screws as fiducial markers localized separately in pCT and the OR. This was conducted following the standard procedure via the StealthStation, which included manually identifying the screw locations in the image space and localizing them in the physical space with a tracked digitizing stylus connected to the StealthStation. Other screw tip locations in pCT not sampled with the digitizing probe were automatically localized with a template-based technique.

For the ground-truth registration, fiducial registration error (FRE) based on the matched 10 screw pairs between the probe and pCT was obtained (FREprobe). To evaluate target registration error (TRE), 4–6 probe-identified screws not used in fiducial-based registration via the StealthStation were selected on or near the lamina to report their root mean squared (RMS) distances (probe vs. pCT; TREprobe). Similarly, RMS distances between the same screw pairs identified in pCT and iSV after iSV registration were reported (pCT vs. iSV; TREiSV). To further assess the iSV reconstruction accuracy (RMSrecon), the iSV surfaces were transformed into pCT space through the ground-truth registration (i.e., fiducial-registration using identified screw locations via the StealthStation). The resulting RMS distances between screws identified by both the probe and iSV were obtained (probe vs. iSV; points around iSV image boundaries were excluded due to the potentially degraded accuracy in these areas). All image processing and data analyses were performed on a Windows computer with due octo-cores (Intel Xeon E5-2650, 2.6 GHz, 32 GB RAM) using MATLAB (R2014a, The Mathworks, Natick, MA, USA).

3   Results

Individual registrations including the 2D MI-based image registration and 3D ICP-based point cloud registration successfully converged within 20 s. The total pipeline including generation of pCT and iSV depth images, iSV reconstruction and combination (Fig. 2), and the 2D and 3D registrations was 2 min. Probe-based registrations typically required about 15–20 min (mostly for manual identification of fiducials in both pCT image space and the OR). Figure 4 compares the iSV-pCT alignment using registrations based on the iSV-to-pCT pipeline with that obtained via the ground-truth probe registration using the StealthStation. Table 1 summarizes the accuracy measures of the registrations and iSV reconstructions.

Table 1. Summary of FRE and TRE of the probe-based registration (FRE_{probe} and TRE_{probe}, respectively), TRE of the iSV registration (TRE_{iSV}), and the iSV reconstruction accuracy (RMS_{recon}) for four spine samples (eight imaging sessions/poses). In the first experiment (Pig 1), independent, probe-identified screw points were not available (N/A) for TRE evaluation.

Acc. (mm)	Pig 1		Pig 2		Pig 3		Pig 4		Avg. (mm)
	(1)	(2)	(1)	(2)	(1)	(2)	(1)	(2)	
FRE_{probe}	0.56	0.50	0.63	0.43	0.58	0.46	0.41	0.46	0.50 ± 0.08
TRE_{probe}	N/A	N/A	0.62	0.67	0.68	0.73	0.56	0.50	0.63 ± 0.08
TRE_{iSV}	N/A	N/A	1.59	1.61	2.15	1.56	1.51	2.17	1.77 ± 0.31
RMS_{recon}	1.53	2.21	1.59	1.60	2.70	2.53	1.84	2.11	2.01 ± 0.44

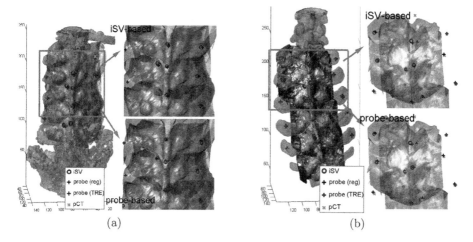

(a)   (b)

Fig. 4. The reconstructed iSV surfaces are combined and overlaid with the surface from pCT using the iSV registration for two cases with representative poses (neutral (1) vs. altered (2)). (a) Pig 2 (1), (b) Pig 3 (2). The iSV-identified screws are compared with those digitized by the probe and found in the pCT using the iSV or ground-truth probe registration (top and bottom insets, respectively). For visualization clarity, not all iSV surfaces are shown (color figure online).

4   Discussion and Conclusion

In this study, we successfully developed a registration pipeline based on pCT and tracked iSV to establish patient registration for image-guided spinal surgery. The registration accuracies as well as the accuracies of the iSV reconstructed surfaces were evaluated using bone-implanted fiducials serving as the "gold standard". The probe had the highest, sub-millimeter accuracy in terms of both FRE and TRE, as expected. The average iSV-based TRE was 1.77 mm based on independent screws located near or within the surgical area of interest, which exceeded the recommended accuracy level of 2 mm [11]. The accuracy performance was comparable to that achieved with ultrasound, although the authors in the ultrasound study reported RMS distances of a same set of points between the ultrasound- and probe-based registrations [2] as opposed to errors between independent, homologous screw tip locations in iSV relative to pCT that were not used for registration as reported here. The average iSV reconstruction accuracy was ~2 mm, comparable to our previous report on human patients [3]. The total computational cost was <2 min (generation of depth projection images, iSV surface reconstructions and combinations, plus registrations).

The current technique is a significant improvement over our previous method because it efficiently combines multiple iSV acquisitions to maximize sampling of the surgical field without involving iSV segmentation. In contrast, our earlier effort was limited to a single iSV surface and required semi-automatic segmentation of bony surfaces for the ICP registration [3]. The registration pipeline described here essentially transformed geometrical surface registration into a topological depth projection image registration, analogously to methods previously applied to the brain [9, 10]. In addition, the shape correspondence using projected 2D images was also analogous to previous studies using surface features [7] or global surface matching [8] for registration in radiotherapy and liver surgery, respectively. However, because a shape model was not available for the porcine spine, some manual input to provide an approximate initial registration in 2D was still necessary, which was a limitation of our study. Regardless, we anticipate that the technique could be further automated, by incorporating a shape model [5] in patient cases. On the other hand, a completely automatic patient registration may not be clinically feasible or desirable, given the potential catastrophic consequences should mis-alignment/mis-registration occur for this surgical specialty [3].

Importantly, the accuracy and efficiency of our iSV-to-pCT registration suggest that the technique has potential to be applied during human procedures. Probe-based registration in spine surgery relies on anatomic landmarks, and typically requires 20–30 min [3] (vs. 2 min, with potential to further reduce manual operations by incorporating a shape model [5]). Intervertebral motion compensation was not necessary in our current study, because both images were acquired at an identical spinal posture. However, the technique developed here that treats the exposed spinal surface as a single unit for registration may effectively serve as an initial starting position for subsequent, more refined registrations at the individual vertebral level. By quantifying the relative differences between the global iSV-to-pCT registration and those obtained from each individual vertebral level, the intervertebral motion can be directly quantified. The accuracy and efficiency performances of the iSV registration suggest the feasibility of this strategy. Results from these investigations will be reported in the future.

If an accurate, robust, and efficient patient registration can be readily achieved with radiation-free, low-cost intraoperative images, application of image-guidance is likely to be broadened within spine surgery. The technique presented here suggests that the iSV technique, with further improvement (e.g., via a shape model to improve automation), may become clinically feasible to provide an effective patient registration in human subjects.

Acknowledgements. This work was supported by the NIH R21 NS078607, The Dartmouth clinical and Translational Science Institute (SYNERGY) under award number KL2TR001088 from the National Center for Advancing Translational Sciences (NCATS) of the NIH (SJ), and the Dow-Crichlow Award (SSL). The content is solely the responsibility of the author(s) and does not necessarily represent the official views of Dartmouth SYNERGY or the NIH. The authors are grateful to Dr. Timothy Schaewe for technical assistance on SteathLink$^{\circledR}$ and help from the Medtronic Navigation (Louisville, CO, USA).

References

1. Nottmeier, E.: A review of image-guided spinal surgery. J. Neurosurg. Sci. **56**(1), 35–47 (2012)
2. Yan, C., Goulet, B., Pelletier, J., Chen, S.S., Tampieri, D., Collins, D.: Towards accurate, robust and practical ultrasound-CT registration of vertebrae for image-guided spine surgery. Int. J. Comput. Assist. Radiol. Surg. **6**(4), 523–537 (2011)
3. Ji, S., Fan, X., Paulsen, K., Roberts, D., Mirza, S., Lollis, S.: Patient registration using intraoperative stereovision in image-guided open spinal surgery. IEEE Trans. Biomed. Eng. **62**(9), 2177–2186 (2015)
4. Kjer, H., Wilm, J.: Evaluation of surface registration algorithms for PET motion correction. B.s. thesis, Technical University of Denmark, Denmark (2010)
5. Rasoulian, A., Rohling, R., Abolmaesumi, P.: Lumbar spine segmentation using a statistical multi-vertebrae anatomical shape + pose model. IEEE Trans. Med. Imaging **32**(10), 1890–1900 (2013)
6. van Kaick, O., Zhang, H., Hamarneh, G., Cohen-Or, D.: A survey on shape correspondence. Comput. Graph. Forum **30**(6), 1681–1707 (2011)
7. Placht, S., Stancanello, J., Schaller, C., Balda, M., Angelopoulou, E.: Fast time-of-flight camera based surface registration for radiotherapy patient positioning. Med. Phys. **39**(1), 4–17 (2012)
8. dos Santos, T., Seitel, A., Kilgus, T., Suwelack, S., Wekerle, A., Kenngott, H., Speidel, S., Schlemmer, H., Meinzer, H., Heimann, T., Maier-Hein, L.: Pose-independent surface matching for intra-operative soft-tissue marker-less registration. Med. Image Anal. **18**(7), 1101–1114 (2014)
9. Sinha, T., Dawant, B., Duay, V., Cash, D., Weil, R., Thompson, R., Weaver, K., Miga, M.: A method to track cortical surface deformations using a laser range scanner. IEEE Trans. Med. Imaging **24**(6), 767–781 (2005)
10. Ji, S., Fan, X., Roberts, D., Hartov, A., Paulsen, K.: Cortical surface shift estimation using stereovision and optical flow motion tracking via projection image registration. Med. Image Anal. **18**(7), 1169–1183 (2014)
11. Cleary, K., Peters, T.: Image-guided interventions: technology review and clinical applications. Annu. Rev. Biomed. Eng. **12**, 119–142 (2010)

Automatic Localisation of Vertebrae in DXA Images Using Random Forest Regression Voting

Paul A. Bromiley[1](✉), Judith E. Adams[2], and Timothy F. Cootes[1]

[1] Imaging Sciences Research Group, University of Manchester, Manchester, UK
{paul.bromiley,timothy.f.cootes}@manchester.ac.uk
[2] Radiology and Manchester Academic Health Science Centre, Central Manchester University Hospitals NHS Foundation Trust, Manchester, UK
judith.adams@manchester.ac.uk

Abstract. We describe a method for automatic detection and localisation of vertebrae in clinical images that was designed to avoid making *a priori* assumptions of how many vertebrae are visible. Multiple random forest regressors were trained to identify vertebral end-plates, providing estimates of both the location and pose of the vertebrae. The highest-weighted responses from each model were combined using a Hough-style voting array. A graphical approach was then used to extract contiguous sets of detections representing neighbouring vertebrae, by finding a path linking modes of high weight, subject to pose constraints. The method was evaluated on 320 lateral dual-energy X-ray absorptiometry spinal images with a high prevalence of osteoporotic vertebral fractures, and detected 92 % of the vertebrae between T7 and L4 with a mean localisation error of 2.36 mm. When used to initialise a constrained local model segmentation of the vertebrae, the method increased the incidence of fit failures from 1.5 to 2.1 % compared to manual initialisation, and produced no difference in fracture classification using a simple classifier.

1 Introduction

Osteoporosis is a common skeletal disorder defined by a reduction in bone mineral density (BMD) resulting in a T-score of <2.5 (i.e. more than 2.5 standard deviations below the mean in young adults), measured using dual energy X-ray absorptiometry (DXA) [1]. It significantly increases the risk of fractures, most commonly occurring in the hips, wrists or vertebrae. Approximately 40 % of postmenopausal Caucasian women are affected, increasing their lifetime risk of fragility fractures to as much as 40 % [1]. Osteoporosis therefore presents a significant public health problem for an ageing population. However, between 30–60 % of vertebral fractures may be asymptomatic and only about one third of those present on images come to clinical attention; they are frequently not noted by radiologists, not entered into medical notes, and do not lead to preventative treatments [2]. Many of these cases involve images acquired for purposes other than assessment for the presence of vertebral fractures, so identification

© Springer International Publishing Switzerland 2016
T. Vrtovec et al. (Eds.): CSI 2015, LNCS 9402, pp. 38–51, 2016.
DOI: 10.1007/978-3-319-41827-8_4

may be opportunistic. However, a recent multi-centre, multinational prospective study [3] found a false negative rate of 34 % for reporting vertebral fractures from lateral radiographs of the thoracolumbar spine. The potential utility of computer-aided vertebral fracture identification systems is therefore considerable. Modern clinical imaging is primarily digital, with images acquired in digital imaging and communications in medicine (DICOM) format and stored on a picture archiving and communication system (PACS). A system that could interface with a PACS, use information from the DICOM header to select images that cover a portion of the spine, automatically segment vertebrae, and detect any abnormal shape would therefore be particularly valuable.

Several authors have investigated the use of methods based on statistical shape models to segment vertebrae in both radiographs, e.g. de Bruijne et al. [4], and DXA images, e.g. Roberts et al. [5]. In recent work [6], the random forest regression voting constrained local model (RFRV-CLM) [7] was applied to DXA images. This approach uses random forest (RF) [8] regressors to predict the locations of landmarks that delineate the vertebrae. Each RF predicts one landmark, and fitting is performed subject to a constraint provided by a global shape model. The RFRV-CLM was shown to be more robust, i.e. suffered from a smaller number of fitting failures on more severely fractured vertebrae, than the active appearance model [9], an important consideration in clinical tasks where pathological cases are most significant. High-resolution RFRV-CLMs require initialisation relatively close to the location of the structure being segmented. The use of multi-stage, coarse-to-fine models can reduce the required initialisation accuracy. However, fully automatic application of such models still requires an initial estimate of the location of each vertebra. This is problematic due to the repetitive nature of vertebrae and the extensive shape differences between normal and pathological anatomy.

A variety of methods that detect potential vertebral candidates have been proposed; see Glocker et al. [10] for references. However, most assume that the number of vertebrae visible in the image is known a priori. This is a significant limitation, particularly when using midline sagittal reformatted images from computed tomography (CT) scans performed for various clinical indicators and not specifically acquired to view the spine, since the region of the body imaged can vary significantly. DXA images acquired for vertebral fracture assessment (VFA) typically cover the anatomy from T4 to L4. However, confounding bony structures, adipose tissue in the abdomen, or variation in the field of view can result in vertebrae being obscured or omitted, leading to fit failures with models that assume a certain number of vertebrae are present and can be accurately located. Several authors have proposed solutions to the more general problem of vertebra localisation where the number present is not known a priori. Klinder et al. [11] described a framework for fully automatic localisation, identification and segmentation of vertebrae in CT images, producing a triangulated surface mesh and a level label for all visible vertebrae. However, a complex chain of processing steps was required. Glocker et al. [10] used RF regressors trained on features from arbitrary, unregistered CT images to predict the locations of all visible vertebral centroids simultaneously, followed by a refinement stage using a probabilistic graphical model. Later work [12] reported that this approach had problems with images featuring pathology or very narrow fields of view, and instead used RF classifiers to generate a probabilistic label map for vertebral centroids, combined with a shape and appearance model to remove false positives.

We describe a method for detecting vertebrae in clinical images, based on RF regressors, that is intended to be robust to obscured or non-present vertebrae. The key idea is to use a set of relatively non-specific regressors trained to predict the location and pose of lower vertebral end-plates. Each regressor detects multiple vertebrae in a query image, and so does not require a specific vertebra to be present and visible. The results are combined using a Hough-style voting array, and the modes of the smoothed array represent potential detections. A graphical approach is then used to find the highest-weighted path through the modes subject to pose constraints. An evaluation on 320 DXA VFA images with a high prevalence of osteoporotic fractures is described in Sect. 3.

2 Method

The algorithm described here was based on our own implementation of Hough forests [13], and used a set of RF regressors, each trained on a different vertebral level, to predict the offset to a distinctive portion of that vertebra given local patches of image features. Figures 1 and 2 show the various stages of the algorithm. Training data consisted of a set of lateral DXA spinal images I with manual annotations $\mathbf{x}_l$ of N points $l = 1 \ldots N$ on each, outlining the vertebrae (see Fig. 1). The two end points of the curve that delineated the lower end plate were extracted. The lower end-plate was used as, of the four sides of the vertebra visible in the lateral view, it tends to exhibit the smallest changes in size and pose when osteoporotic fractures are present. The two reference points were used to calculate the parameters $\boldsymbol{\theta}$ of a similarity registration that transformed the image into a standardised reference frame, such that the reference points were transformed to specific coordinates. The image was then resampled into this frame by applying $I_r(m, n) = I(T_{\boldsymbol{\theta}}^{-1}(m, n))$, where (m, n) specify pixel coordinates. A scaling parameter w_{frame} set the reference frame width in pixels, allowing variation of the resolution.

A set of random displacements $\boldsymbol{d}_j$ was then generated by sampling from a uniform distribution in the range $[-d_{max}, +d_{max}]$ in x and y. Patches of image data of area w_{patch}^2 were extracted from the reference frame images at these displacements, and features $\boldsymbol{f}_j$ extracted from them. Haar-like features were used [14], as they have proven effective for a range of applications and can be calculated efficiently from integral images. The process was repeated with random perturbations in scale and orientation to make the detector locally pose-invariant. The free parameters were chosen to set w_{patch} to twice the length of the lower end-plate and the reference points to relative coordinates $(0.75, 0.25)$ and $(0.75, 0.75)$ in an undisplaced patch i.e. the patch size was equivalent to an entire

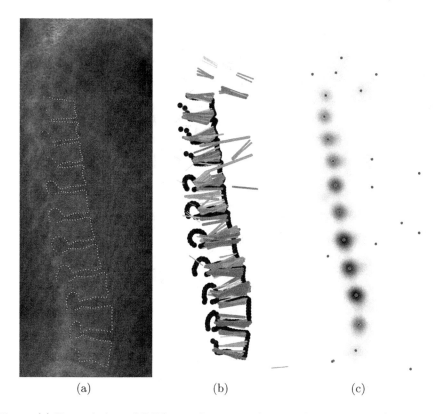

(a)   (b)   (c)

Fig. 1. (a) Example lateral DXA spinal image with manual annotations of 405 points on T7-L4. (b) Top 100 detections from each of the 10 lower end-plate detectors, overlaid on the manual annotations. The hue indicates the vertebral level on which the detector was trained, from T7 (green) to L4 (red), and the saturation and line thickness indicate the weighting. (c) The smoothed Hough voting array produced from the posterior point of the end-plate detections, and the detected modes. (Color figure online)

vertebra plus a border of (approximately, given that vertebrae are not square) one quarter of the end-plate length around each boundary. The resolution was set to 1 mm per pixel, and d_{max} was set to 0.4 of the patch size, so that the patches always covered more of the target vertebra than its neighbours. The pose variation was set to 0.1 rad, the resolution of the search (see below).

A RF was then constructed; each tree was trained on a bootstrap sample of pairs $\{(\boldsymbol{f}_j, \boldsymbol{d}_j)\}$ from the training data using a standard, greedy approach. At each node, a random set of n_{feat} features was chosen by sampling from a uniform distribution of range $1 \ldots N_{MRS}$ and using the result as skip sizes through the feature list. A feature f_i and threshold t that best split the data into two compact groups were chosen by minimising

$$G_T(t) = G(\{\boldsymbol{d}_i : f_i < t\}) + G(\{\boldsymbol{d}_i : f_i \geq t\}) \quad \text{where} \quad G(\{\boldsymbol{d}_i\}) = N_s log|\Sigma|. \quad (1)$$

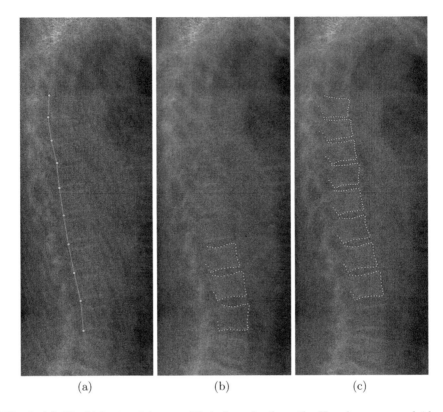

(a)   (b)   (c)

Fig. 2. (a) The highest-weight set of linked modes from the Hough array, overlaid on the original image (see Fig. 1). (b) Example fitted 99-point RFRV-CLM triplet model initialised with the three lowest automatic detections. (c) Concatenated points from the central vertebra in all fitted RFRV-CLM triplet models initialised from the automatic vertebra detections.

$G(S)$ is an entropy measure, N_s is the number of samples and Σ is their covariance matrix. Splitting terminated at either a maximum depth, D_{max}, or a minimum number of samples, N_{min}. The process was repeated to generate a forest of size n_{trees}. Free parameters of the RFs (N_{MRS}, D_{max}, N_{min}, n_{trees}) were set to the values given in the study of Bromiley et al. [6].

To detect vertebrae in a query image, a grid of points covering the image was defined; the resolution of this grid was set to 3 mm. Each of the RF end-plate detectors was applied at each grid location. The required Haar-like features were extracted and passed into the RF, which output a prediction of the displacement to the reference points. The process was repeated with a range of angle and scale variation. Since RF searching is fast, optimisation of free parameters was avoided by using large search ranges: −0.8 to 0.8 rad in steps of 0.1, and scales from 0.1 to 4 in rational/integer steps. For each detector, the predictions were used to vote into a Hough array. Each vote was weighted by the determinant of the covariance matrix of the samples that reached the relevant RF leaf node. The array was then smoothed using a Gaussian kernel of standard deviation (s.d.) 1 mm, to allow mode detection using a 9-way maximum, and the modes detected using exhaustive search. Each mode was a potential end-plate detection.

Vertebrae are repeating structures with considerable similarity in shape between neighbours. Therefore, each RF end-plate detector tended to locate multiple vertebrae across a considerable range of the spine (see Fig. 1). This provided robustness to variations in exactly which vertebrae were visible in the image. A second stage of Hough voting was performed to combine the results from the multiple models and estimate the location and pose of all detected vertebrae[1]. The highest-weighted N_{modes} modes from each detector were used to cast votes into a single Hough array. Each vote was weighted by the length of the line subtended by the two reference points. This had two effects. First, it acted as a shape prior; vertebrae are the largest structures in spinal images that might be delineated by parallel edges, so the weighting aided in elimination of false detections on ribs, humerus etc. Second, it weighted the vote according to the amount of information it contained about the vertebral pose. The array was then smoothed with a Gaussian kernel of s.d. σ_{comb}, and modes were detected. Estimating the location and pose simultaneously would require a four-dimensional array, which would be inefficient in terms of memory requirements, and would require a large N_{modes} to avoid problems with sparsity. Therefore, a two stage approach was adopted. The posterior-most point of the detection was used to vote into a two-dimensional (2D) array. For each detected mode in this array, all votes within $3\sigma_{comb}$ were extracted, and their anterior-most points were used to vote into a second 2D array. This was again smoothed using a Gaussian kernel of s.d. σ_{comb}, and the main mode was detected. σ_{comb} was set to 5 mm, and N_{modes} was set to 100.

The result of the combined Hough voting was a single set of N_m potential lower end-plate detections (see Fig. 1), containing false positives. To initialise a subsequent appearance model, an ordered set of points with no missing vertebrae or false detections was required, and so a graphical method was used to extract the highest-weighted subset of modes subject to pose constraints. This could be performed by optimising over all possible paths through the graph. In practice, it was found to be sufficient to start from the highest-weighted mode in the posterior-point Hough array. The main mode of the corresponding anterior-point Hough array gave an estimate of the vertebral pose. The normals to the vector between these modes specified the local superior and inferior directions of the spine, and a path was extracted by searching in each direction using

$$\underset{\substack{i=1...N_{m,}\\i\neq c}}{\arg\min} \|p_i - p_c\| \ \ s.t. \ w_i > w_t, \ \frac{rot(a_c - p_c, \pm\pi/2).(p_i - p_c)}{|rot(a_c - p_c, \pm\pi/2)||(p_i - p_c)|} > \cos\theta_t, \quad (2)$$

---

[1] This was performed as a separate step for implementation reasons. We have not yet investigated the possibility of performing the search for all RF regressors using a combined array.

where p_i is the location of mode i in the posterior-point Hough array, a_i the corresponding anterior point, c specifies the current mode, w_i is the weight of mode i, w_t and θ_t are thresholds, and $\pm$ specifies the search direction. θ_t was set to twice the angular resolution of the RF search, and w_t was set to the 2σ value of a Gaussian distribution with a s.d. of σ_{comb} and a mean scaled to the height of the highest-weighted mode in the posterior-point Hough array. This eliminated any statistically insignificant modes whilst accounting both for the smoothing applied and the typical width of the distribution of votes contributing to the modes. The result of the search was a set of ordered points that specified the posterior-most points on the lower end-plates; an example is given in Fig. 2. The remaining orientation ambiguity was resolved by assuming that the superior-to-inferior axis of the body corresponded more closely to the direction of increasing image y-coordinate.

The extracted path might have missing detections, posing a problem for initialisation of subsequent shape and appearance models. Therefore, a second stage of searching through the posterior-point array, equivalent to the use of an adaptive threshold, was included. The lengths of the links in the path were compared to normative vertebral heights learned from the training data, assuming that the lowest detection was on L4, and any heights more than 1.5 times that expected were referred for the second search. A threshold w'_t was calculated using the same procedure as w_t, but the 3σ point of the distribution. The values in the posterior-point voting array along the link were analysed at a set of rational steps ($1/2$, $1/3$ and $2/3$ etc.). The set, if any, that had the highest proportional weight, and individual weights higher than w'_t, was added to the path. This procedure was sub-optimal as it assumed a vertebral level assignment and, in future work, we intend to replace it with a robust, shape-model based procedure.

3 Evaluation

The method was evaluated on 320 DXA VFA images scanned on various Hologic (Bedford, MA, USA) scanners[2]. Manual annotations of 405 landmarks were available for each image, covering the vertebrae from T7 to L4 (see Fig. 1). Each of these vertebrae was also classified by an expert radiologist into one of five groups (normal, deformed but not fractured, and grade 1, 2 and 3 fractures according to the Genant definitions [16]).

The automatic initialisation algorithm was applied in a leave-1/4-out procedure, using 3/4 of the data to train the detectors and then applying them to the remaining 1/4. Figure 3 shows the accuracy of the detected lower end-plate points, and the number of such points detected, after the extraction of the linked path and after the additional search to detect missing points in the path. A vertebral level was manually assigned to each detection, by finding the closest manual

---

[2] 44 patients from a previous study [15]; 80 female subjects in an epidemiological study of a UK cohort born in 1946; 196 females attending a local clinic for DXA BMD measurement, for whom the referring physician had requested VFA (approved by the local ethics committee).

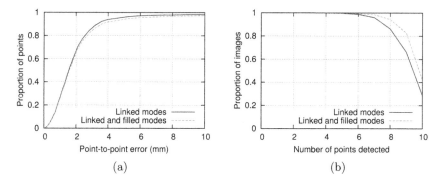

Fig. 3. Cumulative distribution function (CDF) of the P-to-P errors (a) and number of points detected (b) for the 320 DXA images, after path extraction and missing point detection. (Color figure online)

posterior lower end-plate point. Errors are given as the Euclidean distance, in millimetres, between the detected point and the corresponding manual annotation (point-to-point, or P-to-P, error). Additional vertebrae were detected above T7 in many images, and below L4 in some. Since manual annotations were not available for these, detections above the centroid of T7, and below the centroid of L4 plus its height, were removed from the analysis. The proportions of the vertebrae detected at each level are given in Table 1. There is a reduction in the proportion of detections above T10 and for L4, where the vertebrae are obscured by other bony structures. However, over 90 % of the vertebrae were detected at other levels. The additional search to detect missing points resulted in no significant accuracy loss, but a 4.4 % rise in detected points. Nine out of the ten target points were found in 85 % of the images, and at least six were found in 99 % of the images. RF searching was inefficient by design (see Sect. 2) and took 16.7 s per regressor per image on a machine with two Xeon X5670 processors using a single core; the Hough voting based combination of the results and extraction of the linked modes took 1.24 s per image.

The automatically detected lower end-plate points were then used to initialise the fitting of a RFRV-CLM covering a triplet of neighbouring vertebrae, as described in the study of Bromiley et al. [6], and the results compared to those achieved using manual initialisation of the same points. This model covered 99 points (33 on each of the vertebrae in the triplet). For the automatic initialisation, the RFRV-CLM was applied to all triplets of neighbouring initialisation points. The 33 points on the central vertebra were then extracted; no use was made of the overlap of neighbouring models. A vertebral level was manually assigned by comparing the centroid of these points and of the manual annotations for each vertebra. Additional vertebrae above T7 were again removed from the analysis, and errors were calculated for each point as the minimum Euclidean distance to a piecewise linear curve through the manual annotations (point-to-curve or P-to-C error), to compensate for the aperture problem with

Table 1. Statistics of the mean P-to-C errors on each vertebra after RFRV-CLM fitting, using manual and automatic initialisation. Column five gives the %age of vertebrae at each level that had an end-plate detection and, in brackets, a central vertebra from a RFRV-CLM fit assigned to them. Fitting of L4 required L5 to be detected; this is rarely present in DXA VFA images, hence the low percentage of L4 fits.

Vertebral level	Manual initialisation			Automatic initialisation			
	Median (mm)	Mean (mm)	Errors >2 mm (%)	Detected (%)	Median (mm)	Mean (mm)	Errors >2 mm (%)
T7	–	–	–	64.69 (46.87)	0.70	1.19	12.7
T8	0.54	0.72	3.44	87.81 (71.21)	0.53	0.79	4.39
T9	0.49	0.60	2.19	95.63 (88.75)	0.48	0.69	3.17
T10	0.51	0.60	1.56	98.75 (95.63)	0.51	0.67	2.61
T11	0.56	0.70	1.25	100.0 (98.12)	0.55	0.78	2.86
T12	0.59	0.70	1.88	100.0 (99.38)	0.58	0.75	3.14
L1	0.56	0.64	1.25	100.0 (99.38)	0.54	0.62	0.94
L2	0.57	0.63	0.31	100.0 (98.75)	0.57	0.62	0.32
L3	0.56	0.63	0.31	96.88 (79.38)	0.53	0.60	0.0
L4	–	–	–	77.19 (13.13)	0.53	0.60	0.0

dense annotations on extended edges. The mean error over each fitted vertebra was then calculated. The same metric was applied to the manually initialised fits and, for consistency, only those triplets for which all three of the initialisation points were available were included. Therefore, results on T7 and L4 were not available for manual initialisation. Example results from a single triplet model fit, and the concatenated central vertebra points from all triplets, are shown in Fig. 2.

Figures 4 and 5 show CDFs of the mean P-to-C error on manually and automatically initialised RFRV-CLM fits for each vertebral level, and for each vertebral status. Tables 1 and 2 provide statistics derived from these curves, including the percentage of vertebrae with mean P-to-C errors above 2 mm, which gives an indication of the proportion of fit failures. There is little difference between the medians or means for either status or level, indicating that the accuracy of the RFRV-CLM fitting is largely independent of the initialisation as long as

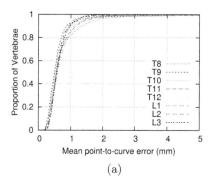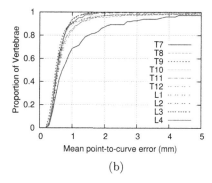

(a)   (b)

Fig. 4. CDFs of the mean P-to-C errors of the 33 points on the central vertebra in each RFRV-CLM triplet model for the 320 DXA images, for each vertebral level, for manual (a) and automatic (b) initialisation. (Color figure online)

Table 2. Statistics of the mean P-to-C errors on each vertebra after RFRV-CLM fitting, using manual and automatic initialisation.

Vertebra status	% age of sample	Manual initialisation			Automatic initialisation			
		Median (mm)	Mean (mm)	Errors >2 mm (%)	Detected (%)	Median (mm)	Mean (mm)	Errors >2 mm (%)
Normal	84.0	0.52	0.60	0.80	78.7 ± 0.8	0.52	0.63	1.38
Deformed	4.6	0.59	0.71	1.74	78.6 ± 3.4	0.58	0.73	2.73
Grade 1	3.5	0.61	0.79	1.14	83.2 ± 4.0	0.64	0.95	7.14
Grade 2	4.5	0.76	0.88	2.63	85.4 ± 3.6	0.77	1.06	6.30
Grade 3	3.5	0.87	1.16	11.49	85.7 ± 4.0	0.88	1.33	13.33

it is within the capture range of the model. The percentage of fitting failures on all detected vertebrae between T8 and L3 increased from 1.5 % for manual initialisation to 2.1 % for automatic, but the increase was larger for fractured vertebrae. However, using the 2 mm threshold, at least 86.7 % of vertebrae were successfully fitted, regardless of status. Importantly, there was no statistically significant variation in the proportion of vertebrae detected with vertebral status i.e. no evidence of bias against detecting fractured or non-fractured vertebrae.

To evaluate the importance of the differences in segmentation accuracy, a simple classifier based on the standard six-point morphometry technique was applied to the results from both manually and automatically initialised RFRV-CLM fits. The anterior H_a, middle H_m, and posterior H_p heights of each vertebra were extracted. A predicted posterior height $H_{p'}$ of each vertebra was also calculated by taking the posterior heights of the closest four annotated vertebrae, multiplying by ratios of vertebral heights in normative data obtained from the study of Leidig-Bruckner and Minne [17], and taking the maximum of the four values (on the basis that fractures reduce vertebral height). This process used the vertebral level assignment derived from the manual annotations for the

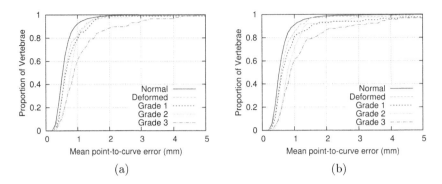

Fig. 5. CDFs of the mean P-to-C errors of the 33 points on the central vertebra in each RFRV-CLM triplet model for the 320 DXA images, for each vertebral status, for manual (a) and automatic (b) initialisation. (Color figure online)

automatically initialised results. Three ratios were then calculated: the biconcavity ratio H_m/H_p, the wedge ratio H_a/H_p, and the crush ratio $H_p/H_{p'}$. The data were whitened by subtracting the median and dividing by the square root of the covariance matrix (estimated using the median absolute deviation). The resulting data for the automatically initialised annotations are shown in Fig. 6, showing clear separation between the normal and fractured vertebrae and, in particular, that deformed vertebrae are displaced from the normal class along a different vector through the space than the fractured vertebrae. However, since only a simple classifier was intended, a threshold was applied to the Euclidean distance between the origin and the point defined by the three height ratios, to classify the vertebrae into non-fractured (normal and deformed) and fractured (grade 1,

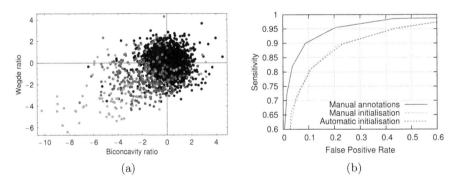

Fig. 6. (a) The whitened biconcavity and wedge ratios used by the simple classifier (black = normal; red = deformed; green, blue, cyan = grade 1, 2, 3 fractures, respectively). (b) ROC curves for classification of the detected vertebrae using the manual annotations, and RFRV-CLM annotations with manual and automatic initialisation. (Color figure online)

2 and 3) classes. Figure 6 shows receiver operating characteristic (ROC) curves produced by varying the threshold. The simple classifier achieves 90 % sensitivity at a false positive rate of 10 % when applied to the manual annotations. Using the manually initialised annotations reduced this to 80 %, largely due to errors on grade 1 fractures, where shape changes can be quite subtle. However, there was no significant difference in classifier accuracy between manual and automatic initialisation.

4   Conclusion

This paper has described a method for automatic detection and localisation of vertebrae in clinical images. The algorithm relies on a set of RF regressors trained to predict the location of vertebral lower end-plates. We have demonstrated that the individual RFs are not specific to the vertebrae they were trained on but instead, due to the similarity of neighbouring vertebrae, respond over a considerable range of the spine. This provides robustness to vertebrae that are obscured or not present. The use of multiple models, and Hough voting to combine their results, provides robustness to fit failures [18]. The failure of any one RF to detect vertebrae will result in responses scattered throughout the voting array. Only locations that result in strong responses from multiple models will result in significant modes. These are detected, and a graphical method applied to find a path through the detections, subject to pose constraints. This can be used to initialise a high-resolution appearance model that provides an accurate segmentation.

The method was evaluated on 320 DXA VFA images with a high prevalence of osteoporotic fractures. Other authors who have studied this problem [10–12] have used CT images that, since the modality is used for a wider range of clinical purposes, show a much larger variation in the region of the spine being imaged and the number of vertebrae visible. The difference in the dimensionality of the images prevents any comparison of localisation accuracy. However, we note that the proportions of vertebrae detected by Glocker et al. [10,12] are similar to the detection rates presented here. Instead, our evaluation focused on using the automatic annotations, and the equivalent manually annotated points, to initialise a RFRV-CLM. This demonstrated no difference in accuracy when the initialisation was within the capture range of the RFRV-CLM. Automatic initialisation led to more fit failures on grade 1 fractures, where the shape change may be subtle. However, the increase was smaller on grade 2 and 3 fractures. A simple classifier was applied, and showed little difference in performance between RFRV-CLM segmentations using manual and automatic initialisation.

One drawback of the algorithm is that it implicitly assumes prior knowledge of an overall image scaling, in the form of the pixel size in mm, although this information is available in the DICOM header for digital clinical images. Another is the relatively simple technique used to extract the path through the modes of the voting array. An appearance model based technique, such as that described in the study of Glocker et al. [12], might prove more robust. Finally, we have not yet evaluated the technique on images showing wide variation in the number of visible vertebrae. These issues will be addressed in future work.

Acknowledgements. This publication presents independent research supported by the Health Innovation Challenge Fund (grant no. HICF-R7-414/WT100936), a parallel funding partnership between the Department of Health and Wellcome Trust. The views expressed in this publication are those of the authors and not necessarily those of the Department of Health or Wellcome Trust.

References

1. Rachner, T., Khosla, S., Hofbauer, L.: Osteoporosis: now and the future. Lancet **377**(9773), 1276–1287 (2011)
2. Cummings, S., Melton, L.: Epidemiology and outcomes of osteoporotic fractures. Lancet **359**(9319), 1761–1767 (2002)
3. Delmas, P., Langerijt, L., Watts, N., Eastell, R., Genant, H., Grauer, A., Cahall, D.: Underdiagnosis of vertebral fractures is a worldwide problem: the IMPACT study. J. Bone Miner. Res. **20**(4), 557–563 (2005)
4. de Bruijne, M., Lund, M., Tankó, L., Pettersen, P., Nielsen, M.: Quantitative vertebral morphometry using neighbour-conditional shape models. Med. Image Anal. **11**(5), 503–512 (2007)
5. Roberts, M.G., Cootes, T.F., Adams, J.E.: Automatic location of vertebrae on DXA images using random forest regression. In: Ayache, N., Delingette, H., Golland, P., Mori, K. (eds.) MICCAI 2012, Part III. LNCS, vol. 7512, pp. 361–368. Springer, Heidelberg (2012)
6. Bromiley, P., Adams, J., Cootes, T.: Localisation of vertebrae on DXA images using constrained local models with random forest regression voting. In: Yao, J., et al. (eds.) CSI 2014. LNCVB, vol. 20, pp. 159–172. Springer, Switzerland (2015)
7. Lindner, C., Bromiley, P., Ionita, M., Cootes, T.: Robust and accurate shape model matching using random forest regression-voting. IEEE Trans. Pattern Anal. Mach. Intell. **37**(9), 1862–1874 (2015)
8. Breiman, L.: Random forests. Mach. Learn. **45**(1), 5–32 (2001)
9. Cootes, T., Edwards, G., Taylor, C.: Active appearance models. IEEE Trans. Pattern Anal. Mach. Intell. **23**(6), 681–685 (2001)
10. Glocker, B., Feulner, J., Criminisi, A., Haynor, D.R., Konukoglu, E.: Automatic localization and identification of vertebrae in arbitrary field-of-view CT scans. In: Ayache, N., Delingette, H., Golland, P., Mori, K. (eds.) MICCAI 2012, Part III. LNCS, vol. 7512, pp. 590–598. Springer, Heidelberg (2012)
11. Klinder, T., Ostermann, J., Ehm, M., Franz, A., Kneser, R., Lorenz, C.: Automated model-based vertebra detection, identification, and segmentation in CT images. Med. Image Anal. **13**(3), 471–482 (2009)
12. Glocker, B., Zikic, D., Konukoglu, E., Haynor, D.R., Criminisi, A.: Vertebrae localization in pathological spine CT via dense classification from sparse annotations. In: Mori, K., Sakuma, I., Sato, Y., Barillot, C., Navab, N. (eds.) MICCAI 2013, Part II. LNCS, vol. 8150, pp. 262–270. Springer, Heidelberg (2013)
13. Gall, J., Lempitsky, V.: Class-specific Hough forests for object detection. In: Proceedings of 2009 IEEE Conference on Computer Vision and Pattern Recognition - CVpPR 2009, pp. 1022–1029. IEEE (2009)

14. Viola, P., Jones, M.: Rapid object detection using a boosted cascade of simple features. In: Proceedings of 2001 IEEE Computer Society Conference on Computer Vision and Pattern Recognition - CVpPR 2001, vol. 1, pp. 511–518. IEEE (2001)
15. McCloskey, E., Selby, P., de Takats, D., Bernard, J., Davies, M., Robinson, J., Francis, R., Adams, J., Pande, K., Beneton, M., Jalava, T., Löyttyniemi, E., Kanis, J.: Effects of clodronate on vertebral fracture risk in osteoporosis: a 1-year interim analysis. Bone **28**(3), 310–315 (2001)
16. Genant, H., Wu, C., van Kuijk, C., Nevitt, M.: Vertebral fracture assessment using a semiquantitative technique. J. Bone Miner. Res. **8**(9), 1137–1148 (1993)
17. Leidig-Bruckner, G., Minne, H.: The spine deformity index (SDI): a new approach to quantifying vertebral crush fractures in patients with osteoporosis. In: Vertebral Fracture in Osteoporosis, pp. 235–252. Osteoporosis Research Group, University of California (1995)
18. Bromiley, P., Schunke, A., Ragheb, H., Thacker, N., Tautz, D.: Semi-automatic landmark point annotation for geometric morphometrics. Front. Zool. **11**(61), 1–21 (2014)

Robust CT to US 3D-3D Registration by Using Principal Component Analysis and Kalman Filtering

Rebeca Echeverría[1,2], Camilo Cortes[1,3], Alvaro Bertelsen[1(✉)], Ivan Macia[1], Óscar E. Ruiz[3], and Julián Flórez[1]

[1] eHealth and Biomedical Applications, Vicomtech-IK4, Donostia, Spain
{ccortes,abertelsen,imacia,jflorez}@vicomtech.org
[2] Universidad Publica de Navarra, Pamplona, Spain
echeverria.64713@e.unavarra.es
[3] Laboratorio de CAD CAM CAE, Universidad EAFIT, Medellín, Colombia
oruiz@eafit.edu.co

Abstract. Algorithms based on the unscented Kalman filter (UKF) have been proposed as an alternative for registration of point clouds obtained from vertebral ultrasound (US) and computerised tomography (CT) scans, effectively handling the US limited depth and low signal-to-noise ratio. Previously proposed methods are accurate, but their convergence rate is considerably reduced with initial misalignments of the datasets greater than 30° or 30 mm. We propose a novel method which increases robustness by adding a coarse alignment of the datasets' principal components and batch-based point inclusions for the UKF. Experiments with simulated scans with full coverage of a single vertebra show the method's capability and accuracy to correct misalignments as large as 180° and 90 mm. Furthermore, the method registers datasets with varying degrees of missing data and datasets with outlier points coming from adjacent vertebrae.

1 Introduction

In the realm of spinal surgery, ultrasound (US) is an attractive imaging modality for image-guided interventions because it is non-invasive, produces no radiation, offers real-time acquisition and has low costs. However, the registration of US intra-operative scans with respect to (w.r.t.) pre-operative scans (e.g. computerised tomography, CT) is challenging because of the limited depth of field, low resolution and reduced signal-to-noise ratio of US scans.

Among the proposed strategies for US to CT registration, the methods based on the unscented Kalman filter (UKF) have proven to effectively handle datasets with incomplete and noisy data. However, the UKF-based methods require a good initial alignment between the CT and US datasets to perform accurate registrations.

In this work, we implement a registration algorithm that addresses the problem of producing a good initial guess of the registration parameters by means

© Springer International Publishing Switzerland 2016
T. Vrtovec et al. (Eds.): CSI 2015, LNCS 9402, pp. 52–63, 2016.
DOI: 10.1007/978-3-319-41827-8_5

of a principal component analysis (PCA) of the point clouds. This good initial guess enables the robust functioning of UKF, unviable otherwise. Our registration algorithm refines the registration parameters obtained from the PCA by implementing an UKF with a modified batch-based point inclusion strategy for its iterations. The proposed algorithm was tested systematically with simulated data, considering scenarios with partial scans of the vertebra and with outlier points coming from adjacent vertebrae, which were not addressed in other works based on the use of the UKF. In all cases, the proposed method obtained remarkable results.

1.1   Related Work

Several methods have been proposed to register CT and US volumes. On one hand, intensity-based methods are interesting because segmentation of the CT and US datasets is avoided. Methods of Lang et al. [1] and Gill et al. [2] are based on the US simulation of the CT volume. Then, the acquired and simulated US are registered by maximizing an intensity similarity metric between them. These methods are able to register datasets with initial misalignments up to 20 mm. In order to avoid US volume reconstruction, Yan et al. [3] propose a method to register a group of US slices to a CT volume. However, such method requires that the initial misalignments between the datasets are smaller than 15 mm to work properly. To overcome limitations of previous approaches, Hacihaliloglu et al. [4] present a method that projects, by using three-dimensional (3D) Radon transform, and aligns local phase-based bone features in the projective space. The quantitative evaluation of such method (initial misalignments of the datasets between ±30 mm and ±15°) proves its accuracy. A general limitation of the reviewed methods is their computational complexity, which impedes their real-time use.

On the other hand, real-time US to CT registration is usually based on point-based registration methods, such as the iterative closest point (ICP) algorithm [5]. In this line of work, Ungi et al. [6] present an algorithm based on the pairing of manually defined landmarks in the CT and US data by using a simplified version of the ICP algorithm. The ICP method, however, is vulnerable to outlier points in the datasets, only accounts for isotropic Gaussian noise on both datasets and it requires a good initial registration guess.

To improve upon ICP, methods based on the Kalman filter have been proposed for registration of point clouds carrying anisotropic noise. In the work of Moghari and Abolmaesumi [7], an UKF-based registration method that is more accurate and robust than the ICP is presented. However, the UKF robustness sharply decreases with low quality (misalignment beyond 30° or 30 mm) in the initially guessed registration. In the work of Talib et al. [8], a linear Kalman filter (LKF) is used to register coplanar points of US snapshots as they are acquired from the patient. The LKF shows good accuracy and response times in the registration if the initial registration guess has misalignments under 5° and 20 mm [8].

Although methods in the works of Moghari and Abolmaesumi [7] and Talib et al. [8] require a good initial alignment between the datasets, such works do not report any action to overcome such an obstacle. In response to the mentioned limitations, we present a complete registration algorithm composed of two stages: (1) a coarse registration stage based on PCA, capable of correcting large misalignments between the CT and US datasets, and (2) a fast fine registration stage based on the UKF, which refines the initial guess from PCA.

2   Materials and Methods

2.1   Registration Problem

The registration problem consists in the statistical estimation of a rigid transformation $\mathbf{T}(\mathbf{R}, \mathbf{t})$ which brings the CT point cloud ($\mathbf{Y} \in \mathbb{R}^{3 \times N}$) and the US points cloud ($\mathbf{U} \in \mathbb{R}^{3 \times M}$) into alignment. $\mathbf{R}$ represents a rotation matrix (belonging to the special orthogonal SO(3) group) parameterized by Euler angles $[\theta_x, \theta_y, \theta_z]$ and $\mathbf{t} = [t_x, t_y, t_z]^T$ is translation vector. Then, the registration problem can be stated as finding $\mathbf{R}$ and $\mathbf{t}$ such that the cost function f is minimized:

$$f = \sum_{i=1}^{M} \left\| \mathbf{c}_i - (\mathbf{R}\mathbf{u}_i + \mathbf{t}) \right\|, \tag{1}$$

where points $\mathbf{c}_i \in \mathbf{Y}$ and points $\mathbf{u}_i \in \mathbf{U}$. Points $\mathbf{c}_i$ are computed as $\mathbf{c}_i = \Psi(\mathbf{Y}, \mathbf{R}\mathbf{u}_i + \mathbf{t})$ where function $\mathbf{c} = \Psi(\mathbf{A}, \mathbf{b})$ finds the point $\mathbf{c}$ in set $\mathbf{A}$ that presents the minimum Euclidean distance to point $\mathbf{b}$. Notice that the CT and US scans: 1. do not sample the same object points, 2. do not have the same sizes, 3. do not completely sample the interest subset, 4. do not only sample the interest subset and may include points from adjacent objects.

2.2   Registration by Using PCA and Kalman Filters

The workflow of the implemented registration algorithm is shown in Fig. 1(a). In the PCA-based registration, the parameters of a coarse registration transformation $\mathbf{T}^0$ are estimated, and then, point cloud $\mathbf{U}$ is transformed as $\mathbf{T}^0\mathbf{U}$. In the UKF-based registration (Fig. 1(b)), point cloud $\mathbf{T}^0\mathbf{U}$ is incrementally transformed as $\mathbf{T}^j\mathbf{T}^{j-1}\dots\mathbf{T}^1\mathbf{T}^0\mathbf{U} = \mathbf{T}^e\mathbf{U}$ where $\mathbf{T}^j$ is the transformation estimated in iteration j of the UKF. $\mathbf{T}^e(\mathbf{R}^e, \mathbf{t}^e)$ minimizes (1).

Coarse Registration Using PCA. A pre-requisite for PCA-based registration is the fact (indeed present in vertebrae cases) that object protrusions and asymmetries exist, which guide the alignment.

Since point clouds $\mathbf{Y}$ and $\mathbf{U}$ sample enough common neighborhoods in the object, we propose to initialize the registration procedure by aligning the principal axes of data sets $\mathbf{Y}$ and $\mathbf{U}$. Let $\mathbf{V}$ and $\mathbf{W}$ be $3 \times 3 \in SO(3)$ matrices containing the principal axes (eigenvectors) of point sets $\mathbf{Y}$ and $\mathbf{U}$, respectively.

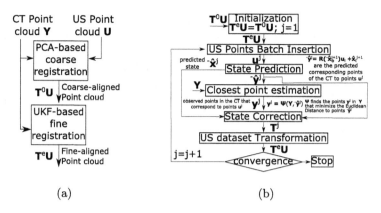

(a)   (b)

Fig. 1. (a) Workflow of the implemented registration algorithm. (b) Workflow of the UKF-based registration.

$\mathbf{V}$ and $\mathbf{W}$ are obtained by singular value decomposition (SVD) of the covariance matrices of their respective point clouds [9]. $\mathbf{V}$ and $\mathbf{W}$ have their orthogonal column vectors sorted in order of descending variance, with determinant $+1$ enforced. $\mathbf{R}$ is given by:

$$\mathbf{R} = \mathbf{V}\mathbf{W}^{T}. \tag{2}$$

The translation vector $\mathbf{t}$ is determined by the distance between the centroid of dataset $\mathbf{Y}$ and the rotated centroid of dataset $\mathbf{U}$:

$$\mathbf{t} = \mathbf{c}_{\mathrm{Y}} - \mathbf{R}\mathbf{c}_{\mathrm{U}}, \tag{3}$$

where $\mathbf{c}_{\mathrm{Y}}$ and $\mathbf{c}_{\mathrm{U}}$ are the centroids of $\mathbf{Y}$ and $\mathbf{U}$ respectively.

PCA determines the direction of each principal axis of the data but allows sign ambiguity. Therefore, the sign of eigenvectors in $\mathbf{W}$ is set so the distance between the point clouds $\mathbf{T}^0\mathbf{U}$ and $\mathbf{Y}$ is minimized. The resulting misalignment between $\mathbf{Y}$ and $\mathbf{T}^0\mathbf{U}$ is deterministic and is independent of any rigid transformation applied on $\mathbf{Y}$ or $\mathbf{U}$.

Fine Registration Using the Unscented Kalman Filter. The implemented UKF formulation is a variant of the one presented in the work of Moghari and Abolmaesumi [7]. To register point clouds $\mathbf{Y}$ and $\mathbf{U}$ using the UKF, points in $\mathbf{U}$ and $\mathbf{Y}$ are regarded as inputs and outputs, respectively, of a multiple-input and multiple-output (MIMO) system. The non-linear system state vector is then $\mathbf{x} = [\theta_x, \theta_y, \theta_z, t_x, t_y, t_z]^T$, which builds transformation matrix $\mathbf{T}(\mathbf{R}, \mathbf{t})$ (Eq. 1). The UFK is comprised by the prediction and correction steps of the estimates of $\mathbf{x}$ (Fig. 1(b)). The a priori and maximum a posteriori estimates of $\mathbf{x}$ in iteration j are denoted as $^{-}\hat{\mathbf{x}}^j$ (predicted) and $\hat{\mathbf{x}}^j$ (corrected), respectively.

Prediction of $\hat{\mathbf{x}}$: In this step, a prediction of the values of the system variables is performed and with such prediction the outputs of the MIMO system are also predicted for a given set of inputs. In the prediction step, the fact that $\mathbf{U}$ is transformed incrementally is considered. Let the state of $\mathbf{U}$ in iteration j of the UKF be denoted by $\mathbf{U}^e$, where $\mathbf{U}^e = \mathbf{T}^e\mathbf{U} = \mathbf{T}^j\mathbf{T}^{j-1}\ldots\mathbf{T}^0\mathbf{U}$. This means that initial matrices $\mathbf{T}^j$ represent relatively large transformations, but, as more iterations are completed, matrices $\mathbf{T}^j$ represent transformations similar to the identity matrix ($\mathbf{I}$). Following this rationale, a reasonable guess of the transformation to be applied in iteration $j+1$ is the one applied in iteration j. Then, the prediction $^-\hat{\mathbf{x}}^{j+1}$ is computed as per (4):

$$^-\hat{\mathbf{x}}^{j+1} = \hat{\mathbf{x}}^j (\forall j \geq 1). \tag{4}$$

Notice that the input for the fine registration method is the transformed dataset $\mathbf{T}^0\mathbf{U}$, which is closely aligned with $\mathbf{Y}$. Therefore, $\hat{\mathbf{x}}^0$ (which may represent a large transformation) is not used to predict $^-\hat{\mathbf{x}}^1$. Instead, $^-\hat{\mathbf{x}}^1$ is initialized such that it represents the identity matrix ($\mathbf{I}$), as proposed in the work of Moghari and Abolmaesumi [7].

Let $\mathbf{u}^{j+1} = \left[\mathbf{u}_1^T, \mathbf{u}_2^T, \ldots, \mathbf{u}_m^T\right]^T = \left[x_1, y_1, z_1, x_2, y_2, z_2, \ldots, x_m, y_m, z_m\right]^T$ be a vector (with size $3m \times 1$) containing the (x, y, z) coordinates of points $\in \mathbf{U}^e$ concatenated vertically, which are used to estimate $\hat{\mathbf{x}}^{j+1}$. To achieve a smooth behavior of the filter, $\mathbf{u}^{j+1}$ is populated keeping a set of points from $\mathbf{U}^e$ previously used in the registration, but adding a new set of points not used before in the estimation of the state vector $\hat{\mathbf{x}}$.

For each point $\mathbf{u}_i \in \mathbf{u}^{j+1}$ a prediction $(^-\hat{\mathbf{y}}_i)$ of its corresponding point in dataset $\mathbf{Y}$ is computed as per (5), where $\mathbf{x}_\theta = \left[\theta_x, \theta_y, \theta_z\right]^T$ and $\mathbf{x}_t = \left[t_x, t_y, t_z\right]^T$. The vector containing the coordinates of the predicted $^-\hat{\mathbf{y}}_i$ points is $^-\hat{\mathbf{y}}^{j+1} = \left[^-\hat{\mathbf{y}}_1^T, \ldots, ^-\hat{\mathbf{y}}_m^T\right]^T$:

$$^-\hat{\mathbf{y}}_i = \mathbf{R}(^-\hat{\mathbf{x}}_\theta^{j+1})\mathbf{u}_i + ^-\mathbf{x}_t^{j+1}. \tag{5}$$

Correction of $\hat{\mathbf{x}}$: The correction of $\hat{\mathbf{x}}$ is based on the minimization of the distances between the predicted $^-\hat{\mathbf{y}}_i$ (5) and the observed $\mathbf{y}_i$ points ($\mathbf{y}_i \in \mathbf{Y}$) that correspond to points $\mathbf{u}_i$. The points $\mathbf{y}_i$ are defined as the observed correspondences in $\mathbf{Y}$ to points $\mathbf{u}_i$. The points $\mathbf{y}_i$ are the ones that present the minimum Euclidean distance to the points $\mathbf{u}_i$ transformed by (5), and therefore, points $\mathbf{y}_i$ are computed as $\mathbf{y}_i = \Psi\left(\mathbf{Y}, ^-\hat{\mathbf{y}}_i\right)$. The vector containing the observed correspondences $\mathbf{y}_i$ is $\mathbf{y}^{j+1} = \left[\mathbf{y}_1^T, \ldots, \mathbf{y}_m^T\right]^T$. Then, $\hat{\mathbf{x}}$ is corrected as per (6), where $\mathbf{K}^{j+1} \in \mathbb{R}^{6 \times 3m}$ is the Kalman gain matrix. $\mathbf{K}$ and the covariance matrices of the noise and state vector are computed as proposed by Moghari and Abolmaesumi [7]:

$$\hat{\mathbf{x}}^{j+1} = ^-\hat{\mathbf{x}}^{j+1} + \mathbf{K}^{j+1}(\mathbf{y}^{j+1} - ^-\hat{\mathbf{y}}^{j+1}). \tag{6}$$

Finally, $\mathbf{T}^{j+1}$ is assembled with the estimated variables in $\hat{\mathbf{x}}^{j+1}$ and it is applied to dataset $\mathbf{U}^e$, $\mathbf{U}^e = \mathbf{T}^{j+1}\mathbf{U}^e$. The prediction and correction steps are repeated until convergence is achieved. Notice that the fact that this algorithm registers point batches $\mathbf{y}_i$ and $\mathbf{u}_i$, which contain m points, does not imply that point clouds $\mathbf{U}$ and $\mathbf{Y}$ must have the same size.

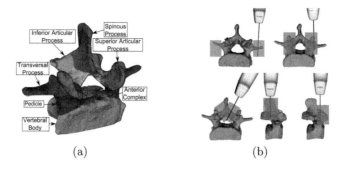

(a)   (b)

Fig. 2. (a) Typical anatomy of a lumbar vertebra. (b) US views to scan it defined in the work of Chin et al. [10]: paramedian sagittal (PS) transverse process view (top left), PS articular process view (top right), PS oblique view (bottom left), transverse spinous process view (bottom centre) and transverse interlaminar view (bottom right).

In contrast to the UKF formulation in the work of Moghari and Abolmae-sumi [7], the size of $\mathbf{u}^{j+1}$ remains constant (batches of points of size $3m \times 1$). In the work of Moghari and Abolmaesumi [7] a point from $\mathbf{U}^e$ is added to $\mathbf{u}^{j+1}$ in each iteration j until convergence is achieved or all points in $\mathbf{U}^e$ have been added to $\mathbf{u}^{j+1}$. Notice that Moghari and Abolmaesumi [7] the inversion of matrices with size $3m \times 3m$, with m increasing in each iteration, is required, which becomes computationally expensive as more iterations are completed [8].

2.3 Evaluation of the Performance of the Registration Algorithm

The performance of our implemented registration algorithm is assessed in the following clinical scenarios:

1. **Base-Case:** When a reasonable quality US scan $\mathbf{U}$ of only the target vertebra is available.
2. **Incomplete US-Scans:** When specific regions of the target vertebra do not appear in $\mathbf{U}$.
3. **Outliers: When regions** belonging to adjacent vertebrae appear in $\mathbf{U}$.

The datasets $\mathbf{U}$ belonging to the mentioned scenarios are generated following the protocol to US-scan lumbar vertebrae proposed in the work of Chin et al. [10]. The various regions of the vertebra (Fig. 2(a)) are scanned from five basic views (Fig. 2(b): 1. paramedian sagittal (PS) transverse process view, 2. PS articular process view, 3. PS oblique view, 4. transverse spinous process view, and 5. transverse interlaminar view.

Then, the datasets $\mathbf{U}$ are created by intentionally failing (or not) in scanning the vertebra in the specified views of the protocol. Table 1 defines the notation that specify the failures in the US acquisition protocol.

The scope of our investigation reaches vertebra vs. vertebra registration. We do not seek to register groups of vertebrae. Notice that algorithms for multiple-vertebra registration must deal with the relative movement among vertebrae as

Table 1. Notation of failures in the US acquisition protocol.

Symbol	Meaning
✓	The scan was completely performed
x	The scan was not performed
I	None of the transverse processes were scanned
II	Transverse process appears disconnected in the scan
III	The right transverse process was not scanned
IV	The superior articular process was not scanned
V	None of the superior articular processes were scanned
VI	The left superior articular process was not scanned
VII	Only the tip of the spinous process was scanned

the patient changes position in CT and US acquisition. Besides, in this work we assume that the vertebra to be registered has been correctly selected in the CT and US volumes by the medical staff.

Datasets Production. The assessment datasets are generated as follows:

(a) A surface model of the vertebra is obtained from a CT scan. We have used the spine surface model available in the work of Lasso et al. [11].
(b) The PLUS software [11] is used to simulate an US scan of (a).
(c) Volume reconstruction and segmentation are effected to produce an US vertebra surface model from (b).
(d) Datasets $\mathbf{Y}$ and $\mathbf{U}$ are populated by vertices of (a) and (c), respectively.
(e) Datasets $\mathbf{U}$ are generated such that they have complete alignment with $\mathbf{Y}$.
(f) True correspondences between points in $\mathbf{U}$ and $\mathbf{Y}$ are known beforehand.

Note that, despite that a surface model is extracted from the CT scan, dataset $\mathbf{Y}$ only consists of the model's vertices and not of its surface patches. Thus, all registrations are performed between pairs of point clouds.

Registration Accuracy. The accuracy of the registration is estimated with the mean target registration error (mTRE) as per (7):

$$\text{mTRE} = \sqrt{\frac{1}{n}\sum_{i=1}^{n}[\mathbf{y}_i - \mathbf{u}_i]^T[\mathbf{y}_i - \mathbf{u}_i]}, \tag{7}$$

with $\mathbf{u}_i$ and $\mathbf{y}_i$ being true corresponding points in $\mathbf{U}$ and $\mathbf{Y}$, respectively, unused during registration. Successful registrations have mTRE $\leq 2\,\text{mm}$. The success rate (SR) percentage is computed as: SR $=$ (number of successful registrations/total number of trials) $\cdot$ 100.

Table 2. Summary of failures in the image acquisition protocol of datasets 0–12 (notation is defined in Table 1).

Dataset	PS transverse process view		PS articular process view		PS oblique view		Transverse spinous process view	Transverse interlaminar view
	Left	Right	Left	Right	Left	Right		
0	✓	✓	✓	✓	✓	✓	✓	✓
1	✓	✓	✓	✓	✓	x	✓	✓
2	✓	✓	✓	✓	x	x	✓	✓
3	x	x	✓	✓	x	x	✓	I
4	✓	II	✓	✓	x	x	✓	III
5	II	x	✓	✓	x	x	✓	III
6	II	II	✓	✓	x	x	✓	I
7	✓	✓	IV	IV	✓	✓	✓	V
8	II	II	x	x	✓	✓	✓	V
9	II	✓	IV	IV	✓	✓	✓	V
10	✓	✓	IV	✓	✓	✓	✓	VI
11	✓	✓	✓	✓	x	x	VII	✓
12	✓	✓	IV	IV	x	x	VII	V

Base-Case Scenario. In this case, a full compliance with the US acquisition protocol is achieved, which generates dataset 0 in Table 2. The region of interest (ROI) of the US scan excludes neighboring vertebrae (Fig. 3). Arbitrary known transformations $\mathbf{Q}$ (translation components in $[-90, 90]$ mm, Euler angles in $[-180, 180]$ degrees) are generated randomly and are applied to $\mathbf{U}$ to test the performance of the registration algorithm. The translation and rotation magnitudes of $\mathbf{Q}$ are chosen to represent worst-case initial misalignments between $\mathbf{U}$ and $\mathbf{Y}$ of clinical scenarios. One hundred (100) runs with UKF alone and additional 100 runs with UKF plus PCA pre-processing are executed.

Incomplete US-Scans Scenario. In this case (datasets 1 to 12), the US scans lack one or more views of the US acquisition protocol. Table 2 specifies the fault (x = "missing" or roman number index of the defect as in Table 1). Grey rows indicate critically low geometric similarity between $\mathbf{U}$ and $\mathbf{Y}$ (e.g. Fig. 3). The scenario tests the robustness of the algorithm w.r.t. low quality datasets. Transformation matrices $\mathbf{Q}$ are applied to $\mathbf{U}$ as in the Base-Case. Each dataset was used in 20 trials.

Fig. 3. Partial US scan datasets (blue point clouds) and reference CT surface model. From left to right: datasets 0 (Base Case), 3, 5 and 8. (Color figure online)

Outliers Scenario. This case (datasets 13–15) has complete US scans but including portions of neighbouring vertebrae (outliers, Fig. 4). The ratio from the number of outlier points to the target vertebra number of points are 0.10, 0.15 and 0.20 for datasets 13, 14 and 15 respectively. Transformation matrices $\mathbf{Q}$ are applied to $\mathbf{U}$ as in the Base-Case. Each dataset was used in 40 trials.

3 Results

Base-Case Scenario. Registration with the UKF alone has a success rate of only 7 %, demonstrating that the Kalman filter alone is unable to handle large initial misalignments. Registration using our PCA pre-processing has a success rate of 100 % (dataset 0 in Table 3), which shows the robustness given by the PCA-based algorithm. For this case, it is clear that the PCA-based method is capable of bringing $\mathbf{U}$ and $\mathbf{Y}$ into a coarse alignment within the convergence region of the UKF-based method. The quality of the alignment between $\mathbf{Y}$ and $\mathbf{T}^0\mathbf{U}$ (i.e. after the PCA-based registration) is central to the success of our method. The minimum misalignment between $\mathbf{Y}$ and $\mathbf{T}^0\mathbf{U}$ is limited by the deviations of the principal axes of $\mathbf{U}$ w.r.t. the principal axes of $\mathbf{Y}$ (Table 4), which depend on the geometrical similarity between $\mathbf{Y}$ and $\mathbf{U}$. Requirements for a high geometrical similarity are: 1. that the ROI defined in the CT data is in agreement with the expected depth of the US scan (i.e. including the vertebral processes and pedicles but leaving out most of the vertebral body), and 2. that the majority of anatomical features sampled in $\mathbf{Y}$ are also included in $\mathbf{U}$.

Incomplete US Scans Scenario. Table 3 shows the registration results for datasets 1 to 12, which correspond to the incomplete US scans (Table 2).

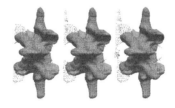

Fig. 4. US scan datasets with outliers (blue point clouds) and reference CT surface model. From left to right: datasets 13, 14 and 15. (Color figure online)

Table 3. Results of the evaluation of the registration algorithm.

Dataset	mTRE (mm)	σ (mTRE)	SR (%)
0	0.7646	0.2197	100
1	0.7060	0.1439	100
2	0.6754	0.1739	100
3	28.3957	1.0697	0
4	0.7871	0.3419	100
5	40.8025	2.7835	0
6	0.8227	0.1794	100
7	0.9403	0.2710	100
8	30.5735	1.2771	0
9	29.5342	1.1585	0
10	0.8511	0.2282	100
11	0.8330	0.1404	100
12	0.8603	0.3095	100
13	0.9122	0.3080	100
14	0.9940	0.4718	100
15	1.3595	0.2699	100

These results show that 8 out of the 12 cases obtained a full success rate (100 %) with all cases obtaining a mTRE below 1 mm. Datasets 3, 5, 8 and 9 obtained a success rate of 0 %. Table 4 shows that the 4 failed registration cases coincide with higher angular deviations between the principal components of $\mathbf{Y}$ and $\mathbf{U}$, which reflect low degree of similarity between $\mathbf{Y}$ and $\mathbf{U}$ and produce poor PCA-based registrations. Sine qua non conditions for registration are (a) the various scans sample conspicuous object features, and (b) salient object features appear in both scans, so unambiguous correspondence permits to span the embedding space $\mathbb{R}^n$ (in this case, $\mathbb{R}^3$). In our algorithm, these preconditions dictate the existence of transverse and articular vertebrae processes in scans $\mathbf{U}$ and $\mathbf{Y}$. None of the successfully registered datasets has a deviation larger than $20°$, which seems to be a tolerable amount to be effectively corrected by the UKF-based algorithm.

Notice that because of the deterministic nature of the PCA, registration trials of the same dataset $\mathbf{U}$ are always coarsely aligned in the same way to $\mathbf{Y}$. Datasets $\mathbf{U}$ that are poorly aligned by the PCA are likely to be inaccurately registered by the UKF-based method because the UKF requires small misalignments between $\mathbf{Y}$ and $\mathbf{T}^0\mathbf{U}$ in order to work properly.

Outliers Scenario. As in the Incomplete US Scans Scenario, if dataset $\mathbf{U}$ contains too many points from adjacent vertebrae, deviations of its principal

Table 4. Deviation (degrees) of the principal axes of the US datasets w.r.t. the reference CT dataset.

Dataset	Axis 1 deviation	Axis 2 deviation	Axis 3 deviation
0	6.4433	13.2106	12.6767
1	5.3957	12.0809	11.6537
2	4.4320	12.3246	12.3582
3	83.443	82.0330	14.1332
4	4.2703	12.5851	12.6444
5	49.7046	51.7842	13.6169
6	3.6261	12.1966	12.6585
7	8.4857	17.1006	15.1288
8	71.4994	72.1479	13.6724
9	26.2153	29.9312	15.2670
10	10.8844	17.6613	13.9660
11	5.3520	14.0130	13.8987
12	5.5425	19.0974	18.3762
13	7.5502	15.5432	13.8587
14	6.4145	14.9550	14.0857
15	8.1677	7.7931	6.4770

axes lead to poor PCA-based registrations. For datasets 13–15, the deviation of the principal axes remained in an adequate range and successful registrations were performed. However, mTRE increased compared to the previously studied scenarios. Notice that, if outlier points are included in $\mathbf{u}^j$, the UKF-based registration estimates a suboptimal transformation $\mathbf{T}^j$, reducing the efficiency and precision of the algorithm.

4   Conclusions

This article presents a two-stage registration algorithm for US and CT 3D point clouds of the vertebrae, which is based on a coarse registration using PCA followed by a fine registration using the Unscented Kalman filter. The PCA-based coarse registration is deterministic and can handle large misalignments between the datasets, as long as both datasets have an appropriate degree of geometrical similarity. In contrast to other UKF-based registration approaches, our algorithm produces an initial alignment between the datasets which is suitable to be improved by the UKF.

The algorithm evaluation was performed in the following scenarios: (a) when an US scan of reasonable quality of the vertebra is available (base-case), (b) when specific regions of the target vertebra are absent in the US scan, and (c) when regions belonging to adjacent vertebrae appear in the US scan. Results show that the proposed algorithm is able to register datasets with initial rotational misalignments within the range $[-180, 180]$ degrees and translational offsets in the range $[-90, 90]$ mm. In the base-case scenario, the registration based on the UKF alone presents a success rate of 7 %. By adding the PCA-based coarse pre-registration, the success rate improves to 100 %, which demonstrates the robustness added by the PCA-based algorithm. The mTRE of successful registrations are: 0.7646 mm in the base-case scenario, 0.8094 mm for incomplete datasets and 1.088 mm for datasets with outliers.

References

1. Lang, A., Mousavi, P., Gill, S., Fichtinger, G., Abolmaesumi, P.: Multi-modal registration of speckle-tracked freehand 3D ultrasound to CT in the lumbar spine. Med. Image Anal. **16**(3), 675–686 (2012)
2. Gill, S., Abolmaesumi, P., Fichtinger, G., Boisvert, J., Pichora, D., Borshneck, D., Mousavi, P.: Biomechanically constrained groupwise ultrasound to CT registration of the lumbar spine. Med. Image Anal. **16**(3), 662–674 (2012)
3. Yan, C., Goulet, B., Tampieri, D., Collins, D.: Ultrasound-CT registration of vertebrae without reconstruction. Int. J. Comput. Assist. Radiol. Surg. **7**(6), 901–909 (2012)
4. Hacihaliloglu, I., Wilson, D., Gilbart, M., Hunt, M., Abolmaesumi, P.: Non-iterative partial view 3D ultrasound to CT registration in ultrasound-guided computer-assisted orthopedic surgery. Int. J. Comput. Assist. Radiol. Surg. **8**(2), 157–168 (2013)
5. Talib, H., Peterhans, M., García, J., Styner, M., Ballester, M.Á.G.: Information filtering for ultrasound-based real-time registration. IEEE Trans. Biomed. Eng. **58**(3), 531–540 (2011)
6. Ungi, T., Moult, E., Schwab, J., Fichtinger, G.: Tracked ultrasound snapshots in percutaneous pedicle screw placement navigation: a feasibility study. Clin. Orthop. Relat. Res. **471**(12), 4047–4055 (2013)
7. Moghari, M., Abolmaesumi, P.: Point-based rigid-body registration using an unscented Kalman filter. IEEE Trans. Med. Imaging **26**(12), 1708–1728 (2007)
8. Talib, H., Peterhans, M., García, J., Styner, M.A., Ballester, M.Á.G.: Kalman filtering for frame-by-frame CT to ultrasound rigid registration. In: Dohi, T., Sakuma, I., Liao, H. (eds.) MIAR 2008. LNCS, vol. 5128, pp. 185–192. Springer, Heidelberg (2008)
9. Salvi, J., Matabosch, C., Fofi, D., Forest, J.: A review of recent range image registration methods with accuracy evaluation. Image Vis. Comput. **25**(5), 578–596 (2007)
10. Chin, K., Karmakar, M., Peng, P.: Ultrasonography of the adult thoracic and lumbar spine for central neuraxial blockade. Anesthesiology **114**(6), 1459–1485 (2011)
11. Lasso, A., Heffter, T., Rankin, A., Pinter, C., Ungi, T., Fichtinger, G.: PLUS: open-source toolkit for ultrasound-guided intervention systems. IEEE Trans. Biomed. Eng. **61**(10), 2527–2537 (2014)

Cortical Bone Thickness Estimation in CT Images: A Model-Based Approach Without Profile Fitting

Oleg Museyko$^{(\boxtimes)}$, Bastian Gerner, and Klaus Engelke

Institute of Medical Physics, University of Erlangen-Nuremberg, Erlangen, Germany
{oleg.museyko,bastian.gerner,klaus.engelke}@imp.uni-erlangen.de

Abstract. Structure of cortical bone is decisive for its strength, and quantification of the structure is crucial for early diagnosis of osteoporosis and monitoring of therapy effect. In three-dimensional computed tomography (CT) images, typically cortical thickness in proximal femur, lumbar vertebrae, and sometimes in distal forearm is estimated. However, resolution of clinical quantitative CT (QCT) scanners is comparable to the cortical thickness, especially for osteoporotic patients, leading to significant partial volume artefacts. A recent model-based approach recovers the cortical bone thickness by numerically deconvolving the image (profile fitting) using an estimated scanner point spread function (PSF) and a hypothesized uniform cortical bone mineralization level (reference density). In this work we provide an essentially analytical unique solution to the model-based cortex recovery problem using few characteristics of the measured profile and thus eliminate the non-linear optimization step for deconvolution. The proposed approach allowed to get rid of the PSF in the model and reduce the sensitivity to errors in the reference density value. Also, run-time and memory effective implementation of the proposed method can be done with the help of a lookup table. The method was compared to an existing approach and to the 50% relative threshold technique by evaluating performance of these three algorithms in a simulated environment with noise and various error levels in the reference density parameter. Finally, accuracy of the proposed algorithm was validated using CT acquisitions of European Forearm Phantom II, a widely used anthropomorphic standard of cortical and trabecular bone compartments that was scanned with various protocols.

1 Introduction

Dual energy X-ray absorptiometry (DXA) is a standard method to measure bone mineral density (BMD) of lumbar vertebrae, which is the best predictor of osteoporotic vertebral fracture. However, DXA cannot differentiate between trabecular and cortical compartments which is important since cortical thickness is an independent contributor to the vertebral bone strength: as shown by Roux et al. [1] it can significantly improve the regression with experimentally measured work to failure and enhance prediction of vertebral fragility. Thus, quantitative CT (QCT) is the method of choice to assess the cortex independently.

© Springer International Publishing Switzerland 2016
T. Vrtovec et al. (Eds.): CSI 2015, LNCS 9402, pp. 64–73, 2016.
DOI: 10.1007/978-3-319-41827-8_6

Measurement accuracy of cortical thickness, BMD and bone mineral content (BMC, i.e. bone mass) in three-dimensional (3D) computed tomography (CT) images is limited by the CT scanner resolution. Typically for clinical quantitative CT (QCT), a voxel size of $0.3 \times 0.3 \times 1 \, \text{mm}^3$ is used which is comparable with the cortical thickness of the lumbar vertebrae, especially by osteoporotic patients (cortical thickness in the middle of the vertebral body is usually below $0.5 \, \text{mm}$). In this case partial volume artefacts become large enough to distort the appearance of the cortical bone. Untill recently, two cortical bone segmentation approaches were commonly used: local adaptive threshold (or 50 %-method) and global threshold. Partial volume artefacts constitute a serious problem for these methods. Thus, the 50 %-method significantly overestimates the thickness of a thin cortex [2] whereas threshold-based techniques [3,4] cannot in general provide an accurate estimation of the whole range of cortex thickness values and require careful choice of thresholds.

A novel approach was proposed in the work of Treece et al. [5], which models the imaging process as a convolution of the imaged bone with the scanner point spread function (PSF) and recovers the cortical bone thickness by numerically deconvolving the given image. Several essential assumptions are made within this model-based approach. First, the cortex is assumed to have a constant density and thus be of a box-shape when plotted along the 1D profile perpendicular to the outer bone surface. The correct estimation of this global constant density (also reference BMD, BMD_{ref}) is the most problematic part of the method. Additionally, the PSF is assumed Gaussian and trabecular density of the bone at one side of the cortex as seen on the profile and soft tissue density at the opposite side are assumed constant for this profile. The standard deviation σ of the Gaussian and the two constant density values are obtained as result of optimization for deconvolution.

Although the model-based approach seems to outperform other methods in estimating the thickness of the "thin" cortex, it is an optimization process which is not guaranteed to converge to the global solution, and its sensitivity to errors in estimation of the model parameters is considerable [6]. On the other hand, the 50 %-method is rather robust and model-independent and cortical BMC-values computed with its help are more accurate than cortical BMD, which is underestimated, and cortical thickness, which is overestimated [2,6].

In this article, the following simple alternative to the model-based deconvolution is proposed for the estimation of the cortical thickness t_c under the model-based assumptions used by Treece et al. [5] as described above:

$$t_c = \frac{\text{BMC}_{\text{cort}}}{\text{BMD}_{\text{ref}}}, \tag{1}$$

where BMC_{cort} is the true BMC of the cortical bone. The main idea is to estimate BMC_{cort} analytically from the profile as measured in the image between two 50 %-points. The purpose of the proposed approach is threefold:

1. Get an analytical solution which allows for comprehensive analysis of the problem and computationally advantageous implementation.

2. Reduce the number of the model parameters.
3. Mitigate cortical thickness estimation errors caused by errors in BMD_{ref}.

2   Materials and Methods

In the following, we will put the center of the cortex to the origin of the profile axis so that the limits of the "real" cortical bone are $-a$ and a (a is unknown). This gives the graph of the "real" cortex as that of the box function with the height BMD_{ref} which is surrounded by two box functions with half-infinite support on both sides of the cortex representing soft tissue ($ST(t)$ with the height b) and trabecular bone compartment ($Tr(t)$ with the box height c, see Fig. 1(a). To avoid unnecessary complications in the formulae and without the loss of generality, we will always assume that "soft tissue" is on the left side of the cortex and "trabecular bone" on the right and $c \geq b = 0$.

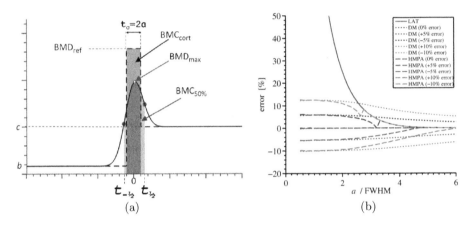

Fig. 1. (a) A profile as a convolution of a piecewise constant cortical function and a Gaussian (scanner PSF), with related notations. (b) Relative thickness estimation error with three algorithms at four error levels in BMD_{ref}: $\pm 5\%$ and $\pm 10\%$ for the range of cortical thickness from "very thin" to "very thick" with Gaussian full width at half maximum (FWHM) equal to 1.5. (Color figure online)

According to the modeled imaging process, the convolution of the piecewise constant function representing the cortex with the imaging PSF equal to $G(t) = \frac{1}{\sqrt{2\pi}\sigma} \exp^{-\frac{t^2}{2\sigma^2}}$ (σ is unknown) produces the ideal measured profile $P(t)$:

$$P(t) = (G * (h + Tr + ST))(t). \tag{2}$$

Using the function $\text{erf}(x) = \frac{2}{\sqrt{\pi}} \int_0^x \exp^{-t^2} dt$ one gets for the model profile:

$$P(t) = \frac{\text{BMD}_{\text{ref}}}{2} \left[\text{erf}\left(\frac{t+a}{\sqrt{2}\sigma}\right) - \text{erf}\left(\frac{t-a}{\sqrt{2}\sigma}\right) \right] + \frac{c}{2} \left[1 + \text{erf}\left(\frac{t-a}{\sqrt{2}\sigma}\right) \right]$$
$$+ \frac{b}{2} \left[1 - \text{erf}\left(\frac{t+a}{\sqrt{2}\sigma}\right) \right]. \tag{3}$$

In the work of Treece et al. [5], the unknown parameters σ, c, and b are recovered as the result of least squares fitting of $P(t)$ with the measured profile, while BMD_{ref} is a model parameter independently estimated from the image data. Here, we propose a method that uses one model parameter, BMD_{ref}, and three parameters measured in the profile (four if $b \neq 0$):

1. c (or $R = \frac{c}{\text{BMD}_{\text{ref}}}$) : mean density of the trabecular part of the profile;
2. BMD_{max} (or $T = \frac{\text{BMD}_{\text{max}}}{\text{BMD}_{\text{ref}}}$) : maximal density value along the profile;
3. $\text{BMC}_{50\%}^{meas}$: BMC-value measured in the profile between cortical boundaries obtained with local adaptive threshold (LAT, also 50%-method).

The values BMD_{max}, c, and b define the 50%-points $t_{-\frac{1}{2}}$ and $t_{\frac{1}{2}}$:

$$P(t_{-\frac{1}{2}}) = \frac{\text{BMD}_{\text{max}} + b}{2}, \quad P(t_{\frac{1}{2}}) = \frac{\text{BMD}_{\text{max}} + c}{2}, \tag{4}$$

where $t_{-\frac{1}{2}}$ lies in the soft tissue compartment (on the "left" side from BMD_{max}) and $t_{\frac{1}{2}}$ – in the trabecular one. Finally, $\text{BMC}_{50\%}^{meas}$ is just an integral of density values between $t_{-\frac{1}{2}}$ and $t_{\frac{1}{2}}$.

2.1   Estimation of the Cortical BMC

Our purpose now is to estimate $\text{BMC}_{50\%}$, i.e., area under the curve (AUC) for the model profile $P(t)$ between two 50%-points, and to compare it with the $\text{BMC}_{\text{cort}} = \text{BMD}_{\text{ref}} \cdot 2a$. Let us denote the primitive of erf(t) as $\text{Er}(t) = \text{terf}(t) + \exp^{-t^2}/\sqrt{\pi}$. Then BMC within two points $-r_1$ and r_2 is the following $\text{AUC}(-r_1, r_2)$:

$$\int_{-r_1}^{r_2} P(t)\, dt = \frac{c\sigma}{\sqrt{2}} \left[\frac{r_1 + r_2}{\sqrt{2}\sigma} + \text{Er}\left(\frac{r_2 - a}{\sqrt{2}\sigma} \right) - \text{Er}\left(\frac{r_1 + a}{\sqrt{2}\sigma} \right) \right] +$$
$$\frac{\text{BMD}_{\text{ref}}\, \sigma}{\sqrt{2}} \left[\text{Er}\left(\frac{r_2 + a}{\sqrt{2}\sigma} \right) - \text{Er}\left(\frac{r_1 - a}{\sqrt{2}\sigma} \right) - \text{Er}\left(\frac{r_2 - a}{\sqrt{2}\sigma} \right) + \text{Er}\left(\frac{r_1 + a}{\sqrt{2}\sigma} \right) \right]. \tag{5}$$

This follows directly from the definitions of $P(t)$ and $\text{Er}(t)$.

We are going to estimate the coordinates r_1 and r_2 of the 50%-points and then substitute them into (5) to get $\text{BMC}_{50\%}$. For this, we first find the ratio $\frac{a}{\sqrt{2}\sigma}$, which we designated as $\bar{a}$, using the equation $P(t_{\text{max}}) = \text{BMD}_{\text{max}}$:

$$\frac{\text{BMD}_{\text{ref}}}{2} \left[\text{erf}\left(\overline{t_{\text{max}}} + \bar{a} \right) - \text{erf}\left(\overline{t_{\text{max}}} - \bar{a} \right) \right] + \frac{c}{2} \left[1 + \text{erf}\left(\overline{t_{\text{max}}} - \bar{a} \right) \right] = \text{BMD}_{\text{max}}, \tag{6}$$

where $\overline{t_{\text{max}}} = t_{\text{max}}/\sqrt{2}\sigma$. The coordinate of the profile peak point, t_{max}, is obtained as an extremal point of the profile curve $(P_t'(t_{\text{max}}) = 0)$: $\overline{t_{\text{max}}} = k/\bar{a}$, where $k = -\frac{1}{4}\ln\left((\text{BMD}_{\text{ref}} - c)/\text{BMD}_{\text{ref}}\right)$. Upon substitution of $\overline{t_{\text{max}}}$ into (6) we obtain an equation for $\bar{a}$ with parameters BMD_{ref}, BMD_{max}, c, and BMD_{max} normalized by BMD_{ref}:

$$\text{erf}\left(k\bar{a}^{-1} + \bar{a} \right) + (R - 1)\text{erf}\left(k\bar{a}^{-1} - \bar{a} \right) - 2T + R = 0. \tag{7}$$

The function on the left hand side of the equation is strictly monotone increasing with respect to $\bar{a}$ and has values of the opposite signs as $\bar{a} \to 0$ and $\bar{a} \to \infty$ and thus has one root only which can be efficiently found with the help of various one-dimensional optimization algorithms.

Having obtained the value of $\bar{a}$, we can estimate the coordinates of the $50\,\%$−points $t_{\pm\frac{1}{2}}$ according to their definition in (4). Here again, we adopt the overline notation $\overline{t_{\pm\frac{1}{2}}}$ for the values $t_{\pm\frac{1}{2}}$ divided by $\sqrt{2}\sigma$:

$$\mathrm{erf}\left(\overline{t_{-\frac{1}{2}}} + \bar{a}\right) + (R-1)\mathrm{erf}\left(\overline{t_{-\frac{1}{2}}} - \bar{a}\right) = T - R, \tag{8}$$

$$\mathrm{erf}\left(\overline{t_{\frac{1}{2}}} + \bar{a}\right) + (R-1)\mathrm{erf}\left(\overline{t_{\frac{1}{2}}} - \bar{a}\right) = T. \tag{9}$$

The function on the left hand side of each of the equations is smooth and has a unique maximum, thus the respective root can be effectively found using one-dimensional (1D) optimization if the search is restricted to the range $(-\infty; \overline{t_{max}})$ for $\overline{t_{-\frac{1}{2}}}$ and $(\overline{t_{max}}; +\infty)$ for $\overline{t_{\frac{1}{2}}}$ (the respective root is unique then).

Now we are in the position to obtain the estimation for the ratio $\frac{\mathrm{BMC}_{50\,\%}}{\mathrm{BMC}_{cort}} =: K$. Denote $\overline{r_1} = \frac{r_1}{\sqrt{2}\sigma} = -\overline{t_{-\frac{1}{2}}}$ and $\overline{r_2} = \frac{r_2}{\sqrt{2}\sigma} = \overline{t_{\frac{1}{2}}}$, then by (5)

$$K = \frac{\mathrm{AUC}(-\overline{r_1}, \overline{r_2})}{2a\mathrm{BMD}_{ref}} = \frac{R}{4\bar{a}}\left[\overline{r_1} + \overline{r_2} + \mathrm{Er}\left(\overline{r_2} - \bar{a}\right) - \mathrm{Er}\left(\overline{r_1} + \bar{a}\right)\right]$$
$$+ \frac{1}{4\bar{a}}\left[\mathrm{Er}\left(\overline{r_2} + \bar{a}\right) - \mathrm{Er}\left(\overline{r_1} - \bar{a}\right) - \mathrm{Er}\left(\overline{r_2} - \bar{a}\right) + \mathrm{Er}\left(\overline{r_1} + \bar{a}\right)\right]. \tag{10}$$

The value of K is then used as a correction factor for $\mathrm{BMC}_{50\,\%}^{meas}$ measured by the $50\,\%$-method, to approximate BMC_{cort} by $\frac{\mathrm{BMC}_{50\,\%}^{meas}}{K}$. Substituting this approximation of BMC_{cort} into (1), we finally obtain the model-based cortical half-thickness:

$$a_{mod} = \frac{\mathrm{BMC}_{50\,\%}^{meas}}{2\mathrm{BMD}_{ref}\,K}. \tag{11}$$

Summarizing, estimation of the cortical thickness is done with the following steps:

1. Obtain $\bar{a}$ as the root of the Eq. (7).
2. Obtain estimated coordinates of the $50\,\%$-points, normalized by $\sqrt{2}\sigma$, as the roots of the Eq. (8), respectively (9).
3. Calculate the BMC correction factor K using (10).
4. Calculate the model-based cortical half-thickness a using (11).

2.2   Hybrid Algorithm and Implementation Details

Given that $a_{50\,\%} \geq a$ (Fig. 1(b)) we add one natural constraint: $a_{mod} \leq a_{50\,\%}$, which, if violated, indicates that $a_{50\,\%}$ by LAT shall be used instead of a_{mod}. Let us call this combined algorithm a hybrid model-based profile analysis (HMPA).

After the profile is set normal to the preliminary segmented periosteal surface and cortical borders are computed, one can use the distance between them as the cortical thickness. However, the thickness value computed this way is over-estimated in general, since even tiny surface roughness renders the profile askew and increases the length of its cortical part. That is why we built a segmentation mask connecting all cortex border points in profiles and measured the thickness at a point as a distance between the outer and inner mask surfaces.

Finally, for the effective implementation one can make use of the fact that there is a functional dependence of the factor K on three parameters only: $T = \mathrm{BMD_{max}}/\mathrm{BMD_{ref}}$, $R = c/\mathrm{BMD_{ref}}$, and $S = b/\mathrm{BMD_{ref}}$. This dependence allows for run-time and size effective implementation as a lookup table.

2.3 Experimental Check of the Accuracy of the Method

The following experiments were conducted to evaluate the method:

1. Simulated profiles for a range of modeled thickness values from 0.5σ up to 7σ. The results of the proposed HMPA-method were compared with that of the 50 %-method [2] and with the deconvolution method (DM) [5]. First, the additive Gaussian noise was simulated corresponding to two exposure levels of 100 and 150 mAs typically used in clinical QCT applications. Second, four levels of the error in $\mathrm{BMD_{ref}}$ were introduced: $\pm 5\,\%$ and $\pm 10\,\%$.
2. CT scans of the European Forearm Phantom (EFP) using Siemens SOMATOM Definition Flash scanner, see examples in Fig. 4. Nine scan protocols were used, which is the number of all combinations of the following scan parameter values: (1) voltage: 120 kV; (2) exposure: 100, 50, and 20 mAs; (3) convolution kernel: B40s (smooth), B50s, and B60s (sharp). Voxel size was $0.3 \times 0.3 \times 1\,\mathrm{mm}^3$ in all reconstructions.

In all these experiments, the ground truth of $\mathrm{BMD_{ref}}$ was known. In practice, one needs to obtain this parameter before starting the cortical thickness estimation algorithm. One can use either simple methods, like 5 % trimmed maximum value in the image, or a more complicated statistical method of Treece et al. [6] for this purpose.

3 Results

The results of cortical thickness estimation with three algorithms (deconvolution, 50 %-method, and the new one) under simulated noise are presented in Fig. 2. Two levels of Gaussian noise were generated roughly corresponding to the noise levels of 150 and 100 mAs, 120 kV, as measured in the calibration phantom.

The effect of over- and underestimation of $\mathrm{BMD_{ref}}$ on the performance of the proposed hybrid method (with analytic estimation (11)) as compared to the deconvolution method (DM) and 50 %-criterion (LAT) is shown in Fig. 1(b).

The proposed algorithm for cortical thickness estimation was implemented within MIAF software [7,8], as well as corresponding binary segmentation of

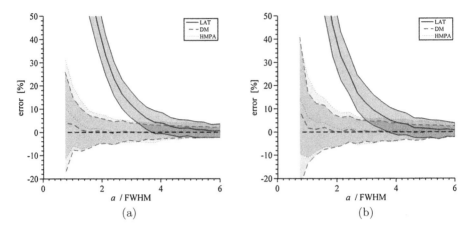

Fig. 2. Relative error of the thickness estimation under simulated noise. For the range of true thickness values (a/FWHM), mean value and standard deviation of the corresponding relative error were computed after three hundred simulations at every value. True reference BMD was used (800 HU), $\sigma = 1.5$, $c = 150$, $b = 0$. (a) Lower noise (30 HU). (b) Higher noise (37 HU)

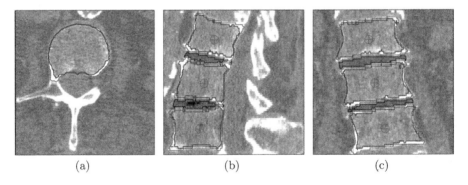

Fig. 3. An example of lumbar spine segmentation of an ex vivo 3D QCT acquisition with voxel size $0.3 \times 0.3 \times 1.3 \, \text{mm}^3$. Periosteal and endosteal cortical borders are shown as well as segmentation of intervertebral disc spaces. Spinous and transverse processes were automatically excluded from the segmentation. (a) L2, axial. (b) L1-L3, sagittal. (c) L1-L3, coronal

the cortex. One example of lumbar spine segmentation for 3D CT acquisition ex vivo is shown in Fig. 3. The results of the EFP segmentation are exemplified in Fig. 4 for two extreme cases: the most noisy one but with highest level of image details and the most smooth one. Finally, the results of cortical thickness estimation based on segmentation of EFP using LAT50, deconvolution, and HMPA methods are summarized in Table 1, where both real BMD_{ref} and "noisy" value of $\text{BMD}_{\text{ref}} \pm 20\%$ were assumed.

4   Discussion

The manuscript presents a model-based approach for the cortical bone segmentation in CT images. Our method shares the main idea and assumption of the constant cortex mineralization with the deconvolution method presented in the works of Treece et al. [5,6]. Both methods give theoretically equivalent results for the ideal profiles and consequently share higher accuracy at the "thin" cortex as compared to the 50 %-method, but also sensitivity to errors in the main model parameter, BMD_{ref}. Exactly this auxiliary parameter, BMD_{ref} distinguishes the parameter set of our method from that of the 50 %-method: BMD_{max}, b, and c. Thus, on the one hand the HMPA-method is the parametric counterpart of the model-based deconvolution method, and on the other hand it is a direct generalization of the 50 %-method to a "thin" cortex case, where the main assumption of the 50 %-method ($\int_{2a}^{\infty} PSF(t)\, dt \approx 0$, see Prevrhal et al. [2]) is not valid. Let us formulate essential differences between the deconvolution method and the proposed one.

First, the method excludes the non-trivial optimization step and gives a solution in the form suitable for analytical investigation (1D root finding steps for $\bar{a}$ and $\overline{t_{\pm\frac{1}{2}}}$ guarantee the correct answer due to nice properties of the corresponding equations). This is achieved due to the usage of few profile metrics instead of the whole curve. Fitting the whole profile curve may be more robust, since not a single value but the whole range is used (see Fig. 2), but on the other hand, optimization for curve fitting is generally subject to local minima, whereas our approach provides a unique solution which allows for effective implementation by means of a lookup table. Moreover, the sensitivity of the deconvolution to errors in BMD_{ref} is greater than that of the new approach, as shown in Fig. 1(b) and Table 1 (for the cases with underestimated BMD_{ref}). Thanks to the lookup table implementation, computation time of the cortical thickness for an EFP acqusition with HMPA, which was less than one minute on a standard PC, was about 20 times less than that with the deconvolution approach.

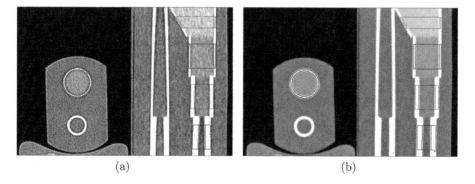

(a)   (b)

Fig. 4. Two CT datasets of the European Forearm Phantom with segmentation contours. For each dataset, two planar reconstructions are shown: axial and sagittal. (a) 120 kV, 20 mAs, sharp kernel B60s. (b) 120 kV, 100 mAs, smooth kernel B40s.

Table 1. Cortical thickness estimation for the European Forearm Phantom (EFP) based on segmentation with local adaptive threshold (LAT), deconvolution (DM), and hybrid model-based profile analysis (HMPA). BMD_{ref} was manually measured in the "cortex" of the shaft.

VOI# (true 2a)	Method	Thickness	100 mAs B40s	B50s	B60s	50 mAs B40s	B50s	B60s	20 mAs B40s	B50s	B60s
1 (0.5 mm)	LAT	$a_{50\%}$,mm	1.58	1.35	1.26	1.60	1.35	1.26	1.60	1.34	1.28
		error,%	216.5	170.3	153.0	220.2	170.6	152.2	220.3	167.9	156.2
	DM	a_{mod}, mm	0.64	0.62	0.63	0.65	0.62	0.65	0.65	0.60	0.62
		error,%	27.4	23.1	25.7	29.4	24.4	29.3	29.6	19.3	23.5
	HMPA	a_{mod}, mm	0.64	0.64	0.65	0.65	0.64	0.66	0.65	0.61	0.65
		error,%	27.7	28.2	30.8	29.3	27.2	31.4	29.7	22.8	29.4
	DM, BMD_{ref} + **20**%	a_{mod}, mm / error,%	0.53	0.50	0.50	0.52	0.50	0.51	0.53	0.49	0.50
		error,%	5.8	-0.7	-0.9	4.9	0.2	2.1	5.8	-2.6	0.0
	HMPA, BMD_{ref} + **20**%	a_{mod}, mm	0.56	0.53	0.54	0.57	0.54	0.55	0.57	0.53	0.54
		error,%	11.4	6.7	7.7	13.2	7.4	10.2	14.3	5.5	8.7
	DM, BMD_{ref} − **20**%	a_{mod}, mm	0.83	0.85	0.86	0.84	0.85	0.86	0.84	0.81	0.83
		error,%	65.4	69.0	71.6	67.9	70.2	71.9	67.8	62.6	66.5
	HMPA, BMD_{ref} − **20**%	a_{mod}, mm	0.81	0.82	0.84	0.83	0.84	0.85	0.83	0.81	0.84
		error,%	62.8	64.0	68.8	65.4	68.1	69.2	65.2	62.4	67.4
2 (1 mm)	LAT	$a_{50\%}$,mm	1.59	1.30	1.20	1.60	1.31	1.23	1.60	1.30	1.19
		error,%	58.7	30.2	20.5	59.5	30.6	22.8	60.5	29.5	18.9
	Deconv	a_{mod}, mm	1.04	1.07	1.02	1.05	1.08	1.03	1.05	1.05	1.00
		error,%	4.3	7.1	1.8	4.9	7.5	2.6	5.3	5.1	0.3
	HMPA	a_{mod}, mm	1.02	0.99	0.97	1.04	1.00	0.98	1.03	0.99	0.95
		error,%	1.8	-0.8	-3.2	3.7	-0.3	-2.4	3.1	-0.6	-4.7
	DM, BMD_{ref} + **20**%	a_{mod}, mm	0.87	0.91	0.89	0.87	0.92	0.90	0.87	0.90	0.89
		error,%	-13.1	-9.5	-10.6	-13.1	-7.8	-9.5	-12.8	-10.4	-11.4
	HMPA, BMD_{ref} + **20**%	a_{mod}, mm	0.83	0.92	0.91	0.83	0.93	0.91	0.84	0.91	0.90
		error,%	-17.2	-8.0	-8.7	-16.6	-7.2	-8.8	-16.4	-9.5	-9.6
	DM, BMD_{ref} − **20**%	a_{mod}, mm	1.27	1.19	1.14	1.28	1.19	1.14	1.28	1.17	1.13
		error,%	26.9	18.6	14.1	27.6	19.4	14.2	28.0	16.8	13.1
	HMPA, BMD_{ref} − **20**%	a_{mod}, mm	1.24	1.08	1.01	1.24	1.08	1.01	1.24	1.08	1.00
		error,%	23.9	8.1	0.6	23.8	8.4	0.6	24.5	8.2	-0.4
	BMD_{ref}, HU		1196	1218	1235	1190	1207	1219	1187	1241	1246

Second, the proposed analytical approach eliminates σ, which is an essential parameter for the deconvolution method. σ may be estimated from phantom measurements but it is a non-trivial and/or not very accurate procedure due to the fact that the CT-scanner PSF is not really a Gaussian, especially for sharp reconstruction kernels, and also since various imaging artefacts, such as field inhomogeneity and beam hardening, will probably lead to somewhat different σ values than those applicable to the in vivo patient acquisitions. Also, additional parameters make the curve fitting more error prone for the noisy profiles in general.

Third, we combine the advantages of an accurate "thin" cortex measurement provided by the model-based approach and robust and accurate estimation of the "thick" cortex provided by the 50 %-method, which is independent of the errors in BMD_{ref}, within a hybrid approach. Essentially, switching to the 50 %-estimation is conservative: the resulting accuracy error is generally not higher than in the case when no 50 %-method was switched on at all.

What is left beyond the scope of the article, is the analysis of real patient data obtained with various resolution levels, such as standard QCT and high-resolution CT (as a ground truth), as it was done by Treece et al. [5]. Note however that high resolution data can be considered as ground truth to only a limited degree since inhomogeneous cortex structure is revealed at high resolution (porosity, adjacent trabeculae etc.) which makes its appearance very different from that at the low resolution. In this view, validation with phantom segmentation may be more informative; phantom measurements in our experiments were rather accurate even for very high noise levels. Finally, sensitivity analysis with respect to errors in parameters was not shown, although it can be easily done using the presented formula for a.

References

1. Roux, J., Wegrzyn, J., Arlot, M., Guyen, O., Delmas, P., Chapurlat, R., Bouxsein, M.: Contribution of trabecular and cortical components to biomechanical behavior of human vertebrae: an ex vivo study. J. Bone Miner. Res. **25**(2), 356–361 (2010)
2. Prevrhal, S., Engelke, K., Kalender, W.: Accuracy limits for the determination of cortical width and density: the influence of object size and CT imaging parameters. Phys. Med. Biol. **44**(3), 751–764 (1999)
3. Buie, H., Campbell, G., Klinck, R., MacNeil, J., Boyd, S.: Automatic segmentation of cortical and trabecular compartments based on a dual threshold technique for in vivo micro-CT bone analysis. Bone **41**(4), 505–515 (2007)
4. Hangartner, T.: Thresholding technique for accurate analysis of density and geometry in QCT, pQCT and μCT images. J. Musculoskelet. Neuronal Interact. **7**(1), 9–16 (2007)
5. Treece, G., Gee, A., Mayhew, P., Poole, K.: High resolution cortical bone thickness measurement from clinical CT data. Med. Image Anal. **14**(3), 276–290 (2010)
6. Treece, G., Poole, K., Gee, A.: Imaging the femoral cortex: thickness, density and mass from clinical CT. Med. Image Anal. **16**(5), 952–965 (2012)
7. Mastmeyer, A., Engelke, K., Fuchs, C., Kalender, W.: A hierarchical 3D segmentation method and the definition of vertebral body coordinate systems for QCT of the lumbar spine. Med. Image Anal. **10**(4), 560–577 (2006)
8. Kang, Y., Engelke, K., Kalender, W.: A new accurate and precise 3-D segmentation method for skeletal structures in volumetric CT data. IEEE Trans. Med. Imaging **22**(5), 586–598 (2003)

Multi-atlas Segmentation with Joint Label Fusion of Osteoporotic Vertebral Compression Fractures on CT

Yinong Wang[1], Jianhua Yao[1(✉)], Holger R. Roth[1], Joseph E. Burns[2],
and Ronald M. Summers[1]

[1] Imaging Biomarkers and Computer-Aided Diagnosis Laboratory,
Department of Radiology and Imaging Sciences, Clinical Center,
National Institutes of Health, Bethesda, USA
{yinong.wang,holger.roth}@nih.gov, {jyao,rsummers}@cc.nih.gov
[2] Department of Radiological Sciences, University of California,
Irvine School of Medicine, Irvine, USA
jburns@uci.edu

Abstract. The precise and accurate segmentation of the vertebral column is essential in the diagnosis and treatment of various orthopedic, neurological, and oncological traumas and pathologies. Segmentation is especially challenging in the presence of pathology such as vertebral compression fractures. In this paper, we propose a method to produce segmentations for osteoporotic compression fractured vertebrae by applying a multi-atlas joint label fusion technique for clinical computed tomography (CT) images. A total of 170 thoracic and lumbar vertebrae were evaluated using atlases from five patients with varying degrees of spinal degeneration. In an osteoporotic cohort of bundled atlases, registration provided an average Dice coefficient and mean absolute surface distance of $92.7 \pm 4.5\%$ and $0.32 \pm 0.13\,\mathrm{mm}$ for osteoporotic vertebrae, respectively, and $90.9 \pm 3.0\%$ and $0.36 \pm 0.11\,\mathrm{mm}$ for compression fractured vertebrae.

1 Introduction

Vertebral compression fractures (VCFs), which often result from osteoporosis, constitute nearly half the number of clinical osteoporotic fractures. Affecting nearly 1.5 million people in the United States each year, these compression fractures can often result in severe and debilitating pain [1]. Loss in height and the deformity of the vertebral body, with associated changes in the curvature of the spine, can result in a reduction in the spine's effectiveness in weight-bearing, movement, and support. VCFs are typically diagnosed via qualitative visual review, using imaging modalities such as radiography and CT. However, clinical time restrictions prevent detailed processing of data and comprehensive characterization of individual fractures using conventional, manual segmentation methods. Automated methods for identifying and segmenting vertebrae have been applied to the characterization of thoracolumbar spine in patients with

T. Vrtovec et al. (Eds.): CSI 2015, LNCS 9402, pp. 74–84, 2016.
DOI: 10.1007/978-3-319-41827-8_7

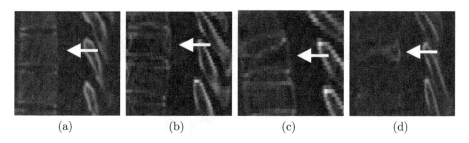

(a)   (b)   (c)   (d)

Fig. 1. Sagittal view of vertebrae with varying severities of vertebral compression fracture (VCF): (a) no VCF; (b) grade 1; (c) grade 2; (d) grade 3. Arrows point to vertebra of interest. Note increasing osteopenia (decreasing bone density) with higher grades.

non-osteopenia spines [2]. However, it has remained unexplored whether similar applications for osteoporotic patients would be of benefit in the evaluation of cases of trauma and pathology such as vertebral compression fractures.

Accurate segmentation of lumbar and thoracic vertebrae can lead to improved identification and quantitative characterization of VCFs, and have potential to guide fracture treatment and management. Additionally, improved segmentation provides a means for extracting features, such as bone density and anatomic landmarks that allow for a better understanding of the integrity of the spine [3]. VCFs are typically graded manually using Genant scoring, which is based on thresholds for percentage height loss relative to adjacent vertebra [4]. Examples of vertebral compression fractures of different levels of severity are shown in Fig. 1.

A number of vertebra segmentation algorithms for computed tomography (CT) images have been proposed. Previous methods that integrated vertebra detection, identification, and segmentation into a single framework were applied primarily to healthy vertebrae [2]. Ibragimov et al. [5] built landmark-based shape representations of vertebrae and aligned models to specific vertebrae in CT images using game theory. An atlas-based method that utilized groupwise segmentation of five vertebrae with majority voting label fusion was proposed by Forsberg [6] to segment healthy vertebrae in a vertebra segmentation challenge[1] [2]. Fusing information from multiple manually segmented atlases allows for greater acuity to be obtained in the visualization of vertebral compression fractures. In this paper, we present a method to produce segmentations of the osteoporotic spine, especially for vertebrae with compression fractures through a multi-atlas local appearance, similarity weighted joint label fusion technique for clinical CT images [7].

2   Methods

We propose a multi-atlas joint label fusion framework for spine segmentation on a vertebral basis (Fig. 2). Each vertebra was localized by the automatic generation

---

[1] http://csi-workshop.weebly.com.

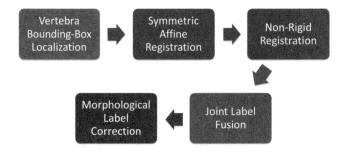

Fig. 2. Workflow for our implementation.

of a bounding box that provided greater local anatomical coherence between images and allowed for more precise image registration. An intensity-based non-rigid B-spline registration technique with affine initialization was used to capture the geometric variability exhibited by vertebrae [8]. Upon completing registration, a set of manually segmented atlases was deformed to the target space using the computed transformations. All transformed atlases were then combined using a joint label fusion technique that utilized local appearance similarity between each registration result to determine the label [7]. Lastly, a morphological label correction step was applied to correct over-segmented results that failed to be properly localized to a single vertebra. This step was used to correct under-segmented results that emerged from the relatively decreased spinal bone density in the osteoporotic test cohort.

2.1 Multi-atlas Registration

The initial location of the vertebra and subsequent bounding box localization was obtained using a fully automatic algorithm reported in the work of Yao et al. [9]. The algorithm is based on adaptive thresholding, watershed, directed graph search, curved reformation, and anatomic vertebra models. The registration was conducted in two stages: symmetric affine transformation for initialization, followed by dense non-rigid registration. Using a floating image I_2 from the atlas and a target image I_1, a displacement field was computed to estimate an affine transformation A that maximized the intensity similarity between floating and target CT images [8]. The resulting output image I was computed by applying $I_1 \doteq I = I_2 \circ A$ where A was then applied to all atlas labels.

After obtaining the initialized affine transformation results, a non-rigid B-spline transformation T was computed that maximized the normalized mutual information (NMI) between the floating and target images [8]. NMI between images I_1 and $I_2 \circ T$ is computed by using their marginal entropies H and joint entropies $H(I_1, I_2 \circ T)$ as a measure of alignment as

$$NMI = \frac{H(I_1) + H(I_2 \circ T)}{H(I_1, I_2 \circ T)}. \tag{1}$$

The non-rigid transformation was then optimized on a global and local scale by maximizing the following cost-function

$$C = (1 - \alpha)\, NMI - \alpha P. \tag{2}$$

The penalty term P uses bending energy to restrict the amount of deformation to achieve physically realistic smooth transformations that penalize only non-rigid registrations [10]:

$$
\begin{aligned}
P = \frac{1}{N} \sum_{\boldsymbol{x} \in \Omega} &\left[\left[\left(\frac{\delta^2 T(\boldsymbol{x})}{\delta x^2} \right)^2 + \left(\frac{\delta^2 T(\boldsymbol{x})}{\delta y^2} \right)^2 + \left(\frac{\delta^2 T(\boldsymbol{x})}{\delta z^2} \right)^2 \right] \right. \\
&+ \left. 2 \cdot \left[\left(\frac{\delta^2 T(\boldsymbol{x})}{\delta xy} \right)^2 + \left(\frac{\delta^2 T(\boldsymbol{x})}{\delta yz} \right)^2 + \left(\frac{\delta^2 T(\boldsymbol{x})}{\delta xz} \right)^2 \right] \right].
\end{aligned}
\tag{3}
$$

Weight factor α controls the penalty term; the default value of $\alpha = 0.005$ was used, which has been shown to work well for medical images [8]. Since the registration methods are computationally heavy, a graphics processing unit (GPU)-accelerated solution, NiftyReg[2] was used. Registration produced a transformed set of floating images and segmentation labels which have been warped to the space of the target images.

Two configurations of atlases were explored in our registration experiments: a single vertebra atlas and a three-vertebra atlas, where a vertebra is bundled with the ones directly above and below. T1 and L5 vertebra were bundled with the nearest two thoracic and lumbar vertebrae, respectively. The bundled atlas was a means to preserve the interface between adjacent vertebrae and to prevent conflicting segmentation.

2.2   Joint Label Fusion

Since individual registrations to multiple atlases following the affine and non-rigid transformations can yield drastically different results, a joint fusion method (JLF) was applied to the labels in order to enforce region coherence. Since all atlases shared common structures and similar appearances, independent errors in the final segmentation result were minimized following JLF [7]. With a measure of registration success for each transformed atlas, a weighted voting scheme achieved optimal label fusion that minimizes the expectation of combined label differences. Joint label fusion achieves consensus segmentation

$$\bar{S}(x) = \sum_{i=1}^{n} w_i(x) S_i(x), \tag{4}$$

based on individual voting weights $w_i(x)$ and segmentations $S_i(x)$. Weights were determined by

$$w_x = \frac{M_x^{-1} \cdot 1_n}{1_n^t M_x^{-1} 1_n}, \tag{5}$$

---

[2] http://cmictig.cs.ucl.ac.uk/wiki/index.php/NiftyReg.

where $1_n = [1; 1; \ldots; 1]$ is a vector of size n and M_x is the pairwise dependency matrix that estimates the likelihood of two atlases both producing wrong segmentations on a per-voxel basis for the target image. The end result was a segmentation determined by the probability distribution of propagated labels provided by multi-atlas registrations.

2.3 Morphological Label Correction

After joint label fusion, post processing measures were taken to correct segmentation error and to refine the boundaries of the binary label result. First, morphological operators and connected components were applied to remove isolated islands and to close holes. Next, collision detection and correction steps were taken to correct segmentations where a voxel was assigned to two vertebrae. A perceptron linear classifier based on the voxel intensity difference and the distance relative to the centers of the vertebrae was applied to determine which vertebra to which the voxel belonged. The weights for intensity difference and distance were set empirically. Finally, a Laplacian level set algorithm was employed to refine the segmentation [11].

3   Experiments and Results

3.1 Dataset

The dataset used in this experiment was obtained from the University of California, Irvine Medical Center. The dataset contained spine CT data from 10 patients, five from a healthy cohort ranging in age from 20 to 34 years (27 ± 5 years), and five from an osteoporotic cohort ranging in age from 59 to 82 years (73 ± 9 years) that have been previously identified to have at least one vertebral compression fracture. The studies were performed with spine CT protocol, with in-plane resolution ranging from 0.31 to 0.45 mm, and slice thickness ranging from 1 to 2 mm.

A total of 170 thoracic and lumbar vertebrae were evaluated. Among them, 16 vertebrae were previously identified with compression fracture (one with grade 1, ten with grade 2, and five with grade 3). All thoracic and lumbar vertebrae were manually segmented to build atlases for the validation our algorithm. Figure 3 shows reconstructed images from the healthy and osteoporotic data sets and their manual segmentations in a sagittal imaging plane.

3.2 Evaluation Methodology

The Dice coefficient (DC) and mean absolute surface distance (ASD) were used for evaluating the accuracy of segmentation. They are defined as

$$DC = \frac{2 \cdot |GT \cap S|}{|GT| + |S|} \times 100\,\%, \tag{6}$$

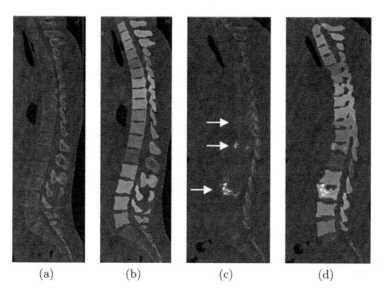

(a)   (b)   (c)   (d)

Fig. 3. Sagittal views of spine atlases used. (a) Healthy spine (20 years old) with (b) manual segmentation. (c) Osteoporotic spine (78 years old) with (d) manual segmentation. Arrows point to fractured vertebrae.

$$ASD = \frac{1}{|V_S|} \sum_{i=1}^{|V_S|} \|d_i\left(V_s, V_{GT}\right)\|, \tag{7}$$

where GT and S refer to the ground truth and the computed segmentations respectively, V refers to the volume, and d_i refers to the distance between the nearest surface voxels of each label [12]. The vertebrae were partitioned into four substructures using the algorithm in the work of Yao et al. [3]: vertebral body (VB), left transverse process (LTP), right transverse process (RTP) and spinous process (SP). Performance was evaluated on both the whole vertebra and the vertebral body substructure.

Performance was evaluated for either using healthy or osteoporotic cases as atlases. We compared three experimental setups: (1) use of healthy vertebrae as atlases to segment the osteoporotic vertebrae with compression fractures (H2D), (2) use of the osteoporotic vertebrae as atlases for segmentation of osteoporotic vertebrae (D2D), and (3) use of a three-vertebra bundled atlas using osteoporotic data (BD2D). A leave-one-vertebra-out scheme was adopted in the second and third experiments.

3.3   Results

Experiments were conducted to assess the segmentation of healthy and osteoporotic vertebrae and vertebrae with compression fracture. Figure 4 shows the visual segmentation result at each step of the process. Individual registrations

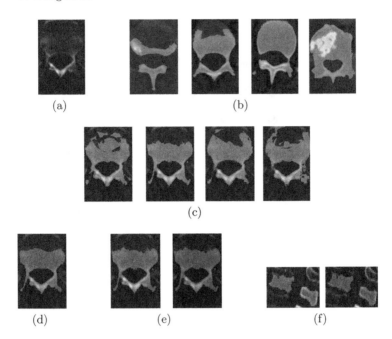

Fig. 4. Segmentation results at each step of the process: (a) Original image; (b1) − (b4) atlas labels; (c1) − (c4) registration results; (d) ground truth segmentation; (e1),(f1) joint label fusion; (e2),(f2) corrected result in axial and sagittal views.

using GPU-based NiftyReg were completed with a runtime of 5 minutes each, with an additional 5 minutes for the label fusion [8]. Table 1 lists the characteristics (volume and density) of osteoporotic vertebrae at different grades of compression fracture and the segmentation performance in different experimental setups.

BD2D setup performed better than both H2D and D2D especially for fractured vertebrae as shown in Table 1, suggesting that the bundled osteoporotic atlases provided the best registration results. However, the performance on grade 3 compression fractures was not on the same level as those of grades 1 and 2. A paired t-test showed statistically significant improvement in the DC and mean ASD when using BD2D instead of H2D atlas in all metrics of segmentation performance ($p < 0.001$).

Table 2 shows the segmentation performance on both the whole vertebra and the vertebral body using the three groups of atlases before and after morphological label correction. While the DC was higher for the whole vertebra for all atlas registration groups, the mean ASD performed better on just the vertebral body substructure. Depending on the atlas and the segmentation performance metric used, the morphological label correction improved results over the label fusion alone. However, using BD2D, the improvements seen in the DC and mean ASD in both the whole vertebra and vertebra body substructure were statistically significant ($p < 0.05$).

Table 1. Comparison of upper thoracic (UT), lower thoracic (LT), lumbar (L), non-fracture (NF), grades $1-3$ (G1, G2, G3) compression fracture, VCF, and all vertebrae. Mean and standard deviation (in parenthesis) of segmentation volume (cm^3), density (HU), Dice coefficient (DC) (%) and absolute surface distance (ASD) (mm) of refined (-r) H2D, D2D, and BD2D setups are reported. Best performing methods are bolded.

	No Vert	Vol.	Den.	DC H2D-r	DC D2D-r	DC BD2D-r	ASD H2D-r	ASD D2D-r	ASD BD2D-r
UT	30	21	259	90.6	91.3	92.5	0.33	0.32	0.29
		(3.7)	(48)	(4.7)	(4.9)	(1.5)	(0.16)	(0.15)	(0.06)
LT	30	33	274	92.4	91.9	93.0	0.34	0.37	0.34
		(6.7)	(96)	(3.6)	(3.4)	(2.8)	(0.10)	(0.13)	(0.10)
L	25	56	267	91.5	93.5	92.5	0.42	0.37	0.35
		(8.1)	(86)	(10.5)	(4.5)	(7.7)	(0.40)	(0.35)	(0.21)
NF	69	36	254	92.0	92.6	93.0	0.35	0.34	0.31
		(16)	(52)	(7.1)	(4.4)	(4.7)	(0.27)	(0.24)	(0.14)
G1	1	22	216	88.3	92.4	92.2	0.31	0.34	0.39
G2	10	31	259	91.0	92.3	92.6	0.32	0.30	0.29
		(11)	(41)	(2.7)	(1.3)	(1.1)	(0.07)	(0.05)	(0.04)
G3	5	39	465	86.2	86.1	87.6	0.55	0.53	0.50
		(16)	(160)	(3.8)	(3.0)	(3.6)	(0.09)	(0.08)	(0.08)
VCF	16	33	321	89.3	90.4	**91.0**	0.39	0.37	**0.36**
		(12)	(134)	(3.7)	(3.5)	**(3.2)**	(0.13)	(0.12)	**(0.11)**
All	85	35	267	91.5	92.1	**92.7**	0.36	0.35	**0.32**
		(15)	(78)	(6.6)	(4.3)	**(4.5)**	(0.25)	(0.23)	**(0.13)**

4 Discussion

The multi-atlas joint label fusion segmentation method presented in this paper provides a robust framework for the segmentation and analysis of osteoporotic spine and vertebral compression fractures. Compared to prior literature which used multi-atlas joint label fusion techniques for healthy spine [2], our method produced similar or better performance, as measured by DC, for both non-fractured osteoporotic vertebrae (93.0 %) and compression fractured vertebrae (91.0 %). A similar pattern was observed in the mean ASD where we obtained a mean ASD of 0.31 mm and 0.36 mm for non-fractured and fractured vertebrae, respectively. The same five osteoporotic cases were re-evaluated by the techniques used in the work of Yao et al. [13]. The two best performing methods, one of which was not fully-automated and used statistical shape model deformation and B-spline relaxation [14], and one similar to ours that used multi-atlas registrations on bundles of five vertebrae with basic majority voting label fusion [6], produced similar overall DC of 89.8 % and 89.7 % and ASD of 0.64 mm

Table 2. Mean and standard deviation of Dice coefficient (DC) (%) and absolute surface distance (ASD) (mm) for whole vertebra and vertebral body (VB) using JLF of H2D, D2D, BD2D and refined results. Two statistical tests were conducted: comparison of (1) each atlas type with its refined (-r) segmentations and (2) H2D-r and D2D-r with BD2D-r. Varying levels of significance in the first test are marked by asterisks, where $*$ indicates $p \leq 0.05$, $**$ $p \leq 0.01$, and $***$ $p \leq 0.001$. Significance of $p \leq 0.05$ in the second test is indicated by §.

	DC	DC_VB	ASD	ASD_VB
H2D	91.2 (6.8)	88.0 (21.1)	0.35 (0.17)	0.33 (0.14)
H2D-r	91.5* (6.6)	88.7** (18.3)	0.36 (0.25)	0.32 (0.11)
D2D	92.0 (4.4)	89.2 (17.7)	0.33 (0.16)	0.31 (0.14)
D2D-r	92.1 (4.3)	89.4*** (17.7)	0.35 (0.23)	0.32*** (0.15)
BD2D	92.5 (4.4)	89.5 (17.9)	0.31 (0.10)	0.30 (0.09)
BD2D-r	92.7**§ (4.5)	89.7**§ (18.0)	0.32*§ (0.13)	0.30***§ (0.10)

and 0.86 mm respectively. Our technique, which utilized multi-atlas registrations on bundles of three vertebrae with joint label fusion based on local similarity appearance with a weighting scheme and additional morphological label corrections, performed at a DC of 92.7 % and ASD of 0.32 mm.

Certain metrics in our algorithm can be selected and further optimized to improve performance. In image registration, the local normalized correlation coefficient (LNCC) could be used instead of NMI within NiftyReg [8], assuming that a linear relationship exists between the intensities of the voxels of the floating and target images. The weight factor α can be varied to determine the best value to use on CT images, as the default value was optimized for intermodality registrations of medical images. In addition, the cases chosen for these experiments may not have fully captured the variability of morphology in the osteoporotic population. More cases and optimized atlas selection could produce a segmentation algorithm than can be applied to a more robust population of osteoporotic individuals.

Based on results in Tables 1 and 2, segmentation performance on grade 3 compression fractures was not as high as those on grades 1 and 2. One potential reason for this is the markedly elevated intensities observed in the grade 3 VCFs as a result of injected surgical cement in three of the five fractured vertebrae. Additional fractured vertebrae are necessary to increase and test the robustness of the algorithm, as there were only 16 VCFs total, of which only one grade 1 in the test cohort.

The average DC was higher when evaluating the whole vertebrae than on a single vertebral body. However, the opposite was true when examining the mean ASD. This is likely the result of evaluating smaller and less variable regions at the surface of the vertebral body rather than more variable regions across the entire vertebra.

5 Conclusion

In this paper, we present a robust method for segmenting osteoporotic compression fractures. Despite significantly greater variability in the morphology of compression fractured spines, we have shown that optimization of existing techniques for non-osteopenia spines can yield similar or better performance for segmentation of osteoporotic spines. With these improved segmentations, morphological features of osteoporotic compression fractured vertebrae can be better characterized for clinical applications. The extraction of features through an improved segmentation result may also provide means for better treatment and management of spinal disease.

Acknowledgements. This research was supported in part by the Intramural Research Program of National Institutes of Health Clinical Center.

References

1. Riggs, B., Melton III, L.: The worldwide problem of osteoporosis: insights afforded by epidemiology. Bone **17**(5 Suppl.), 505–511 (1995)
2. Yao, J., Li, S.: Report of vertebra segmentation challenge in 2014 MICCAI Workshop on computational spine imaging. In: Yao, J., et al. (eds.) CSI 2014. LNCVB, vol. 20, pp. 247–259. Springer, Switzerland (2015)
3. Yao, J., Burns, J., Getty, S., Stieger, J., Summers, R.: Automated extraction of anatomic landmarks on vertebrae based on anatomic knowledge and geometrical constraints. In: Proceedings of 11th IEEE International Symposium on Biomedical Imaging, ISBI 2014, pp. 397–400. IEEE (2014)
4. Genant, H., Wu, C., van Kuijk, C., Nevitt, M.: Vertebral fracture assessment using a semiquantitative technique. J. Bone Miner. Res. **8**(9), 1137–1148 (1993)
5. Ibragimov, B., Likar, B., Pernuš, F., Vrtovec, T.: Shape representation for efficient landmark-based segmentation in 3-D. IEEE Trans. Med. Imaging **33**(4), 861–874 (2014)
6. Forsberg, D.: Atlas-based registration for accurate segmentation of thoracic and lumbar vertebrae in CT data. In: Yao, J., et al. (eds.) CSI 2014. LNCVB, vol. 20, pp. 49–59. Springer, Switzerland (2015)
7. Wang, H., Suh, J., Das, S., Pluta, J., Craige, C., Yushkevich, P.: Multi-atlas segmentation with joint label fusion. IEEE Trans. Pattern Anal. Mach. Intell. **35**(3), 611–623 (2013)
8. Modat, M., Ridgway, G., Taylor, Z., Lehmann, M., Barnes, J., Hawkes, D., Fox, N., Ourselin, S.: Fast free-form deformation using graphics processing units. Comput. Methods Programs Biomed. **98**(3), 278–284 (2010)
9. Yao, J., óConnor, S., Summers, R.: Automated spinal column extraction and partitioning. In: Proceedings of 3rd IEEE International Symposium on Biomedical Imaging, ISBI 2006, pp. 390–393. IEEE (2006)
10. Rueckert, D., Sonoda, L., Hayes, C., Hill, D., Leach, M., Hawkes, D.: Nonrigid registration using free-form deformations: application to breast MR images. IEEE Trans. Med. Imaging **18**(8), 712–721 (1999)

11. Hui, H., Jionghui, J.: Laplacian operator based level set segmentation algorithm for medical images. In: Proceedings of 2nd International Congress on Image and Signal Processing, CISP 2009, pp. 1–5. IEEE (2009)
12. Dice, L.: Measures of the amount of ecologic association between species. Ecology **26**(3), 297–302 (1945)
13. Yao, J., Burns, J., Forsberg, D., Seitel, A., Rasoulian, A., Abolmaesumi, P., Hammernik, K., Urschler, M., Ibragimov, B., Korez, R., Vrtovec, T., Castro-Mateos, I., Pozo, J., Frangi, A., Summers, R., Li, S.: A multi-center milestone study of clinical vertebral CT segmentation. Comput. Med. Imaging Graph. **49**, 16–28 (2016)
14. Castro-Mateos, I., Pozo, J., Lazary, A., Frangi, A.: 3D vertebra segmentation by feature selection active shape model. In: Yao, J., et al. (eds.) CSI 2014. LNCVB, vol. 20, pp. 241–245. Springer, Switzerland (2015)

Statistical Shape Model Construction of Lumbar Vertebrae and Intervertebral Discs in Segmentation for Discectomy Surgery Simulation

Rabia Haq[1(✉)], Joshua Cates[2], David A. Besachio[3], Roderick C. Borgie[3], and Michel A. Audette[1]

[1] Old Dominion University, Norfolk, USA
{rhaqx001,maudette}@odu.edu
[2] University of Utah, Salt Lake City, USA
cates@sci.utah.edu
[3] Naval Medical Center Portsmouth, Portsmouth, USA
{david.besachio,roderick.borgie}@med.navy.mil

Abstract. Discectomy procedure simulations require patient-specific and robust three-dimensional representation of vertebral and intervertebral disc structures, as well as existing pathology, of the lumbar spine. Prior knowledge, such as expected shape and variation within a sample population, can be incorporated through statistical shape models to optimize the image segmentation process. This paper describes a framework for construction of statistical shape models (SSMs) of nine L1 vertebrae and eight L1-L2 intervertebral discs from computed tomography and magnetic resonance (MR) images respectively. The generated SSMs are utilized as a reference for knowledge-based priors to optimize coarse-to-fine multi-surface segmentation of vertebrae and intervertebral discs in volumetric MR images. Correspondence between instances within each model has been established using entropy-based energy minimization of particles on the image surfaces, which is independent of any reference bias or surface parameterization techniques. The resulting shape models faithfully capture variability within the first seven principal modes.

1 Introduction

According to the Global Burden of Disease study [1,2], lower back pain is the single leading cause of disability worldwide. Imaging studies indicate that 40 % of patients suffering from chronic back pain showed symptoms of intervertebral disc degeneration (IDD) [3]. Primary treatment for lower back pain consists of non-surgical treatment methods. If non-surgical treatments are ineffective, a surgical procedure may be required to treat IDD, a procedure known as spinal discectomy. Approximately 300,000 discectomy procedures, over 90 % of all spinal surgical procedures [4,5], are performed each year in the United States alone, totaling up to $11.25 billion in cost per year.

© Springer International Publishing Switzerland 2016
T. Vrtovec et al. (Eds.): CSI 2015, LNCS 9402, pp. 85–96, 2016.
DOI: 10.1007/978-3-319-41827-8_8

Discectomy procedure simulation requires patient-specific and robust three-dimensional (3D) representation of vertebral and intervertebral disc structures, as well as existing pathology, of the lumbar spine. Although lumbar vertebral structures have high variability, the prominent features of the bone are consistent within a sample population. This facilitates the incorporation of a statistical shape model with expected variations into a volumetric image segmentation framework. Low image resolution and image artifacts, such as image noise, make biomedical volumetric image segmentation a challenge. Ambiguous image intensity results in incorrect, or even disconnected, boundary detection of the structure of interest. Prior knowledge, such as expected shape and variance within a sample population, can be incorporated through statistical shape models to optimize the image segmentation process.

This paper describes a framework for the construction of statistical shape models (SSMs) of L1 vertebrae and L1-L2 intervertebral discs from computed tomography (CT) and magnetic resonance (MR) images of respectively of healthy subjects. The generated SSMs are utilized as a reference for knowledge-based priors to optimize segmentation of vertebrae and intervertebral discs in volumetric MR images. These shape models can be incorporated into a controlled-resolution deformable segmentation model of the lumbar spine. Incorporation of strong shape priors would facilitate quantification and analysis of shape variations across healthy subjects. It is aimed as a tool for improving spine segmentation results that can be utilized as part of an anatomical input to an interactive spine surgery training simulator, especially a discectomy procedure [6].

Statistical shape models from nine L1 vertebrae and eight L1-L2 intervertebral discs have been generated to be utilized as shape priors during spine segmentation from volumetric MR images. Correspondence between instances within each model has been established using entropy-based point placement on the image surfaces [7–9], which is independent of any reference bias or surface parameterization techniques. The rest of the paper is as follows: Sect. 2 provides an overview of the correspondence and active shape model construction methods; Sect. 3 describes the initial shape model results for vertebrae and intervertebral discs. Finally, Sect. 4 presents a conclusion and future improvements of the implemented method.

2   Method

2.1   Image Dataset and Preprocessing

Datasets provided by the SpineWeb initiative have been utilized for generating shape models of an L1 vertebra and an L1-L2 intervetebral disc. Volumetric CT scans of healthy subjects, along with binary masks, of nine anonymized patients [10] were used for model construction of L1 vertebra. The CT scans and binary masks had a resolution of $0.2 \times 0.3 \times 1 \, mm^3$. In addition, expert segmentations of the L1-L2 interveterbral disc of eight anonymized patients, with $2.0 \times 1.25 \times 1.25 \, mm^3$ resolution [11], were preprocessed as input to the correspondence and shape model construction method.

These binary images were initially aligned along the first principal mode, and any aliasing artifacts were removed during image preprocessing. The fast marching method was applied to generate distance maps of the binary images, which were used for 3D surface reconstruction and establish correspondence between instances of both vertebra and disc shape models.

2.2   Correspondence Establishment

Correspondence establishment is the process of finding a set of points on one two-dimensional (2D) contour or 3D surface that can be mapped to the same set of points in another image. Anatomically meaningful and correct correspondences are of utmost importance, as they ensure correct shape parametrization and shape representation. This can be achieved by co-registering manual landmarks onto the shape boundary in 2D shape space but is challenging in 3D space. Anatomical landmarks are points of correspondence on each shape that match within a sample population [12], which may be manually or automatically placed. Correspondence landmarking may entail identifying matching parts between 3D anatomical structures, which is challenging due to inherent variability within geometry or shape of the anatomical structure across a population [13,14]. Therefore, landmark placement to establish correspondence for robust statistical analysis is a significant task.

According to Heimann et al. [13], a number of methods for correspondence establishment are feasible, where a generic template mesh is registered onto a set of instances through model-to-model or model-to-image registration to achieve a set of instances with automatic point-to-point correspondences through distance [15]. However, this method introduces a bias through selection of a reference topology [16,17]. To mitigate the reference bias, Rasoulian et al. [18,19] utilized forward group-wise registration to establish probabilistic point-to-point correspondences to generate 3D training shapes of L2 vertebrae. Similarly, Mutsvangwa et al. [20] employed rigid and non-rigid registration of pointsets, and implemented a probabilistic principal component analysis (PCA) to mitigate outlier effects of a 3D scapula model. Vrtovec et al. [21] established correspondences through a hierarchical elastic mesh-to-image registration of an extracted reference across 25 lumbar vertebral image volumes. Kaus et al. [22] rigidly aligned a reference triangular mesh to training shapes and then utilized discrete deformable models to locally adapt the reference mesh to segmented volumes, thus propagating the reference pointset across 32 vertebral images. Lorenz et al. [23] performed curvature-adaptive landmark-guided warping and mesh relaxation of a reference mesh across a set of 31 lumbar vertebral image volumes for 3D statistical model construction. Becker et al. [24] parameterized 14 lumbar vertebral shapes to a rectangle by utilizing a graph embedding method, and reduced mesh distortion using energy minimization-based adaptive resampling. Heitz et al. [25] also implemented non-rigid b-spline based warping to construct models of C6 and C7 cervical vertebrae. This list is a reference of 3D vertebral and intervertebral disc statistical shape models and is by no means exhaustive. In contrast, 3D shape variability of intervertebral discs is less explored in the literature. Peloquin et al. [26] constructed a statistical shape model of 12 L3-L4 intervertebral discs from signed distance maps of manually segmented binary images.

This research focuses on the refinement of a correspondence technique introduced by Cates et al. [7,8] that is independent of structure parameterization or a reference bias. The utilized technique employs a two-stage framework, with soft correspondence establishment in the first stage, and correspondence optimization across all instances of the shape space in the second stage. Soft correspondence is established by automatically placing homologous points on the shape surface through an iterative, hierarchical splitting strategy of particles, beginning with a single particle. A 3D surface can be sampled using a discrete set of N points that are considered random variables $Z = (X_1, \ldots, X_N)$ drawn from a probability density function (PDF) $p(X)$. Denoting a specific shape realization of this PDF as $z = (x_1, x_2, \ldots, x_N)$, the amount of information contained in each point is the differential entropy of the PDF function $p(x)$, which is estimated as the logarithm of its expectation $\log\{E(p(x))\}$, $E(\cdot)$ estimated by Parzen windowing. The cost function C becomes

$$C\{x_1, \ldots, x_N\} = -H(P^i) = \sum_j \log \frac{1}{N(N-1)} \sum_{k \neq j} p(x_j)$$

$$= \sum_j \log \frac{1}{N(N-1)} \sum_{l \neq j} G(x_j - x_l, \sigma_j), \qquad (1)$$

where G is an isotropic Gaussian kernel with standard deviation σ_j. These dynamic particles have repulsive forces that interact within their circle of influence limited through the Gaussian kernel until a steady state is achieved, and are constrained to lie on shape surface through gradient descent in the tangent plane.

These correspondences are further optimized by entropy-based energy minimization of particle distribution along gradient descent by balancing the negative entropy of a shape instance with the positive entropy of the entire shape space encompassing all instances (known as an ensemble) [27]. Consider an ensemble ϵ consisting of M surfaces, such as $\epsilon = (z_1, z_2, \ldots, z_M)$, where points are ordered according to correspondences between these surface pointsets. A surface z_k can be modeled as an instance of a random variable Z, where the following cost function is minimized:

$$Q = H(Z) - \sum_k H(P_k). \qquad (2)$$

The cost function Q favors a compact representation of the ensemble and assumes a normal distribution of particles along the shape surface. Hence, $p(z)$ is modeled parametrically with a Gaussian distribution with covariance Σ. This ensemble entropy term can be represented as

$$H(z) \approx \frac{1}{2} \log \|\Sigma\| = \frac{1}{2} \Sigma_k \lambda_k, \qquad (3)$$

where λ_k are ensemble covariance eigenvalues. This process optimally repositions the particles of the shapes within the ensemble to generate robust shape representations with uniformly-distributed particles.

ShapeWorks[1] was used to establish dense correspondences of 16,384 homologous points on nine L1 vertebral instances, and 4,038 points on eight L1-L2 intervertebral disc instances. The ensemble shapes were respectively normalized according to centroid-referred coordinates, and were further aligned during the correspondence optimization process through iterative Procrustes analysis [28]. Statistical shape models were respectively generated for an L1 vertebra and L1-L2 disc using these point clouds in the manner summarized in Sect. 2.3.

2.3 Construction of a Statistical Shape Model

The shape of an object is the geometrical information that remains after effects of translation, rotation and scaling have been filtered [29]. Statistical shape model capturing variations within L1 vertebrae and L1-L2 intervertebral disc population have been constructed using PCA [30].

The generalized mean shape $\bar{X}$ and covariance matrix Σ_X can be calculated for the datasets. Assuming that the training dataset covers a set of closely related shapes, correlation between shape points can be represented by a multivariate Gaussian distribution. PCA is utilized to extract the principal modes, which represent data correlation along principal directions within the dataset, to reduce problem dimensionality.

Each eigenvector ϕ_i represents the modes of variation within the training dataset, and the corresponding eigenvalue λ_i captures the amplitude of variation within the corresponding eigenvector, with the largest λ corresponding to the largest deformation in corresponding modes. The eigenvalues of Φ are sorted in descending order such that $\lambda_i > \lambda_{i+1}$ and the largest t eigenvalues and corresponding eigenvectors are kept so that $\Phi_t = (\phi_1, \phi_2, \ldots, \phi_t)$. A sample shape X can be approximated as a linear combination of the mean shape and first t modes of variation represented by $X = \bar{X} + b_t \Phi_t$, where b_t is a t-dimensional vector representing modes of variation. Assuming the mean shape $\bar{X}$ is located at the origin, three standard deviations of λ_i capture expected shape variability with a 99.7 % confidence interval.

The calculated average shape and expected variations can be incorporated within the discrete deformable simplex model segmentation [6, 31–33] to constraint the model variability and faithfully capture structure boundary in presence of image artifacts and noise.

3 Results

3.1 Shape Mean and Variance Evaluation

Figure 1 is a graphical representation of dense correspondence-based mean shape of the L1 vertebrae and L1-L2 intervertebral discs. Both mean shapes look qualitatively normal. Figure 2 illustrates the changes in the shapes along the first three principal modes of variation by 3σ for vertebrae and intervertebral discs. The

---

[1] http://www.sci.utah.edu/software/shapeworks.html.

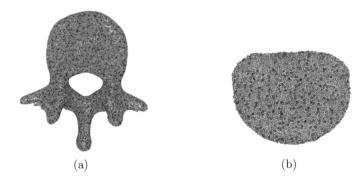

(a)   (b)

Fig. 1. Correspondence-based mean shapes. (a) Mean L1 vertebra shape from a population of nine instances, viewed from inferior. (b) Mean L1-L2 intervertebral disc shape from a population of eight instances, viewed from superior.

first mode for both shape models mainly captures scaling across the population. The maximum vertebral variability (16 mm) is observed at the inferior and superior articular processes and the spinous process. The second and third modes in the vertebral model capture variation and scaling in the transverse processes and foramen size respectively. In contrast, the first mode of the intervertebral disc model varies maximally by 7 mm. The second principal mode captured stretching in the lateral parts of the disc, and the third mode captured rotational effects in the lateral part of the disc respectively.

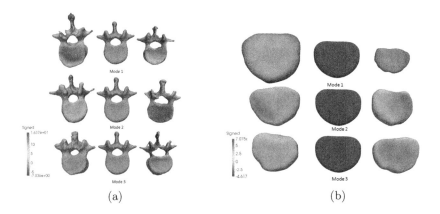

(a)   (b)

Fig. 2. Graphical representation of shape model variability (in mm) captured by the first three principal modes ($-3\sigma \leftarrow$ mean $\rightarrow +3\sigma$) of (a) L1 vertebra, viewed from superior (b) L1-L2 intervertebral disc, viewed from superior. Red corresponds to the maximum outward signed distance (mm) from the mean shape, while blue corresponds to the maximum inward signed distance (mm) from the mean shape. (Color figure online)

3.2 Statistical Shape Model Evaluation

Shape model correspondences and the constructed statistical models may be evaluated through established metrics, such as model compactness, generalization ability, and specificity [14]. A robust statistical model should have low generalization ability, low specificity and high compactness for the same number of modes. Compactness is the ability of the model to use a minimum number of parameters to faithfully capture shape variance within the dataset. This may be calculated as the cumulative variance captured by the first m number of modes

$$C(m) = \sum_{i=1}^{m} \lambda_i, \qquad (4)$$

where λ_i is the largest eigenvalue of the i-th mode. Figure 3 graphically illustrates the compactness of the statistical models as a function of the number of modes required to capture 100 % of the variation across the population. Each principal mode represents a distinct shape variation amongst the shape population. Both shape models were able to capture variance within the first seven principal modes, with 39.45 % variance of the vertebra model, and 71.04 % disc shape variation captured within the first principal mode respectively. The generalized ability of the statistical model to represent new, unseen instances of a new shape that are not present in the training dataset was evaluated by performing leave-one-out experiments. Vertebra and disc statistical shape models were generated using all training samples except one, which was considered the test sample. This test sample was then reconstructed using the statistical shape model, and the root-mean-square (RMS) distance and Hausdorff distance errors were calculated between the reconstructed sample and the original test sample after rigid registration. This method was repeated over the entire vertebra and disc datasets respectively, to calculate an average and worst measure of error for both statistical models. Generalization ability $G(m)$, and its associated standard error $\sigma_{G(m)}$ can be mathematically represented as

$$G(m) = \frac{1}{n} \sum_{i=1}^{n} \mathbb{D}_i(m), \qquad \sigma_{G(m)} = \frac{\sigma}{\sqrt{n-1}}, \qquad (5)$$

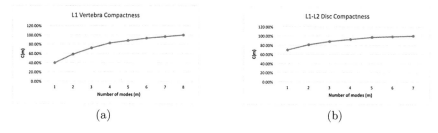

(a)   (b)

Fig. 3. Compactness ability of (a) L1 vertebra (b) L1-L2 intervertebral disc shape models. 100 % of the variation was captured within the first seven modes for both models.

where $\mathbb{D}_i(m)$ is the RMS or Hausdorff distance error between the test sample and the instantiated shape, n is the number of shapes (i.e. nine L1 vertebrae and eight L1-L2 discs in our study) and σ is the standard deviation of $G(m)$.

Model specificity is the measure of a model to only instantiate instances that are valid and similar to those in the training dataset. To measure our statistical models' specificity, $(n-1)$ instances where randomly generated within $[-3\lambda, +3\lambda]$ using our statistical models, and compared to the closest shape in the training dataset. Specificity $S(m)$ and its standard error $\sigma_{S(m)}$ have been calculated as

$$S(m) = \frac{1}{n}\sum_{j=1}^{n}\mathbb{D}_j(m), \qquad \sigma_{S(m)} = \frac{\sigma}{\sqrt{n-1}}, \qquad (6)$$

where n is the number of samples, $\mathbb{D}_i(m)$ is the RMS distance error between a randomly generated instance and its nearest shape within the training dataset, and σ is the standard deviation of $S(m)$.

Results of the vertebra model generalization ability are presented in Fig. 4(a) and (b). For the first mode of variation, the average reconstruction error for an unseen instance is 0.47 mm with a confidence interval of 0.03 mm, with an initial Hausdorff distance of 8.2 mm. This error converges to 0.4 mm with worst mean error of 7.6 mm. Our vertebra models cumulative specificity error is 1.43 mm in seven principal modes with negligible standard error. Our vertebra model results are comparable with those in the literature. Vrtovec et al. [21] model is more compact, capturing 52 % variability within the first principal mode. Rasoulian et al. [18] capture $G(m)$ RMS error of 0.95 mm, with Hausdorff error of 9 mm within the first principal mode, which is decreased to 0.8 mm RMS and 7.5 mm after seven modes. Their model is worse in generalization and specificity,

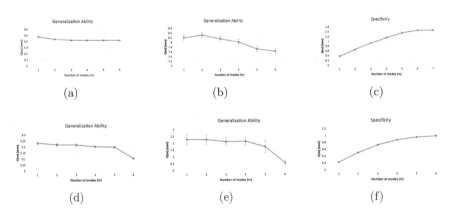

Fig. 4. Generalization ability and specificity of L1 vertebra and L1-L2 intervertebral disc shape models. Errorbars indicate standard error. (a) – (c) L1 vertebra: (a) generalization (RMS), (b) generalization (Hausdorff), and (c) specificity. (d) – (f) L1-L2 intervertebral disc: (d) generalization (RMS), (e) generalization (Hausdorff), and (f) specificity.

but outperforms in model compactness (capturing 60 % in the first mode). Our statistical model outperforms Kaus et al. [22] whos model reported 1.66 mm mean error after 20 modes, with 30 % first mode compactness, constructed with 32 (L1-L4) vertebral training shapes.

Our intervertebral disc model is able to represent unseen instances with an initial RMS error of 0.23 mm, and Hausdorff distance of 2.24 mm, which converges to 0.1 mm RMS error and 0.5 mm worst error after six principal modes. As depicted in Fig. 4(d) and (e), mode 5 attributes a spike in the distance errors. This may be caused by a singular variation within a training sample captured by this mode. The overall effect of this variation is reduced by mode 6, as demonstrated by a reduction in the $G(m)$ error. The disc model specificity captures cumulative 1.0 mm RMS error within six modes. Peloquin et al. [26] present comparable results for model compactness of 14 L3-L4 discs, capturing 70 % variability within the first mode. They presented a leave-one-out analysis to determine which samples influenced model outliers, demonstrating that PCs > 4 had higher influence on the mean shape of the model.

Overall, the compact model transitions coherently, with a tradeoff between compactness and the ability to faithfully represent new training shapes. Some outliers in the first principal mode can be noted in the variant vertebral shape. These outliers may be reduced by increasing the size of the population dataset, as well as exploring probabilistic PCA instead of simple PCA, which may better account for any outliers in the model. Moreover, large variability exists between the nine vertebrae instances, leading to large variability in the L1 vertebral shape model itself, as seen in Fig. 2. An increase in the training dataset would lead to a more robust and faithful vertebral model better able to represent variability within a population.

4   Future Work and Conclusion

The current shape models can be improved by increasing the size of the training dataset. Moreover, probabilistic PCA can be implemented to capture outliers in the vertebral shape model in presence of a small training size.

This paper quantifies inter-patient 3D shape variation of an L1 vertebra and an L1-L2 intervertebral disc of the lumbar spine. The constructed shape models have been shown to faithfully capture variance within a population with few particle outliers, capturing 100 % variability within the first seven modes. The main advantage of this correspondence method is the lack of a reference bias, as it places particles on the implicit shape surface independent of prior surface parameterization. It also iteratively performs alignment during the correspondence optimization phase in order to mitigate error introduced by shape misalignment.

The calculated strong shape prior knowledge will be incorporated within a multi-surface, multi-resolution simplex deformable segmentation model of lumbar vertebrae and intervertebral discs. The shape models can be registered to the volumetric images, and set as a template meshes that are allowed to deform and capture the structure boundary while constraining the model according to expected variation. The inherent regularization and surface smoothness parameters in the discrete simplex model enforce mesh smoothness, mitigating the effects of shape model noise. These shape forces can be integrated in a controlled-resolution segmentation pipeline to faithfully capture structure boundary in presence of image artifacts, improving on our previous segmentation results [6].

References

1. Luoma, K., Riihimäki, H., Luukkonen, R., Raininko, R., Viikari-Juntura, E., Lamminen, A.: Low back pain in relation to lumbar disc degeneration. Spine **25**(4), 487–492 (2000)
2. Global Burden of Disease Study: Global, regional, and national incidence, prevalence, and years lived with disability for 301 acute and chronic diseases and injuries in 188 countries, 1990–2013: a systematic analysis for the Global Burden of Disease Study 2013. Lancet 386(9995), pp. 743–800 (2015)
3. Freemont, A., Watkins, A., Le Maitre, C., Jeziorska, M., Hoyland, J.: Current understanding of cellular and molecular events in intervertebral disc degeneration: implications for therapy. J. Pathol. **196**(4), 374–379 (2002)
4. Atlas, S., Deyo, R.: Evaluating and managing acute low back pain in the primary care setting. J. Gen. Intern. Med. **16**(2), 120–131 (2001)
5. An, H., Anderson, P., Haughton, V., Iatridis, J., Kang, J., Lotz, J., Natarajan, R., Oegema Jr., T., Roughley, P., Setton, L., Urban, J., Videman, T., Andersson, G., Weinstein, J.: Introduction: disc degeneration: summary. Spine **29**(23), 2677–2678 (2004)
6. Haq, R., Aras, R., Besachio, D., Borgie, R., Audette, M.: 3D lumbar spine intervertebral disc segmentation and compression simulation from MRI using shape-aware models. Int. J. Comput. Assist. Radiol. Surg. **10**(1), 45–54 (2015)
7. Cates, J., Fletcher, P., Whitaker, R.: Entropy-based particle systems for shape correspondence. In: Pennec, X., Joshi, S. (eds.) Proceedings of MICCAI Workshop on Mathematical Foundations of Computational Anatomy, MFCA 2006, pp. 90–99 (2006)
8. Datar, M., Cates, J., Fletcher, P.T., Gouttard, S., Gerig, G., Whitaker, R.: Particle based shape regression of open surfaces with applications to developmental neuroimaging. In: Yang, G.Z., Hawkes, D., Rueckert, D., Noble, A., Taylor, C. (eds.) MICCAI 2009, Part II. LNCS, vol. 5762, pp. 167–174. Springer, Heidelberg (2009)
9. Harris, M., Datar, M., Whitaker, R., Jurrus, E., Peters, C., Anderson, A.: Statistical shape modeling of cam femoroacetabular impingement. J. Orthop. Res. **31**(10), 1620–1626 (2013)
10. Ibragimov, B., Likar, B., Pernuš, F., Vrtovec, T.: Shape representation for efficient landmark-based segmentation in 3-D. IEEE Trans. Med. Imaging **33**(4), 861–874 (2014)
11. Chen, C., Belavy, D., Zheng, G.: 3D intervertebral disc localization and segmentation from MR images by data-driven regression and classification. In: Wu, G., Zhang, D., Zhou, L. (eds.) MLMI 2014. LNCS, vol. 8679, pp. 50–58. Springer, Heidelberg (2014)
12. Dryden, I., Mardia, K.: Statistical Shape Analysis. Wiley, New York (1998)
13. Heimann, T., Meinzer, H.: Statistical shape models for 3D medical image segmentation: a review. Med. Image Anal. **13**(4), 543–563 (2009)

14. Styner, M.A., Rajamani, K.T., Nolte, L.P., Zsemlye, G., Székely, G., Taylor, C.J., Davies, R.H.: Evaluation of 3D correspondence methods for model building. In: Taylor, C.J., Noble, J.A. (eds.) IPMI 2003. LNCS, vol. 2732, pp. 63–75. Springer, Heidelberg (2003)

15. Davies, R., Twining, C., Cootes, T., Waterton, J., Taylor, C.: A minimum description length approach to statistical shape modeling. IEEE Trans. Med. Imaging **21**(5), 525–537 (2002)

16. Ma, J., Lu, L., Zhan, Y., Zhou, X., Salganicoff, M., Krishnan, A.: Hierarchical segmentation and identification of thoracic vertebra using learning-based edge detection and coarse-to-fine deformable model. In: Jiang, T., Navab, N., Pluim, J.P.W., Viergever, M.A. (eds.) MICCAI 2010, Part I. LNCS, vol. 6361, pp. 19–27. Springer, Heidelberg (2010)

17. Clogenson, M., Duff, J., Luethi, M., Levivier, M., Meuli, R., Baur, C., Henein, S.: A statistical shape model of the human second cervical vertebra. Int. J. Comput. Assist. Radiol. Surg. **10**(7), 1097–1107 (2015)

18. Rasoulian, A., Rohling, R., Abolmaesumi, P.: Group-wise registration of point sets for statistical shape models. IEEE Trans. Med. Imaging **31**(11), 2025–2034 (2012)

19. Hufnagel, H., Pennec, X., Ehrhardt, J., Ayache, N., Handels, H.: Generation of a statistical shape model with probabilistic point correspondences and the expectation maximization-iterative closest point algorithm. Int. J. Comput. Assist. Radiol. Surg. **2**(5), 265–273 (2008)

20. Mutsvangwa, T., Schwartz, C., Roux, C.: An automated statistical shape model developmental pipeline: application to the human scapula and humerus. IEEE Trans. Biomed. Eng. **62**(4), 1098–1107 (2015)

21. Vrtovec, T., Tomaževič, D., Likar, B., Travnik, L., Pernuš, F.: Automated construction of 3D statistical shape models. Image Anal. Stereol. **23**(2), 111–120 (2004)

22. Kaus, M., Pekar, V., Lorenz, C., Truyen, R., Lobregt, S., Wesse, J.: Automated 3-D PDM construction from segmented images using deformable models. IEEE Trans. Med. Imaging **22**(8), 1005–1013 (2003)

23. Lorenz, C., Krahnstover, N.: Generation of point-based 3D statistical shape models for anatomical objects. Comput. Vis. Image Underst. **77**(2), 175–191 (2000)

24. Becker, M., Kirschner, M., Fuhrmann, S., Wesarg, S.: Automatic construction of statistical shape models for vertebrae. In: Fichtinger, G., Martel, A., Peters, T. (eds.) MICCAI 2011, Part II. LNCS, vol. 6892, pp. 500–507. Springer, Heidelberg (2011)

25. Heitz, G., Rohlfing, T., Maurer Jr., C.: Statistical shape model generation using nonrigid deformation of a template mesh. In: Fitzpatrick, J., Reinhardt, J. (eds.) Proceedings of SPIE Medical Imaging 2005: Image Processing Conference, SPIE Proceedings, vol. 5747, pp. 1411–1421. SPIE (2005)

26. Peloquin, J., Yoder, J., Jacobs, N., Moon, S., Wright, A., Vresilovic, E., Elliott, D.: Human L3L4 intervertebral disc mean 3D shape, modes of variation, and their relationship to degeneration. J. Biomech. **47**(10), 2452–2459 (2014)

27. Cates, J.E., Fletcher, P.T., Styner, M.A., Hazlett, H.C., Whitaker, R.T.: Particle-based shape analysis of multi-object complexes. In: Metaxas, D., Axel, L., Fichtinger, G., Székely, G. (eds.) MICCAI 2008, Part I. LNCS, vol. 5241, pp. 477–485. Springer, Heidelberg (2008)

28. Gower, J.: Generalized procrustes analysis. Psychometrika **40**(1), 33–51 (1975)

29. Kendall, D.: The diffusion of shape. Adv. Appl. Probab. **9**(3), 428–430 (1977)

30. Cootes, T., Taylor, C., Cooper, D., Graham, J.: Training models of shape from sets of examples. In: Proceedings of 1992 British Machine Vision Conference, BMVC 1992, pp. 9–18. BMVA Press (1992)

31. Gilles, B., Magnenat-Thalmann, N.: Musculoskeletal MRI segmentation using multi-resolution simplex meshes with medial representations. Med. Image Anal. **14**(3), 291–302 (2010)
32. Delingette, H.: General object reconstruction based on simplex meshes. Int. J. Comput. Vis. **32**(2), 111–146 (1999)
33. Schmid, J., Kim, J., Magnenat-Thalmann, N.: Robust statistical shape models for MRI bone segmentation in presence of small field of view. Med. Image Anal. **15**(1), 155–168 (2011)

Automatic Intervertebral Discs Localization and Segmentation: A Vertebral Approach

Amir Jamaludin[1]([✉]), Meelis Lootus[1], Timor Kadir[2], and Andrew Zisserman[1]

[1] University of Oxford, Oxford, UK
{amirj,meelis,az}@robots.ox.ac.uk
[2] Mirada Medical, Oxford, UK
timor.kadir@mirada-medical.com

Abstract. This paper describes an automatic system for intervertebral discs (IVDs) localization and segmentation in three-dimensional magnetic resonance imaging scans. The system builds upon the localization and segmentation system first introduced by Lootus et al. with several improvements to the localization step. The system was trained on T1 and T2 scans of 341 patients obtained from various sources. The proposed system achieved a mean localization error of 1.1 ± 0.6 mm and a mean Dice overlap coefficient of 84.0 ± 1.5 % on the 15 training data of the challenge on IVD localization and segmentation at the 3rd MICCAI Workshop & Challenge on Computational Methods and Clinical Applications for Spine Imaging - MICCAI–CSI2015.

1 Introduction

The objective of this work is the automated localization and segmentation of intervertebral discs (IVDs), and to this end we propose a system that was first presented in the work of Lootus et al. [1] and improve it with ideas from the work of Jamaludin et al. [2]. The whole system comprises five main steps: 1. vertebrae detection and labelling, 2. corner localization of detected vertebrae, 3. detection of the extent of the vertebrae in sagittal slices, 4. IVDs segmentation via graph cuts, and 5. localization of IVDs centres.

2 Methodology

2.1 Vertebrae Detection and Labelling

To detect and label the vertebrae, we use the detection and labelling scheme proposed by Lootus et al. [3] which uses a combination of a deformable part model (DPM) detector [4] and labelling via graphical model. The input to this stage is a three-dimensional (3D) magnetic resonance (MR) volume and the output is a series of approximate bounding boxes with the vertebrae labels from T11 to the combined sacrum (S1 and S2). The detector uses two different groups of histogram of oriented gradients (HOG) templates one for the combined sacrum

© Springer International Publishing Switzerland 2016
T. Vrtovec et al. (Eds.): CSI 2015, LNCS 9402, pp. 97–103, 2016.
DOI: 10.1007/978-3-319-41827-8_9

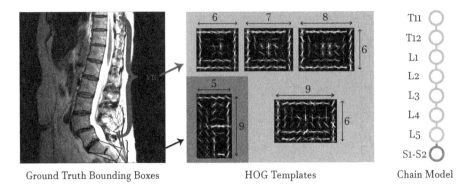

Ground Truth Bounding Boxes   HOG Templates   Chain Model

Fig. 1. Examples of the ground truth bounding boxes that were used to train the HOG templates models are shown here in cell units where one cell is made up of 8×8 pixels. Only one template was trained for the sacrum while four different templates of varying ratio were trained for the other vertebrae.

(S1-S2) and the other for T11-L5 vertebrae detections. The graphical model is a chain graph with eight vertices, one for each vertebra (T11 to S1-S2), with the edges describing the geometrical relationships of one vertebra and the next. Both the HOG templates and geometrical relationships of the vertices are trained with annotated ground truth bounding boxes with labels as described in the work of Lootus et al. [3]. Examples of annotated ground truths, the trained HOG templates, and the graph of the chain model can be seen in Fig. 1 while an example of the input and output can be seen in Fig. 2.

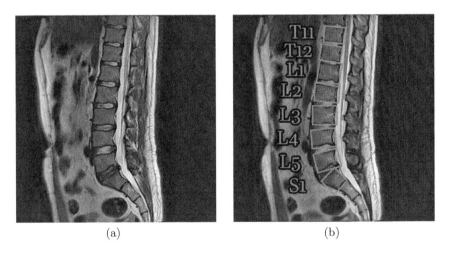

(a)   (b)

Fig. 2. (a) A midsagittal slice of the 3D MR scan (input). (b) The same scan superimposed with the bounding boxes and their corresponding labels (output). Note: the S1-S2 bounding box is truncated to just S1.

2.2 Corner Localization

We then refine the localization of these bounding boxes such that the resulting quadrilaterals are more consistent and tightly fit the vertebrae. This is achieved by regressing to the corner points of the vertebrae contained in the bounding boxes. We adapt the supervised descent method (SDM) by Xiong et al. [5] originally developed for the detection of facial landmarks. Implementation details and experimentation results of the regression of the corner points can be found in the work of Jamaludin et al. [2]. Examples of corner localized vertebrae with corresponding bounding box inputs can be seen in Fig. 3.

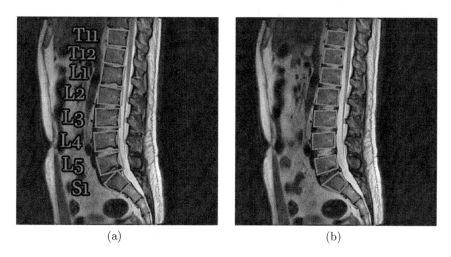

(a)   (b)

Fig. 3. (a) Input. (b) Output. Note: the quadrilaterals are tighter in terms of fit compared to the original bounding boxes.

2.3 Detection of the Extent of the Vertebrae

All the previous steps are performed on each sagittal slice of the scan, however, it is also necessary to determine the vertebra start and end. This is important since the positions of the vertebrae in a scan are initially unknown and there exist slices which contain only partial volumes of the vertebrae, largely containing other non-vertebral tissue. Such partial vertebrae are problematic because they should be considered to be part of the background class during segmentation. To this end we utilise a binary classifier to distinguish non-vertebrae and vertebrae quadrilaterals.

We follow the method proposed by Chatfield et al. [6], where the steps are: 1. dense scale-invariant feature transform feature extraction over the quadrilaterals, 2. Fisher vector encoding of the features, 3. spatial tiling of the features in the image and 4. classification via linear support vector machines. This is done on a per slice basis on every slice where the quadrilaterals are classified as either vertebra or non-vertebra. Examples can be seen in Fig. 4.

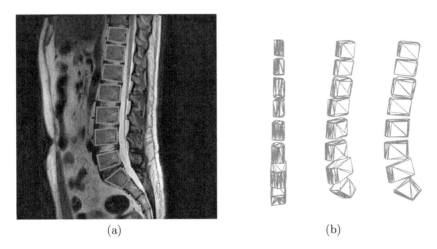

(a)   (b)

Fig. 4. (a) Tight quadrilaterals of the midsagittal slice (input). (b) Triangular mesh plots made from quadrilaterals in the 3D volume that were classified as vertebrae (output). The plots shown is of a single scan but at three different orientations.

2.4   IVD Segmentation

We follow the segmentation scheme proposed by Lootus et al. [3] which uses a standard graph cuts algorithm. We therefore segment twice, once for the vertebrae and then once more for the IVDs. The placement of the foreground and background seeds are automatically generated according to tight quadrilaterals similar to the work of Lootus et al. [3]. This two-step segmentation proves to be better than segmenting the IVDs directly from the quadrilaterals due to the fact that accurate foreground seed placement is less demanding than vertebrae segmentation.

There are two main differences between our implementation and that discussed in the work of Lootus et al. [3]. First, the seeds are set to be the biggest at the midsagittal point, determined from the extent detector, and smallest at the sagittal edge of the vertebrae extent. Also, for the IVD segmentation, we combine the sagittal segmentation with its coronal segmentation by flipping the third axis of the 3D volume with the first axis and segmenting it again. The joint segmentation result is the final IVDs segmentation. Example segmentations of the vertebrae and IVDs can be seen in Fig. 5.

2.5   Localization of IVDs Centres

To localize the IVDs centres we combine three different localization predictions: 1. the centroid of adjacent vertebrae corner points, 2. a linear regression of adjacent vertebrae corner points, and 3. the centroid of segmented binary mask of each IVD.

The first localization prediction is the centroid of the corner points of adjacent vertebrae to a specific IVD. We assume that this centroid is a close approximation

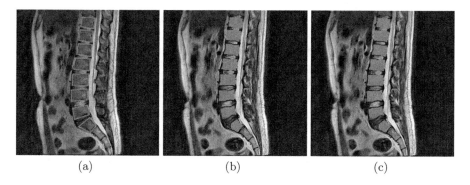

(a)   (b)   (c)

Fig. 5. (a) Tight quadrilaterals of the midsagittal slice, now classified as either vertebra or non-vertebra according to extent detector (input). For (b) vertebrae segmentation and (c) IVD segmentation are shown the resulting segmentation masks.

to the centroid of the IVD since an IVD will be bounded by the adjacent vertebrae. The second localization prediction is essentially the output of a linear regressor using the corner points as features. The linear regressor is trained by leave-one-out cross validation of the whole training set. The final localization prediction is the centroid of the segmentation binary mask. All three predictions are then averaged to give the final localization prediction. Through experimentations, we found averaging the three predictions give us a more accurate prediction overall. Example of IVDs centres localization can be seen in Fig. 6.

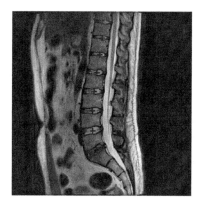

Fig. 6. Shown is a single sagittal slice and the predicted IVDs centres. In practice, the localization predictions predict the centres in 3D space.

3   Results

Results for the corner localization and the extent detector can be seen in the work of Jamaludin et al. [2]. To test our segmentation and IVD localization we use the 15 training data provided as part of the challenge on IVD localization and segmentation [7] at the 3rd MICCAI Workshop &Challenge on Computational Methods and Clinical Applications for Spine Imaging - MICCAI–CSI2015. As per the challenge we use mean and standard deviation of the results to the ground truth for the localization task and the mean Dice overlap for the segmentation task. Results can be seen in Table 1. Besides the 15 training data provided we also tested our approach with the five test data provided in the challenge. For segmentation, we obtain a dice overlap of $82.3 \pm 3.2\%$ and an absolute distance of 1.57 ± 0.20 mm. Similarly for localization, we achieve a mean localization of 1.02 ± 0.47 mm. Our localization results on the challenge dataset is good and the system manages to achieve sub-voxel accuracy on average. However, our segmentation results can be improved upon, possibly by means of a true 3D graph cut segmentation algorithm.

Table 1. Localization and segementation results.

Task	Mean ± STD	Median	Min	Max
Localization (mm)	1.1 ± 0.6	1.0	0.2	2.9
Segmentation (Dice, %)	84.0 ± 1.5	84.2	79.8	86.4

4   Conclusion

This paper has presented an automatic IVDs localization and segmentation system. The proposed system managed to achieve good localization and segmentation accuracy on the challenge data which is impressive considering the system was mostly trained on a totally different dataset. This indicates the robustness of our system.

Acknowledgements. We are grateful for discussions with Prof. Jeremy Fairbank, and Dr. Jill Urban. This work was supported by the RCUK CDT in Healthcare Innovation (EP/G036861/1). The data used in this research was obtained during the EC FP7 project HEALTH-F2-2008-201626.

References

1. Lootus, M., Kadir, T., Zisserman, A.: Automated radiological grading of spinal MRI. In: Yao, J., et al. (eds.) CSI 2014. LNCVB, vol. 20, pp. 119–130. Springer, Switzerland (2015)
2. Jamaludin, A., Kadir, T., Zisserman, A.: Automatic Modic changes classification in spinal MRI. In: Vrtovec, T., et al. (ed.) Proceedings of 3rd MICCAI 2015 Workshop & Challenge on Computational Methods and Clinical Applications for Spine Imaging, MICCAI-CSI 2015, pp. 14–26 (2015)

3. Lootus, M., Kadir, T., Zisserman, A.: Vertebrae detection and labelling in lumbar MR images. In: Yao, J., et al. (eds.) CSI 2013. LNCVB, vol. 17, pp. 219–230. Springer, Switzerland (2014)
4. Felzenszwalb, P., Girshick, R., McAllester, D.: Cascade object detection with deformable part models. In: Proceedings of 2010 IEEE Conference on Computer Vision and Pattern Recognition, CVPR 2010, pp. 2241–2248. IEEE (2010)
5. Xiong, X., de la Torre, F.: Supervised descent method and its applications to face alignment. In: Proceedings of 2013 IEEE Conference on Computer Vision and Pattern Recognition, CVPR 2013, pp. 532–539. IEEE (2013)
6. Chatfield, K., Lempitsky, V., Vedaldi, A., Zisserman, A.: The devil is in the details: an evaluation of recent feature encoding methods. In: Proceedings of 2011 British Machine Vision Conference, BMVC 2011, pp. 76.1–76.12. BMVA Press (2011)
7. Chen, C., Belavy, D., Yu, W., Chu, C., Armbrecht, G., Bansmann, M., Felsenberg, D., Zheng, G.: Localization and segmentation of 3D intervertebral discs in MR images by data driven estimation. IEEE Trans. Med. Imaging 34(8), 1719–1729 (2015)

Challenge (Automatic Intervertebral Disc Localization and Segmentation from 3D T2 MRI Data)

Segmentation of Intervertebral Discs in 3D MRI Data Using Multi-atlas Based Registration

Chunliang Wang[1,2] and Daniel Forsberg[1,2(✉)]

[1] Sectra, Linköping, Sweden
daniel.forsberg@sectra.com
[2] Center for Medical Image Science and Visualization, Linköping University,
Linköping, Sweden
chunwan@kth.se

Abstract. This paper presents one of the participating methods to the intervertebral disc segmentation challenge organized in conjunction with the 3rd MICCAI Workshop & Challenge on Computational Methods and Clinical Applications for Spine Imaging - MICCAI–CSI2015. The presented method consist of three steps. In the first step, vertebral bodies are detected and labeled using integral channel features and a graphical parts model. The second step consists of image registration, where a set of image volumes with corresponding intervertebral disc atlases are registered to the target volume using the output from the first step as initialization. In the final step, the registered atlases are combined using label fusion to derive the final segmentation. The pipeline was evaluated using a set of $15 + 10$ T2-weighted image volumes provided as training and test data respectively for the segmentation challenge. For the training data, a mean disc centroid distance of 0.86 mm and an average DICE score of 91 % was achieved, and for the test data the corresponding results were 0.90 mm and 90 %.

1 Introduction

Lower back pain is considered as one of the most common neurological ailments in the United States and as such costs associated to lower back pain form a significant portion of the total annual spending on healthcare. Degeneration of intervertebral discs (IVDs), as caused by aging, trauma, mechanical load, nutritional or genetic factors, is a common underlying cause of lower back pain. The degree of degeneration is typically assessed by means of magnetic resonance imaging (MRI), given the superior ability of MRI to distinguish between soft tissues and its absence of ionizing radiation. Because of significant inter-observer variation in grading IVD degeneration and constantly increasing workloads for radiologists, more and more research is devoted to develop computer assisted diagnosis systems to support the radiologists in their work and thereby improving the diagnostic process [1]. A crucial initial step in such a system is an accurate segmentation of the IVDs.

Over the last years, a number of different methods have been proposed for segmentation of IVDs [1–6]. The performance ranges from a mean DICE score

© Springer International Publishing Switzerland 2016
T. Vrtovec et al. (Eds.): CSI 2015, LNCS 9402, pp. 107–116, 2016.
DOI: 10.1007/978-3-319-41827-8_10

of a mediocre 74 % to an impressive 92 %. However, a drawback of some referenced methods is the limitation to two-dimensional (2D) image data, as typically given by the mid-sagittal slice of an image volume covering the lumbar spine. In addition, thus far no comparison between methods has been possible since all have been evaluated on different data sets. To this end, that is promoting three-dimensional (3D) segmentation of IVDs along with enabling a valid comparison of different methods, an IVD segmentation challenge was set up and organized in conjunction with the 3rd MICCAI Workshop & Challenge on Computational Methods and Clinical Applications for Spine Imaging - MICCAI–CSI2015.

In this paper, we present one of the challenge participants of said challenge. As such, the presented method is capable of both localizing and segmenting IVDs in MRI data. The method builds upon earlier work as presented by Lootus et al. [7] for vertebral body detection and labeling in MRI data and by Forsberg [8] for multi-atlas based segmentation of vertebrae in computed tomography data. The two approaches are combined and adapted to the task of localization and segmentation of IVDs in MRI data. Results are presented and discussed as pertaining to the training and test data provided for the challenge.

2   Materials and Methods

2.1   Image Data

The image data provided for training/testing and initial/final evaluation consisted of MRI data from 15 respectively 10 subjects, where each subject had been scanned with a 1.5 T scanner (Siemens Magnetom Sonata, Siemens Healthcare, Erlangen, Germany) and form a subset of the data used in the work of Chen et al. [2]. The image data consisted of sagittal T2-weighted turbo spin echo image volumes with a spatial resolution of $2.00 \times 1.25 \times 1.25\,\mathrm{mm}^3$ and a size of $39 \times 305 \times 305$ or $48 \times 304 \times 304$. The IVDs have been manually segmented using the original sagittal images. Examples of the image data and ground truth segmentations are given in Fig. 1.

2.2   Segmentation Pipeline

The proposed segmentation pipeline consists of the following three components, detection and labeling of vertebral bodies, multi-atlas based segmentation per IVD and finally label fusion. Note that the presented method is a 3D-based method providing an accurate segmentation in 3D, even though the initial detection and labeling step is performed on individual 2D images.

2.3   Detection and Labeling

Detection and labeling of vertebrae is a challenge of its own and a number of methods have been presented in recent years. In our pipeline, it was decided to mimic the approach presented by Lootus et al. [7]. However, we employed aggregated channel features [9] coupled with an AdaBoost classifier for detection of the

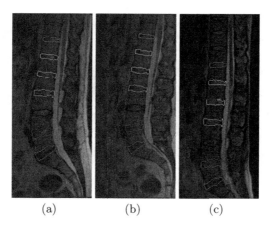

(a)   (b)   (c)

Fig. 1. Example of data used for the evaluation along with ground truth segmentations.

individual vertebrae. The reasons for not choosing the deformable parts model based on histogram of oriented gradients, as employed by Lootus et al. [7], were twofold. Firstly, it did not perform as well as the chosen approach, and secondly, it was more computationally demanding. Similar to the work of Lootus et al. [7], two different detectors were trained, one general vertebra detector and one for the fused S1 and S2 segments of the sacrum. To remove a significant portion of the false positive detections, a greedy non-maxima suppression algorithm was employed. In order to improve the performance of the detector, by increasing the number of detections, a set of sagittal slices (the three mid-sagittal slices) were fed as input to the vertebra detector. The individually detected objects are then combined using a pictorial structures model [10], further removing false positive detections along with labeling the detected vertebra. The object vertebra detectors along with the graphical parts model had previously been trained on a separate data set. Figure 2 provides a few examples depicting the output from the detection and labeling step.

The output from the detection and labeling consisted of a pair of y and z coordinates along with a label for each detected and labeled vertebra (assuming a coordinate system where x goes from right to left, y anterior to posterior and z inferior to superior). Corresponding x coordinates for each detection and labeling were simply set to the x coordinate of the mid-sagittal slice in the data set. Note that this works well as long as the orientation of the image volume is parallel with the spinal column and the subject has limited spinal deformities in the coronal plane.

2.4   Multi-atlas Based Segmentation

The output from the previous step provided a set of landmarks denoting the centerpoints of vertebra T11 to L5 along with the centerpoint of sacrum S1-S2. These centerpoints were used to provide rough estimates of the centerpoints of the corresponding IVDs, simply by using the midpoint between the centerpoints

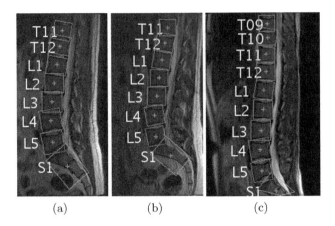

(a)   (b)   (c)

Fig. 2. Example results from the detection and labeling of vertebra. The detection and labeling works well even in cases where the sacrum is not fully depicted (c).

of two consecutive vertebrae. This served as input to the image registration in which a registration per disc was performed by extracting a sub-block (sized $40 \times 96 \times 96$ voxels, determined empirically to ensure a good coverage of each disc) of the data from each volume centered around the respective centerpoints of each disc. Note that for a general segmentation pipeline, the size of the sub-blocks should preferably be set in millimeters and with the possible extension to scale the size depending on sex, age and length of the patient. Each disc of the image data to segment is registered with multiple atlases. The registration was executed in two steps, where an initial affine registration was performed to account for differences in size and pose, and where a subsequent deformable registration was applied to account for local differences in shape. In both cases, local phase-based image registration approaches were applied.

Affine Registration. The affine phase-based registration was defined as an L_2 norm:

$$\epsilon^2 = \frac{1}{2} \sum_k \sum_{\mathbf{x} \in \Omega} c_k(\mathbf{x}) \left[\nabla \varphi_k(\mathbf{x})^T B(\mathbf{x}) \mathbf{p} - \Delta \varphi_k(\mathbf{x}) \right]^2, \tag{1}$$

where φ_k refers to the local phase-difference in orientation $\hat{\mathbf{n}}_k$ between the two images to be registered, c_k is a measure of certainty related to φ_k, and $B(\mathbf{x})\mathbf{p}$ corresponds to a linear parameterization of the local displacement $\mathbf{d}(\mathbf{x})$. A more detailed description is found in the works of Hemmendorff et al. [11] and Eklund et al. [12], and provides details on the employed graphics processing unit (GPU) implementation.

Deformable Registration. Similarly, as for the affine registration, a voxel-wise L_2 norm based upon local phase-differences was defined for the deformable counterpart:

$$\epsilon^2(\mathbf{x}) = \sum_k \left[c_k(\mathbf{x}) \mathbf{T}(\mathbf{x}) \left(\varphi_k(\mathbf{x}) \hat{\mathbf{n}}_k - \mathbf{u}(\mathbf{x}) \right) \right]^2. \tag{2}$$

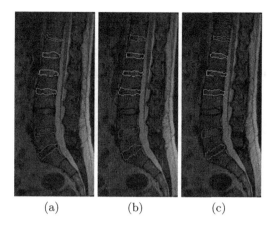

(a)   (b)   (c)

Fig. 3. Example results from the atlas-based registration. The individual segmentations as provided by the atlas-based segmentation are highly irregular and far from perfect, for example note the top disc in (a).

In this case, φ_k and c_k are as before, and $\mathbf{T}$ refers to local structure tensor.

Solving for $\mathbf{u}$ provides a voxel-wise update field $\mathbf{u}(\mathbf{x})$, which can be iteratively regularized and added to the final displacement field $\mathbf{d}$. Details on the registration algorithm can be found in the works of Knutsson and Andersson [13], and Forsberg et al. [14,15] for the employed GPU implementation.

Examples of output from the whole atlas-based segmentation step are shown in Fig. 3.

2.5   Label Fusion

The final step is to merge the labels of the multiple deformed atlases into a single label volume. In this case, a modified majority voting has been employed for label fusion, where instead of a standard majority vote only a minimum number of votes were required to render a valid segmentation. The reason for this approach was that since the discs are well-separated, it is only the background that provides a competing label. The minimum number of votes required for a segmentation was set to five, a number which was empirically determined. Example visualizations of the final segmentations are given in Fig. 4.

2.6   Evaluation

Given that 15 data sets were available for training, including ground truth data, a leave-one-out evaluation was performed for the training data in which one data set is segmented using the 14 others as atlases. This is then repeated for each available data set. Both IVD localization and segmentation results were included in the evaluation. For the evaluation on the test data, all 15 data sets were used as atlases.

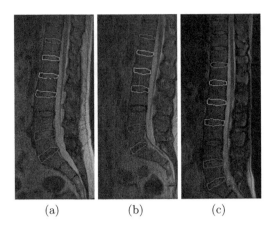

(a)   (b)   (c)

Fig. 4. Example results from the final step of label fusion. Previous irregularities are now gone and no apparent errors in the final segmentations are visible.

The evaluation of the test data was performed in a two-step process, with five data sets released prior to the challenge for an off-site evaluation and with remaining five data sets released on the day of the challenge for an on-site evaluation. The challenge organizers only provided results in terms of mean disc centroid distance and DICE score.

Localization. For each segmented disc, the disc centroid distance was computed as the Euclidean distance between the centroid of the ground truth IVD and the centroid of the segmented IVD obtained from the presented method. Based upon the disc centroid distance a disc localization was considered as successful if the distance was less than 2 mm.

Segmentation. The ground truth data was compared with the segmentations obtained from the multi-atlas based segmentation using the DICE score. The DICE score is defined as:

$$DICE = \frac{2 * |GT \cap S|}{|GT| + |S|}, \tag{3}$$

where GT and S refer to the ground truth and the computed segmentations respectively, and $|\ldots|$ denotes the number of voxels, i.e. no respect was given to the anisotropic resolution.

To complement the agreement measure of the DICE score, false negative (FN) and false positive (FP) ratios were also computed as:

$$FN = \frac{|GT \setminus S|}{|GT|} \tag{4}$$

respectively

$$FP = \frac{|S \setminus GT|}{|S|}. \tag{5}$$

Table 1. Average DICE score, and false negative (FN) and false positive (FP) ratios per disc for the training data.

Disc	DICE	FN	FP
T11/T12	0.89 ± 0.03	0.10 ± 0.04	0.11 ± 0.05
T12/L1	$0.91 \perp 0.02$	0.09 ± 0.02	0.09 ± 0.04
L1/L2	0.91 ± 0.03	0.09 ± 0.04	0.10 ± 0.04
L2/L3	0.92 ± 0.01	0.08 ± 0.03	0.07 ± 0.02
L3/L4	0.92 ± 0.02	0.07 ± 0.03	0.08 ± 0.03
L4/L5	0.92 ± 0.02	0.08 ± 0.03	0.08 ± 0.02
L5/S1	0.89 ± 0.03	0.09 ± 0.04	0.12 ± 0.05

3 Results

3.1 Training Data

The mean disc centroid distance was 0.86 ± 0.45 mm. Only three disc centroid distances were larger than 2 mm (2.05, 2.91 and 2.06 respectively) providing an IVD detection rate of 97%.

The average achieved DICE score was 0.91 ± 0.01 along with an average FN and FP of 0.08 ± 0.02 and 0.09 ± 0.02 respectively. Detailed results per disc and subject are given in Tables 1 and 2 respectively.

Table 2. Average DICE score, and false negative (FN) and false positive (FP) ratios per subject for the training data.

Subject	DICE	FN	FP
1	0.91 ± 0.02	0.09 ± 0.03	0.10 ± 0.01
2	0.91 ± 0.02	0.07 ± 0.02	0.10 ± 0.04
3	0.91 ± 0.01	0.09 ± 0.03	0.08 ± 0.02
4	0.89 ± 0.05	0.09 ± 0.06	0.14 ± 0.05
5	0.92 ± 0.02	0.09 ± 0.03	0.06 ± 0.04
6	0.92 ± 0.03	0.09 ± 0.05	0.06 ± 0.02
7	0.91 ± 0.03	0.08 ± 0.01	0.11 ± 0.05
8	0.92 ± 0.02	0.10 ± 0.03	0.06 ± 0.02
9	0.93 ± 0.01	0.09 ± 0.01	0.06 ± 0.01
10	0.93 ± 0.01	0.07 ± 0.02	0.06 ± 0.02
11	0.90 ± 0.03	0.08 ± 0.04	0.12 ± 0.03
12	0.92 ± 0.01	0.04 ± 0.02	0.12 ± 0.02
13	0.88 ± 0.02	0.11 ± 0.02	0.13 ± 0.05
14	0.91 ± 0.01	0.10 ± 0.04	0.07 ± 0.02
15	0.91 ± 0.02	0.08 ± 0.02	0.10 ± 0.04

3.2   Test Data

For the off-site evaluation the mean disc centroid distance was 0.81 ± 0.42 mm and a detection rate of 97 %. Corresponding results for the on-site evaluation was 0.99 ± 0.78 mm and a detection rate of 80 %. The achieved DICE score was 0.90 ± 0.03 for both the off-site and on-site evaluation.

4   Discussion

In this paper, we have presented one of the methods participating in the IVD segmentation challenge, organized in conjunction with MICCAI–CSI2015, a method relevant for both robust IVD detection and accurate IVD segmentation. The method has been evaluated using training and testing data provided by the challenge organizers. Performance was assessed using disc centroid distance, the DICE score along with computing the ratios of false negatives and false positives (the latter two only computed for the training data).

The presented method achieved a mean disc centroid distance of 0.86 ± 0.45 mm, with a success rate of 97 % given a threshold of 2 mm for the training data. This can be compared with a mean disc centroid distance of 2.08 mm as reported by Ghosh and Chaudhary [3] for the 2D case, 1.23 mm by Law et al. [4] and $1.6 - 2.0$ mm by Chen et al. [2] (both the latter for the 3D case). As such, the presented results are superior to earlier results. Note that the results obtained for the on-site evaluation was somewhat lower than for the training data and for off-site evaluation.

In terms of segmentation accuracy, the presented method performs on par with current state-of-the-art methods for IVD segmentation. For example, Michopoulou et al. [5] achieved an impressive mean DICE score of 0.92, however, only for segmentation of 2D image data and using manual interaction for performing the initial atlas-based registration. Similar DICE scores were presented in the work of Law et al. [4], but again only for 2D image data. Neubert et al. [16] presented an extension of their initial work [6] using multi-level statistical model and achieved a mean DICE score of 0.91 on 3D data.

In Tables 1 and 2 it can be noted that the segmentation accuracy is stable over both discs and subjects, i.e. there exists no failed cases and any future improvements are, thus, rather related to fine-tuning of parameters than making major changes in the presented pipeline. The ratios of false negatives and false positives show that there appear to be an equal distribution of under- and over-segmentation between discs and subjects.

Limitations of the presented results are given by the small size of the data set employed for the evaluation along with its homogeneity. Further, the data set lacks in cases of degenerated IVDs, hence, it is difficult to foresee the performance of the presented segmentation pipeline on more clinically relevant data, including a variety of degenerated IVDs. Another limitation is given by the dependence of the registration step on the detection and labeling step. A missed vertebra in-between other vertebrae can be handled with some additional heuristics to account for long distance between detected vertebra. In the case the detection and labeling is off by one or two labels, i.e. in the case when S1-S2 is missed and instead L5-S1 is labeled as S1-S2, the segmentation is still expected to perform well but neglects to segment the most inferior IVD.

In all, the presented method along with the evaluation results, a mean disc centroid distance of 0.86 ± 0.45 mm and an average DICE score of 0.91 for the training data, show that robust localization and accurate segmentation of IVDs are achievable.

Acknowledgements. The work of D.F. was partially funded by the Swedish Innovation Agency (VINNOVA), grant 2014-01422.

References

1. Oktay, A., Albayrak, N., Akgul, Y.: Computer aided diagnosis of degenerative intervertebral disc diseases from lumbar MR images. Comput. Med. Imaging Graph. **38**(7), 613–619 (2014)

2. Chen, C., Belavy, D., Yu, W., Chu, C., Armbrecht, G., Bansmann, M., Felsenberg, D., Zheng, G.: Localization and segmentation of 3D intervertebral discs in MR images by data driven estimation. IEEE Trans. Med. Imaging **34**(8), 1719–1729 (2015)

3. Ghosh, S., Chaudhary, V.: Supervised methods for detection and segmentation of tissues in clinical lumbar MRI. Comput. Med. Imaging Graph. **38**(7), 639–649 (2014)

4. Law, M., Tay, K., Leung, A., Garvin, G., Li, S.: Intervertebral disc segmentation in MR images using anisotropic oriented flux. Med. Image Anal. **17**(1), 43–61 (2013)

5. Michopoulou, S., Costaridou, L., Panagiotopoulos, E., Speller, R., Panayiotakis, G., Todd-Pokropek, A.: Atlas-based segmentation of degenerated lumbar intervertebral siscs from MR images of the spine. IEEE Trans. Biomed. Eng. **56**(9), 2225–2231 (2009)

6. Neubert, A., Fripp, J., Engstrom, C., Schwarz, R., Lauer, L., Salvado, O., Crozier, S.: Automated detection, 3D segmentation and analysis of high resolution spine MR images using statistical shape models. Phys. Med. Biol. **57**(24), 8357–8376 (2012)

7. Lootus, M., Kadir, T., Zisserman, A.: Vertebrae detection and labelling in lumbar MR images. In: Yao, J., et al. (eds.) CSI 2013. LNCV, vol. 17, pp. 219–230. Springer, Switzerland (2014)

8. Forsberg, D.: Atlas-based registration for accurate segmentation of thoracic and lumbar vertebrae in CT data. In: Yao, J., et al. (eds.) CSI 2014. LNCVB, vol. 20, pp. 49–59. Springer, Switzerland (2015)

9. Dollár, P., Tu, Z., Perona, P., Belongie, S.: Integral channel features. In: Proceedings of 2009 British Machine Vision Conference, BMVC 2009, pp. 91.1–91.11. BMVA Press (2009)

10. Felzenszwalb, P., Huttenlocher, D.: Pictorial structures for object recognition. Int. J. Comput. Vis. **61**(1), 55–79 (2005)

11. Hemmendorff, M., Andersson, M., Kronander, T., Knutsson, H.: Phase-based multidimensional volume registration. IEEE Trans. Med. Imaging **21**(12), 1536–1543 (2002)

12. Eklund, A., Andersson, M., Knutsson, H.: Phase based volume registration using CUDA. In: Proceedings of 2010 IEEE International Conference on Acoustics, Speech and Signal Processing, ICASSP 2010, pp. 658–661. IEEE (2010)
13. Knutsson, H., Andersson, M.: Morphons: segmentation using elastic canvas and paint on priors. In: Proceedings of 12th IEEE International Conference on Image Processing, ICIP 2005, vol. 2, pp. 1226–1229. IEEE (2005)
14. Forsberg, D.: Robust image registration for improved clinical efficiency: using local structure analysis and model-based processing. Ph.D. thesis, Linköping University, Sweden (2013)
15. Forsberg, D., Eklund, A., Andersson, M., Knutsson, H.: Phase-based non-rigid 3D image registration - from minutes to seconds using CUDA. In: Proceedings of Joint MICCAI Workshop on High Performance and Distributed Computing for Medical Imaging - HP/DCI 2011 (2011)
16. Neubert, A., Fripp, J., Engstrom, C., Crozier, S.: Segmentation of lumbar intervertebral discs from high-resolution 3D MR images using multi-level statistical shape models. In: Yao, J., et al. (eds.) CSI 2013. LNCVB, vol. 17, pp. 173–183. Springer, Switzerland (2014)

Deformable Model-Based Segmentation of Intervertebral Discs from MR Spine Images by Using the SSC Descriptor

Robert Korez[✉], Bulat Ibragimov, Boštjan Likar, Franjo Pernuš, and Tomaž Vrtovec

University of Ljubljana, Faculty of Electrical Engineering, Ljubljana, Slovenia
{robert.korez,bulat.ibragimov,bostjan.likar,franjo.pernus, tomaz.vrtovec}@fe.uni-lj.si

Abstract. Gradual degeneration of intervertebral discs of the lumbar spine is one of the most common causes of low back pain. A fully automatic, accurate and robust segmentation of intervertebral discs in magnetic resonance (MR) images is therefore a prerequisite for the computer-aided diagnosis and quantification of intervertebral disc degeneration. In this paper, we propose an automated framework for intervertebral disc segmentation from MR spine images, in which intervertebral disc detection is performed by a landmark-based approach and segmentation by a deformable model-based approach using the self-similarity context (SSC) descriptor. The performance was evaluated on three publicly available databases of MR spine images that represent the training, on-line and on-site testing data for the intervertebral disc localization and segmentation challenge in conjunction with the 3rd MICCAI Workshop & Challenge on Computational Methods and Clinical Applications for Spine Imaging - MICCAI–CSI2015, yielding an overall mean Euclidean distance of 2.4, 1.7 and 2.2 mm for intervertebral disc localization, and an overall mean Dice coefficient of 92.5, 91.5 and 92.0 % for intervertebral disc segmentation for training, on-line and on-site testing data, respectively.

1 Introduction

The vertebral column is a complex anatomical construct, composed of vertebrae and intervertebral discs that are supported by robust spinal ligaments and muscles. During life, all components undergo degenerative changes and morphologic alterations, and although for most individuals such changes do not represent a problem, in some cases they may eventually cause severe, chronic and debilitating low back pain, which is an insidious problem recognized as a biopsycho-social syndrome [1,2]. The complex process begins due to an anatomical or biological event and afterwards it is transformed by psychological and social factors into a chronic illness. Despite the high prevalence of low back pain and significant burden to the society, its etiology remains unclear. The main diagnostic challenge is to locate the pain generator, and the degenerated intervertebral disc has been identified to be capable of acting as such [3]. In clinical practice, magnetic

© Springer International Publishing Switzerland 2016
T. Vrtovec et al. (Eds.): CSI 2015, LNCS 9402, pp. 117–124, 2016.
DOI: 10.1007/978-3-319-41827-8_11

resonance (MR) is the imaging modality of choice for diagnosing intervertebral disc degeneration as precise information on soft tissues is needed. In addition to the non-invasive nature of this modality, MR depicts many important features of the intervertebral disc, including disc height, annulus fibrosus contours and persistence of water in the nucleus pulposus [4]. A fully automatic, accurate and robust segmentation of intervertebral discs in MR images is therefore a prerequisite for the computer-aided diagnosis and quantification of intervertebral disc degeneration that could be also used for computer-assisted planning and simulation in spinal surgery.

In recent years, several automated and semi-automated methods focusing on three-dimensional (3D) intervertebral disc (or space) segmentation have been developed for computed tomography (CT) and MR images. Neubert et al. [5] proposed an automated approach to extract 3D lumbar and thoracic intervertebral discs from MR images using statistical shape analysis and registration of gray level intensity profiles. Kelm et al. [6] introduced an approach that combines local object detection based on iterative marginal space learning with a global probabilistic prior model to obtain an oriented bounding box around the intervertebral disc for a case-adaptive segmentation in MR images. Chen et al. [7] proposed a fully automatic method for localizing and segmenting 3D intervertebral discs from MR images, where the two problems were solved in a unified data-driven regression and classification framework. Korez et al. [8] initialized a 3D parametric model of the intervertebral disc space in the form of a truncated elliptical cone, which was then in an optimization procedure incrementally deformed by adding parameters that provided a more detailed morphometric description of the observed shape, and aligned to the observed intervertebral disc space in CT images to obtain the final segmentation. Recently, Haq et al. [9] initialized a simplex active surface mesh in the sagittal plane of a patient MR volume and allowed it to deform using weak shape priors to capture the intervertebral disc boundary.

In this paper, we present an automated framework for intervertebral disc segmentation from MR spine images that is based on deformable models augmented by the self-similarity context (SSC) descriptor. The framework was tested on images that represent training, on-line and on-site testing data for the intervertebral disc localization and segmentation challenge in conjunction with the 3rd MICCAI Workshop & Challenge on Computational Methods and Clinical Applications for Spine Imaging - MICCAI–CSI2015.

2   Methodology

2.1   Intervertebral Disc Detection

Successful segmentation of intervertebral discs depends on accurate and robust initialization, which can be formulated as a disc detection and labeling task. Thoroughly investigated landmark-based approaches proved to be efficient in detecting various structures, as they can consider global image information and therefore distinguish among locally similar structures such as vertebrae or intervertebral discs [10]. Each intervertebral disc is described by five landmarks that belong to its mid-plane and represent, respectively, the mid-point and most superior, inferior, anterior and posterior points of the disc. The appearance information of each landmark is described by Haar-like features, which effectively capture intensity inhomogeneity and complex neighborhood of that landmark in MR images, and can be rapidly computed from integral image representation [11]. The shape information is described by pairwise spatial relationships among landmarks that belong to the same disc. The optimal landmark positions correspond to the best agreement between the appearance and shape model.

2.2 Intervertebral Disc Segmentation

Mean Shape Model of the Intervertebral Disc. Let set $\mathcal{I}$ contain 3D images of the thoracolumbar spine, where each image is assigned a series of binary masks representing reference segmentations of each individual thoracolumbar intervertebral disc from level T11–T12 to L5–S1. To extract a shape model of each intervertebral disc from each image in $\mathcal{I}$, the marching cubes algorithm is applied to each binary mask, resulting in a 3D face-vertex mesh consisting of vertices with triangle connectivity information. In order to establish pointwise correspondences among vertices of the same intervertebral level, the nonrigid transformation among sets of vertices is recovered using coherent point drift algorithm [12]. Finally, the generalized Procrustes alignment is used to remove translation, rotation and scaling from corresponding meshes, yielding the mean shape model of each intervertebral disc, represented by a 3D mesh $\mathcal{M} = \{\mathcal{V}, \mathcal{F}\}$ of $|\mathcal{V}|$ vertices and $|\mathcal{F}|$ faces (i.e. triangles). The mean shape models of individual intervertebral discs are used for intervertebral disc segmentation in an unknown 3D image.

Deformable Model-Based Segmentation by Using the SSC Descriptor. The results of the landmark-based intervertebral disc detection (Sect. 2.1) initialize intervertebral disc segmentation, which is achieved by adapting the mean shape model to intervertebral disc boundaries in the unknown image. For this purpose, we propose an iterative mesh deformation technique that moves mesh vertices to their optimal locations using the SSC descriptor [13] while preserving the underlying intervertebral space shape [14,15].

By displacing each mesh vertex $\boldsymbol{v}_i$; $i = 1, 2, \ldots, |\mathcal{V}|$ along its corresponding mesh vertex normal $\boldsymbol{n}(\boldsymbol{v}_i)$, a new candidate mesh vertex $\boldsymbol{v}_i^*$ is found in each k-th iteration:

$$\boldsymbol{v}_i^* = \boldsymbol{v}_i + \delta \arg\max_{j_i \in \mathcal{J}} \Big\{ F\big(\boldsymbol{v}_i, \boldsymbol{v}_i + \delta\, j_i\, n(\boldsymbol{v}_i)\big) - D\,\delta^2\, j_i^2 \Big\}\, \boldsymbol{n}(\boldsymbol{v}_i), \qquad (1)$$

where δ is the length of the unit displacement, set

$$\mathcal{J} = \{-j, -j+1, \ldots, j-1, j\}; \quad j = \left\lfloor \frac{J-1}{1-K} \cdot k + \frac{1 - J \cdot K}{1-K} \right\rfloor, \qquad (2)$$

represents the search profile along $n(c_i)$, which is of size $2J+1$ at initial iteration $k = 1$ and three at final iteration $k = K$, and $\lfloor \cdot \rfloor$ denotes the ceil operator. Furthermore, the parameter D controls the tradeoff between the response of the boundary detection operator

$$F(v_i, v_i') = \frac{g_{\max}\left(g_{\max} + \|g_W(v_i')\|\right)}{g_{\max}^2 + \|g_W(v_i')\|^2} \langle n(v_i), g_W(v_i')\rangle, \tag{3}$$

and the distance from v_i to $v_i + \delta j_i\, n(v_i)$, where $g_{\max}$ is the estimated mean amplitude of intensity gradients at intervertebral disc boundaries, $\|\cdot\|$ denotes the vector norm, $\langle \cdot, \cdot \rangle$ denotes the dot product, and g_W is the image appearance operator at candidate mesh vertex location c_i':

$$g_W(v_i') = \left(1 + \alpha C(v_i') + (1 - \alpha)R(v_i')\right) g(v_i'), \tag{4}$$

where α is the weighting parameter, $C(c_i') \in [0,1]$ is the continuous response to the Canny edge operator [16], $R(v_i') \in [-1,1]$ is the continuous response to the random forest regression model [17] (with $R(v_i') = 1$ indicating that the location of v_i' corresponds to appearance characteristics of intervertebral disc boundaries and $R(v_i') = -1$ indicating the opposite), and $g(v_i')$ is the image intensity gradient at v_i'. The important characteristics of each mesh vertex v_i; $i = 1, 2, \ldots, |\mathcal{V}|$ that are used for the random forest regression are described by a 26-dimensional feature vector defined as $(I_{v_i}, SSC_{v_i}, G_{v_i}, g(v_i), \varphi(v_i))$:

- $I_{v_i} = (I(v_i), I(v_i)^2, I(v_i)^3, \sqrt[2]{I(v_i)}, \sqrt[3]{I(v_i)})$,
- SSC_{v_i} is a 12-dimensional SSC descriptor [13] obtained from patch-based self-similarities that aim to find the geometrical and structural context around each mesh vertex v_i,
- $G_{v_i} = (\|g(v_i)\|, \|g(v_i)\|^2, \|g(v_i)\|^3, \sqrt[2]{\|g(v_i)\|}, \sqrt[3]{\|g(v_i)\|})$,

where $I(v_i)$ is the image intensity at v_i, $g(v_i)$ is the image intensity gradient at v_i, and $\varphi(v_i)$ is the angle between $n(v_i)$ and $g(v_i)$ [18].

Once new candidate mesh vertices v_i^* are detected, mesh $\mathcal{M} = \{\mathcal{V}, \mathcal{F}\}$ is reconfigured in each k-th iteration by minimizing the weighted sum E of energy terms $E_{\text{ext}} + \beta E_{\text{int}}$, where β is the weighting parameter. The external energy E_{ext} attracts mesh $\mathcal{M}$ to new mesh vertices v_i^*, $i = 1, 2, \ldots, |\mathcal{V}|$ (1), that are located on intervertebral disc boundaries:

$$E_{\text{ext}} = \sum_{i=1}^{|\mathcal{V}|} w_i^* \left\langle v_i^* - v_i, \frac{g_W(v_i^*)}{\|g_W(v_i^*)\|} \right\rangle^2, \tag{5}$$

where $|\mathcal{V}|$ is the number of mesh vertices, g_W is the image appearance operator (4), and $w_i^* = \max\{0, F(c_i, c_i^*) - D\,\delta^2\,j_i^2\}$; $i = 1, 2, \ldots, |\mathcal{V}|$, are weights that are defined according to the obtained j_i (1) to give a greater influence to more promising locations of mesh vertices. The internal energy E_{int} restricts the flexibility of mesh $\mathcal{M}$ by penalizing the deviation between deformation vertices $\mathcal{V}$ and mean vertices $\mathcal{V}^m$:

$$E_{\text{int}} = \sum_{i=1}^{|\mathcal{V}|} \sum_{j \in \mathcal{N}_i} \left\| \left(\boldsymbol{v}_i - \boldsymbol{v}_j \right) - \left(sR \left(\boldsymbol{v}_i^m - \boldsymbol{v}_j^m \right) + \boldsymbol{t} \right) \right\|^2 \qquad (6)$$

where $\boldsymbol{v}_i$ and $\boldsymbol{v}_i^m$ are vertices from sets $\mathcal{V}$ and $\mathcal{V}^m$, respectively, $\mathcal{M}^m = \{\mathcal{V}^m, \mathcal{F}^m\}$ represents the mean shape model of the observed intervertebral disc (Sect. 2.2), and $\mathcal{N}_i$ is the set of vertices neighboring to $\boldsymbol{v}_i$ (or $\boldsymbol{v}_i^m$, since the topology is preserved). The scaling factor s, rotation matrix R and translation vector $\boldsymbol{t}$ that align mesh vertices $\boldsymbol{v}_i$ to mean vertices $\boldsymbol{v}_i^m$ are determined prior to calculation of (6) by using the Procrustes alignment.

3   Experiments and Results

The proposed automated framework for intervertebral disc segmentation was evaluated (by applying a leave-one-out evaluation scheme) on the publicly available databases of MR spine images that represent training, on-line and on-site testing data for the intervertebral disc localization and segmentation challenge in conjunction with MICCAI–CSI2015. The training, on-line and on-site testing data consist of 15, 5 and 5 sagittally reconstructed MR images of the thoracolumbar spine with a total of 105, 35 and 35 thoracolumbar intervertebral discs from 15, 5 and 5 subjects, respectively. Furthermore, the in-plane voxel size was of 1.25 mm × 1.25 mm, cross-sectional thickness was of 2 mm, and a reference segmentation binary mask was available for each intervertebral disc in the training data.

All experiments were executed on a personal computer with Intel Core i5 processor at 3.2 GHz and 16 GB of memory without a graphics processing unit. The detection of all seven intervertebral discs in the database of training images (i.e. levels from T11–T12 to L05–S01) took on average around 1.4 min, while

Table 1. Summary of intervertebral disc segmentation results on the training data in terms of mean symmetric surface distance (MSD), root-mean-square symmetric surface distance (RMSSD), maximal symmetric surface distance (MaxSD) and Dice coefficient (DICE), reported as mean ± standard deviation.

Intervertebral level	MSD (mm)	RMSSD (mm)	MaxSD (mm)	DICE (%)
T11–T12	0.46 ± 0.18	0.86 ± 0.27	4.05 ± 1.37	90.84 ± 3.29
T12–L01	0.44 ± 0.12	0.83 ± 0.16	4.08 ± 1.13	92.21 ± 1.65
L01–L02	0.45 ± 0.13	0.87 ± 0.19	4.48 ± 1.08	92.75 ± 1.87
L02–L03	0.45 ± 0.10	0.87 ± 0.16	4.02 ± 1.17	93.17 ± 1.22
L03–L04	0.44 ± 0.11	0.82 ± 0.14	3.94 ± 0.94	93.73 ± 1.12
L04–L05	0.48 ± 0.19	0.89 ± 0.26	4.17 ± 1.47	92.97 ± 2.09
L05–S01	0.48 ± 0.34	0.89 ± 0.54	3.91 ± 1.72	92.01 ± 4.39
All levels	**0.46 ± 0.18**	**0.86 ± 0.28**	**4.09 ± 1.31**	**92.52 ± 2.64**

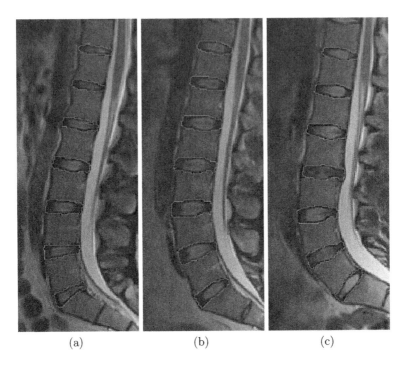

(a)   (b)   (c)

Fig. 1. An example of intervertebral disc segmentation results (in yellow) in comparison to reference segmentation (in red) for three ((a), (b) and (c)) randomly selected MR spine images from the database (mid-sagittal view only). (Color figure online)

the segmentation of each individual intervertebral disc took on average around 30 s. An important aspect of the segmentation process is its dependence on several parameters. Therefore, we analysed the sensitivity of the algorithm against changes in parameters, and based on images in the training database, optimal values were set to $\delta = 0.25$ mm and $D = 5.0$ mm^{-2} (1), $J = 35$ and $K = 15$ (2), $g_{max} = 75$ (3), $\alpha = 0.25$ (4), and $\beta = 30$. Since the total energy E is a sum of quadratic terms, the minimization problem was efficiently solved by the conjugate gradient method.

The detection performance of the proposed framework was evaluated by the Euclidean distance (ED), computed between the detected and corresponding reference landmarks, while the segmentation performance was evaluated by the mean symmetric surface distance (MSD), root-mean-square symmetric surface distance (RMSSD), maximal symmetric surface distance (MaxSD) and Dice coefficient (DICE), computed between the resulting 3D meshes and corresponding reference segmentation binary masks. On the training data, the overall detection performance (mean ± standard deviation) was ED = 2.35 ± 0.98 mm, and the overall segmentation performance was MSD = 0.46 ± 0.18 mm, RMSSD = 0.86 ± 0.28 mm, MaxSD = 4.09 ± 1.31 mm and DICE = 92.52 ± 2.64 % for the proposed framework. Detailed results for segmentation at individual intervertebral levels are presented in Table 1. Furthermore, on the on-line and on-site testing data, the overall detection performance was ED $= 1.74 \pm 0.88$ mm and 2.18 ± 0.82 mm, and the overall segmentation performance was DICE $= 91.5 \pm 2.3\%$ and $92.0 \pm 1.9\%$, respectively. An example of the resulting segmentation for three randomly selected MR thoracolumbar spine images is shown in Fig. 1.

4 Conclusion

In this paper, we presented an automated framework for intervertebral disc segmentation from MR spine images, in which detection of intervertebral discs was performed by a landmark-based approach, and segmentation of intervertebral discs was performed by a deformable model-based approach using the SSC descriptor. The performance was evaluated on three publicly available databases of MR spine images that represent the training, on-line and on-site testing data for the intervertebral disc localization and segmentation challenge in conjunction with MICCAI–CSI2015.

Acknowledgements. This work was supported by the Slovenian Research Agency (ARRS) under grants P2-0232, J2-5473 and J7-6781.

References

1. Negrini, S., Bonaiuti, D., Monticone, M., Trevisan, M.: Medical causes of low back pain. In: Slipman, C., et al. (eds.) Interventional Spine: An Algorithmic Approach, pp. 803–811. Saunders Elsevier, Philadelphia (2008)
2. Prescher, A.: Anatomy and pathology of the aging spine. Eur. J. Radiol. **27**(3), 181–195 (1998)
3. Sizer, P., Phelps, V., Matthijs, O.: Pain generators of the lumbar spine. Pain Pract. **1**(3), 255–273 (2001)
4. An, H., Anderson, P., Haughton, V., Iatridis, J., Kang, J., Lotz, J., Natarajan, R., Oegema, T., Roughley, P., Setton, L., Urban, J., Videman, T., Andersson, G., Weinstein, J.: Introduction: disc degeneration: summary. Spine **29**(23), 2677–2678 (2004)
5. Neubert, A., Fripp, J., Engstrom, C., Schwarz, R., Lauer, L., Salvado, O., Crozier, S.: Automated detection, 3D segmentation and analysis of high resolution spine MR images using statistical shape models. Phys. Med. Biol. **57**(24), 8357–8376 (2012)
6. Kelm, B., Wels, M., Zhou, S., Seifert, S., Suehling, M., Zheng, Y., Comaniciu, D.: Spine detection in CT and MR using iterated marginal space learning. Med. Image Anal. **17**(8), 1283–1292 (2013)
7. Chen, C., Belavy, D., Yu, W., Chu, C., Armbrecht, G., Bansmann, M., Felsenberg, D., Zheng, G.: Localization and segmentation of 3D intervertebral discs in MR images by data driven estimation. IEEE Trans. Med. Imaging **34**(8), 1719–1729 (2015)

8. Korez, R., Likar, B., Pernuš, F., Vrtovec, T.: Parametric modeling of the intervertebral disc space in 3D: application to CT images of the lumbar spine. Comput. Med. Imaging Graph. **38**(7), 596–605 (2014)
9. Haq, R., Aras, R., Besachio, D., Borgie, R., Audette, M.: 3D lumbar spine intervertebral disc segmentation and compression simulation from MRI using shape-aware models. Int. J. Comput. Assist. Radiol. Surg. **10**(1), 45–54 (2015)
10. Ibragimov, B., Likar, B., Pernuš, F., Vrtovec, T.: Shape representation for efficient landmark-based segmentation in 3-D. IEEE Trans. Med. Imaging **33**(4), 861–874 (2014)
11. Ibragimov, B., Prince, J., Murano, E., Woo, J., Stone, M., Likar, B., Pernuš, F., Vrtovec, T.: Segmentation of tongue muscles from super-resolution magnetic resonance images. Med. Image Anal. **20**(1), 198–207 (2015)
12. Myronenko, A., Song, X.: Point set registration: coherent point drift. IEEE Trans. Pattern Anal. Mach. Intell. **32**(12), 2262–2275 (2010)
13. Heinrich, M.P., Jenkinson, M., Papież, B.W., Brady, S.M., Schnabel, J.A.: Towards realtime multimodal fusion for image-guided interventions using self-similarities. In: Mori, K., Sakuma, I., Sato, Y., Barillot, C., Navab, N. (eds.) MICCAI 2013, Part I. LNCS, vol. 8149, pp. 187–194. Springer, Heidelberg (2013)
14. Weese, J., Kaus, M.R., Lorenz, C., Lobregt, S., Truyen, R., Pekar, V.: Shape constrained deformable models for 3D medical image segmentation. In: Insana, M.F., Leahy, R.M. (eds.) IPMI 2001. LNCS, vol. 2082, pp. 380–387. Springer, Heidelberg (2001)
15. Korez, R., Ibragimov, B., Likar, B., Pernuš, F., Vrtovec, T.: A framework for automated spine and vertebrae interpolation-based detection and model-based segmentation. IEEE Trans. Med. Imaging **34**(8), 1649–1662 (2015)
16. Canny, J.: A computational approach to edge detection. IEEE Trans. Pattern Anal. Mach. Intell. **8**(6), 679–698 (1986)
17. Breiman, L.: Random forests. Mach. Learn. **45**(1), 5–32 (2001)
18. Zheng, Y., Barbu, A., Georgescu, B., Scheuering, M., Comaniciu, D.: Four-chamber heart modeling and automatic segmentation for 3-D cardiac CT volumes using marginal space learning and steerable features. IEEE Trans. Med. Imaging **27**(11), 1668–1681 (2008)

3D Intervertebral Disc Segmentation from MRI Using Supervoxel-Based CRFs

Hugo Hutt$^{(\boxtimes)}$, Richard Everson, and Judith Meakin

University of Exeter, Exeter, UK
{hwh202,r.m.everson,j.r.meakin}@exeter.ac.uk

Abstract. Segmentation of intervertebral discs from three-dimensional magnetic resonance images is a challenging problem with numerous medical applications. In this paper we describe a fully automated segmentation method based on a conditional random field operating on supervoxels. A mean Dice score of $90 \pm 3\%$ was obtained on data provided for the intervertebral disc localisation and segmentation challenge in conjunction with the 3$^{\rm rd}$ MICCAI Workshop & Challenge on Computational Methods and Clinical Applications for Spine Imaging - MICCAI–CSI2015.

1   Introduction

Segmentation of intervertebral discs in three-dimensional (3D) magnetic resonance (MR) images is an important step in many applications, but remains a difficult problem for automated computational methods. In this paper we report a fully automated method and evaluate it on data provided for the intervertebral disc localisation and segmentation challenge in conjunction with the 3$^{\rm rd}$ MICCAI Workshop & Challenge on Computational Methods and Clinical Applications for Spine Imaging - MICCAI–CSI2015. The approach described here is adapted from a method for segmentation of vertebrae from MR imaging and computerised tomography (CT) data that we introduced in the works of Hutt et al. [1,2]. The method is based on a conditional random field operating on supervoxels and incorporating a classifier and distance metric learned on sparse supervoxel features. Compared to our previous work, the most notable difference is that we do not use any location features for intervertebral disc segmentation. In Sect. 2 we give a brief description of the main components of the method, before presenting the segmentation results.

2   Methods

2.1   Supervoxels

We formulate the segmentation problem as one of assigning class labels to *supervoxels* (groups of similar voxels). Operating on supervoxels enables more descriptive features to be extracted over the supervoxel regions and greatly reduces computational complexity compared to operating directly on the individual voxels

© Springer International Publishing Switzerland 2016
T. Vrtovec et al. (Eds.): CSI 2015, LNCS 9402, pp. 125–129, 2016.
DOI: 10.1007/978-3-319-41827-8_12

of the images. To generate supervoxels for a volume, we use a modified version of simple linear iterative clustering (SLIC) [3] which results in supervoxels with approximately equal *physical* extent in all directions. We determine the supervoxel parameters empirically by searching for the maximum supervoxel size that still preserves almost all object boundaries in the training images.

2.2 Multi-scale Dictionary Learning

We aim to characterise the supervoxels by extracting descriptive features from them which can be used to learn a model from training data to estimate the class label (i.e. disc or background). We next describe our supervoxel features, which are obtained by encoding and pooling the responses from learned multi-scale dictionaries of linear filters.

To learn the dictionaries, we first construct a Gaussian pyramid representation for each of the training volumes by successive smoothing and downsampling by a factor of 2. We then randomly sample $100\,000$ patches of dimension $5 \times 5 \times 5$ voxels from each pyramid level of the training images and reshape them into vectors $\{\mathbf{v}_i\}_{i=1}^M$. The sampled vectors are whitened and then encoded into a separate dictionary of filters corresponding to each pyramid level using *sparse coding* [4]. For the results given in this paper we used 3-level pyramids and learned a separate dictionary of 128 filters at each level of the training pyramids. This results in a set of dictionaries which are able to capture large-scale structure in the volumes due to being learned over multiple scales, but are also very efficient to compute.

To obtain the final supervoxel features for a volume, patches are first sampled densely over the pyramid using a step-size of 2 voxels. The sampled patches are then encoded using non-linear functions of the linear filter responses, given by

$$\mathbf{u}_i = \max\left\{0, \left[-\mathbf{D}, \mathbf{D}\right]^\top \mathbf{v}_i\right\}, \tag{1}$$

where $\left[-\mathbf{D}, \mathbf{D}\right]$ is a matrix formed by column-wise concatenation of the dictionary $\mathbf{D}$ of learned filters.[1] Features corresponding to different levels of the pyramid are concatenated into a single vector at each location. The densely extracted features are then aggregated within each supervoxel using a max pooling operation and ℓ_2-normalised to unit length.

2.3 CRF with Learned Potentials

Given the set of supervoxel feature vectors for a volume, we define a *conditional random field* (CRF) over the supervoxels that relates the features to the underlying class labels. The resulting model promotes spatial consistency of the labels and enables segmentation to be carried out very efficiently using graph cut algorithms.

---

[1] Separate dictionaries are used to encode patches at different levels of the pyramid.

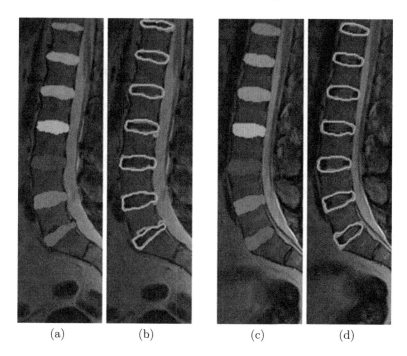

(a)   (b)   (c)   (d)

Fig. 1. (a), (c) Segmentation results overlaid onto a mid-sagittal slice from two subjects (numbers 2 and 10, respectively). (b), (d) Overlap between the CRF segmentations (cyan) and manual annotations (magenta). (Color figure online)

The CRF defines a conditional distribution over the supervoxel class labels $\mathbf{x}$ given the features $\mathbf{y}$ and can be formulated in terms of an energy function. The energy function is a sum over a unary data term and a pairwise smoothness term:

$$E(\mathbf{x}, \mathbf{y}) = \underbrace{\sum_{i \in \mathcal{S}} \psi(\mathbf{y}_i \mid x_i)}_{\text{Data term}} + \lambda \underbrace{\sum_{i \in \mathcal{S}} \sum_{j \in \mathcal{N}_i} \phi(\mathbf{y}_i, \mathbf{y}_j \mid x_i, x_j)}_{\text{Smoothness term}}, \qquad (2)$$

where $\mathcal{S}$ is the set of supervoxels and $\mathcal{N}_i$ are the neighbours of supervoxel i. The constant λ controls the relative importance of the data and smoothness terms. The data term of the CRF is defined as the negative log likelihood of the supervoxel feature vector given the class label:

$$\psi(\mathbf{y}_i \mid x_i) = - \log \Big(P(\mathbf{y}_i \mid x_i) \Big). \qquad (3)$$

The likelihood $P(\mathbf{y}_i \mid x_i)$ is the probability estimate for the supervoxel given by a learned support vector machine (SVM) classifier. We train the SVM on labelled supervoxel examples using a generalised RBF kernel, given by

$$K(\mathbf{y}_i, \mathbf{y}_j) = \exp \Big(- \gamma (\mathbf{y}_i - \mathbf{y}_j)^\top \mathbf{M} (\mathbf{y}_i - \mathbf{y}_j) \Big), \qquad (4)$$

where γ is an overall kernel width parameter. The matrix $\mathbf{M}$ defines a pseudo-metric between supervoxel features which we learn from training data using the large margin nearest neighbour (LMNN) [5] algorithm. The smoothness term of the CRF incorporates the learned distance metric as follows

$$\phi(\mathbf{y}_i, \mathbf{y}_j \mid x_i, x_j) = \begin{cases} \exp\left(-(\mathbf{y}_i - \mathbf{y}_j)^\top \mathbf{M}(\mathbf{y}_i - \mathbf{y}_j)\right) & \text{if } x_i \neq x_j \\ 0 & \text{otherwise} \end{cases}, \quad (5)$$

which penalises neighbouring supervoxels that have similar feature vectors and are assigned to different classes.

We compute soft estimates (max-marginals) for the supervoxels $P(x_i \mid \mathbf{y}_i)$ from the CRF and obtain the final voxel-level segmentation by thresholding the max-marginals after smoothing with a Gaussian filter.

Table 1. Segmentation results on the training dataset. The table shows the Dice score (%) and average absolute surface distance (ASD) (mm) for each individual subject. The final column gives the median value over all subjects.

Subject	1	2	3	4	5	6	7	8	9	10	11	12	13	14	15	Med.
Dice	91	93	89	84	93	92	89	92	92	94	87	90	89	90	92	91
ASD	0.54	0.40	1.22	1.37	0.34	0.45	0.72	0.40	0.44	0.35	0.95	0.63	0.59	0.54	0.45	0.54

3   Results

The method was evaluated on a dataset consisting of T2-weighted turbo spin echo MR images from 25 different subjects provided for the MICCAI–CSI2015 intervertebral disc localisation and segmentation challenge [6].[2] Each image contains intervertebral discs of the lower spine from T11 to L5. A total of 7 discs in each image have been manually annotated. The complete dataset is split into an initial training dataset consisting of 15 subjects and two test datasets each consisting of 5 subjects.

Leave-one-out testing was used to evaluate the performance of the method on the training dataset. At each iteration the model was learned on the 14 training subjects and then evaluated on the single held out subject. The process was repeated for all subjects, thus ensuring that the training and test data were always from separate subjects. For each test subject, parameters, such as λ, were learned using leave-one-out cross validation on the 14 training subjects; here too, the validation subject was always separate from the remaining 13 training subjects. The average value of λ over all leave-one-out iterations was 0.67, while the average values of the SVM regularisation and kernel parameters were $C = 5.24$ and $\gamma = 0.52$. The execution time for processing a single volume after learning was approximately 6 min using an Intel Core i5 2.50 GHz machine with 8 GB of RAM.

The segmentations were evaluated using the Dice score and average absolute surface distance (ASD); the results on the training dataset are summarised in

---

[2] Available from the SpineWeb: http://spineweb.digitalimaginggroup.ca.

Table 1. The mean Dice score on the training dataset was $90 \pm 3\%$ and the mean ASD was 0.63 ± 0.32 mm. On the two test datasets the mean Dice scores were $90 \pm 4\%$ and $91 \pm 3\%$; the mean ASD values were 1.24 ± 0.24 mm and 1.19 ± 0.20 mm. Figure 1 provides a visual comparison, for single slices of the 3D segmentation, between example automatic segmentations and manual annotations.

4 Conclusion

We described a method for automated segmentation of intervertebral discs from MR imaging data based on a conditional random field on supervoxels. The method was shown to obtain accurate and consistent results on the challenge data, with each volume taking approximately 6 min to segment. An advantage of our approach is its generality, which means it can be applied to segment different structures without fundamental change to the model. This is illustrated by the consistently good performance of the method on the intervertebral disc dataset, along with previous vertebra segmentation results obtained on MR imaging and CT data.

Acknowledgements. We are grateful to the organisers of the challenge and to the SpineWeb initiative for making the data available.

References

1. Hutt, H., Everson, R., Meakin, J.: Segmentation of lumbar vertebrae slices from CT images. In: Yao, J., et al. (eds.) CSI 2014. LNCVB, vol. 20, pp. 61–71. Springer, Switzerland (2015)
2. Hutt, H., Everson, R., Meakin, J.: 3D segmentation of the lumbar spine from MRI using supervoxel-based CRFs. Technical report, University of Exeter, UK (2015)
3. Achanta, R., Shaji, A., Smith, K., Lucchi, A., Fua, P., Süsstrunk, S.: SLIC superpixels compared to state-of-the-art superpixel methods. IEEE Trans. Pattern Anal. Mach. Intell. **34**(11), 2274–2282 (2012)
4. Olshausen, B., Field, D.: Emergence of simple-cell receptive field properties. Nature **381**(6583), 607–609 (1996)
5. Weinberger, K., Saul, L.: Distance metric learning for large margin nearest neighbor classification. J. Mach. Learn. Res. **10**, 207–244 (2009)
6. Chen, C., Belavy, D., Yu, W., Chu, C., Armbrecht, G., Bansmann, M., Felsenberg, D., Zheng, G.: Localization and segmentation of 3D intervertebral discs in MR images by data driven estimation. IEEE Trans. Med. Imaging **34**(8), 1719–1729 (2015)

Automatic Intervertebral Disc Localization and Segmentation in 3D MR Images Based on Regression Forests and Active Contours

Martin Urschler[1,2(✉)], Kerstin Hammernik[1], Thomas Ebner[1], and Darko Štern[1,2]

[1] Institute for Computer Graphics and Vision, BioTechMed,
Graz University of Technology, Graz, Austria
{urschler,hammernik,ebner,stern}@icg.tugraz.at
[2] Ludwig Boltzmann Institute for Clinical Forensic Imaging, Graz, Austria

Abstract. We introduce a fully automatic localization and segmentation pipeline for three-dimensional (3D) intervertebral discs (IVDs), consisting of a regression-based prediction of vertebral bodies and IVD positions as well as a 3D geodesic active contour segmentation delineating the IVDs. The approach was evaluated on the data set of the challenge in conjunction with the 3rd MICCAI Workshop & Challenge on Computational Methods and Clinical Applications for Spine Imaging - MICCAI–CSI2015, that consists of 15 magnetic resonance images of the lumbar spine with given ground truth segmentations. Based on a localization accuracy of 3.9 ± 1.6 mm, we achieve segmentation results in terms of the Dice similarity coefficient of 89.1 ± 2.9 % averaged over the whole data set.

1 Introduction

Due to reduced physical activity and working conditions of modern office jobs low back pain (LBP) resembles a very important health problem in the developed countries. It is a leading cause of disability affecting work performance and well-being. Clinical studies indicate correlation between LBP and intervertebral disc (IVD) degeneration [1]. A widely used imaging modality for examining IVD degeneration is magnetic resonance (MR) imaging (MRI), since it provides excellent soft tissue contrast without the need for ionizing radiation. In the diagnosis of MR images of the lumbar spine automatic IVD identification and extraction of quantitative measures of IVD geometry and appearance is of high interest. However, development of such automatic methods for accurate and objective IVD localization and segmentation is challenging and still represents an important research area [2–5]. To objectively compare and analyze IVD segmentation approaches, efforts like the challenge *Automatic Intervertebral Disc (IVD) Localization and Segmentation from 3D T2 MRI Data* in conjunction with the 3rd MICCAI Workshop & Challenge on Computational Methods and Clinical Applications for Spine Imaging - MICCAI–CSI2015 are necessary and crucial for potential future application in clinical practice.

© Springer International Publishing Switzerland 2016
T. Vrtovec et al. (Eds.): CSI 2015, LNCS 9402, pp. 130–140, 2016.
DOI: 10.1007/978-3-319-41827-8_13

In this work we present our novel automatic IVD center localization and segmentation approach. It consists of a machine learning step to predict center locations of both vertebral bodies and IVDs as well as an image processing pipeline to segment IVDs given the located spine landmarks. Segmentation is based on geodesic active contours formulated as convex energy functional. We evaluate our method on the 15 MRI data sets from the MICCAI–CSI2015 challenge and report localization errors and Dice similarity coefficients (DSC) with respect to the provided IVD ground truth segmentations.

2   Methods

Our proposed IVD segmentation algorithm is built upon a powerful machine learning based landmark localization step using regression forests [6,7] together with a high-level Markov random field (MRF) model of the global configuration of the relative landmark positions [8]. After landmark prediction, we attach a three-step image processing pipeline for segmentation. First, we roughly segment vertebral bodies based solely on image gradient information, followed by a merging of pairs of adjacent vertebral bodies to single objects to initialize IVD segmentation. Finally, we formulate the IVD segmentation problem as a convex geodesic active contour optimization task based on edges resembling geometrical similarity to the shape of IVDs. Enabled by the robustness of previous localization, this latter segmentation step requires no a priori information on appearance but only a very rough shape prior. The main algorithm steps are shown in Fig. 1.

2.1   Preprocessing

Since the input MRI data sets contain slightly different absolute intensity values and some of the volumes show intensity inhomogeneities, we first perform an automatic Retinex theory based inhomogeneity correction step similar to the

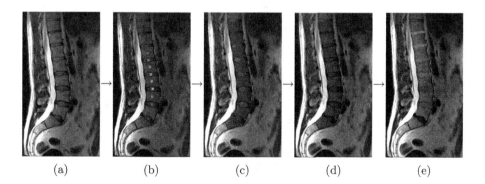

| (a) | (b) | (c) | (d) | (e) |

Fig. 1. Algorithm overview. The 3D MR input images (a) are processed by spinal landmark localization (b), vertebral body segmentation (c), merging of vertebral bodies to initialize IVD segmentation (d) and final voxel-wise IVD labeling (e).

work of Ma et al. [9] to remove the smooth bias field due to this imaging artifact. To derive more similar intensity distributions among the MRI data, we additionally apply histogram matching ignoring background voxels as determined by thresholding [10].

2.2 Spinal Landmark Localization Using Regression Forests

Our approach for localization of vertebrae and IVD centers is based on local appearance information of vertebrae and IVDs in spine images. Inspired by the localization method proposed by Donner et al. [8], we use a Hough forest (HF) [11] to generate probability maps $p_l(\boldsymbol{x})$ for each landmark l being at location $\boldsymbol{x}$. Due to the similar, repeating appearance of spinal landmarks, a global geometric model implemented as an MRF with a dynamic programming based solver is used to select the most probable configuration of landmark positions from the set of candidate positions, thus correctly labeling vertebrae and IVDs.

Candidate Position Generation - Hough Forest. For each landmark l we train a HF from manually annotated locations. Each HF consists of K trees with a maximum depth D. Training starts at the root node using all voxels inside a certain radius r around the landmark position. Our node split functions, passing a voxel either to the left or right child node, are based on Haar-like features. The feature response is calculated as the difference between the mean intensity of two cuboids, whose positions are defined relatively to the voxel position. At each node split, T random thresholds, a pool of F random feature boxes with a maximum distance $d_{f,max}$ from the voxel position and a maximum size $s_{f,max}$ are generated. The respective combination of feature and threshold, which maximizes an Information Gain criterion, is used as the node split function and stored in the split node. In a leaf node we calculate a histogram of the voting vectors

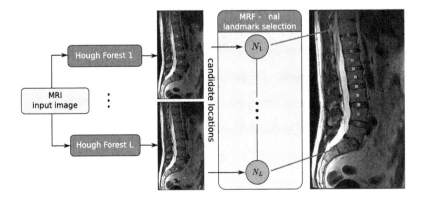

Fig. 2. Overview of the localization pipeline. The colors of the candidate locations indicate the strength of the HF response, where red corresponds to a high value. (Color figure online)

of all voxels arriving at the node and store one single voting vector derived from the maximum of this histogram.

During testing, a random subset of all voxels in an image is pushed through the previously trained trees. All resulting voting vectors from the leaf nodes are summed up in an accumulator data structure, which can be interpreted as probabilities $p_l(\boldsymbol{x})$ of the landmark l being located at position $\boldsymbol{x}$. Using non-maxima suppression we select for each landmark the N strongest local maxima of $p_l(\boldsymbol{x})$ as candidate locations (see Fig. 2).

Candidate Selection - Geometric Model. To select the best candidate for each spinal landmark according to a global geometric model, an MRF is used based on the landmark candidate positions from the previous regression forest step. An MRF is an undirected graph with L nodes and E edges, where each node N_l in the graph corresponds to one landmark. The edges e, connecting the nodes in the graph, are modeling geometric relationships between the landmarks. In our MRF graph only the nodes of neighboring spinal landmarks are connected, thus each vertebral body is connected to its adjacent IVDs and vice versa. Solving the MRF means to select for each node a candidate such that the function

$$\Phi = \prod_{l=1}^{L} \Phi(N_l) \prod_{e=1}^{E} \Phi_n(N_{e_1}, N_{e_2}), \tag{1}$$

based on a product of all node potentials $\Phi(N_l)$ and edge potentials $\Phi_n(N_{e_1}, N_{e_2})$, is maximized. The node potentials $\Phi(N_l)$ are set to the accumulator value $p_l(\boldsymbol{x})$ obtained in the previous step. The edge potentials between nodes N_{e_1} and N_{e_2} and candidate locations c_1 and c_2 are defined as

$$\Phi_n(N_{e_1}, N_{e_2}) = \begin{cases} \Phi_e^x(N_{e_1}, N_{e_2}) \cdot \Phi_e^d(N_{e_1}, N_{e_2}), & \text{if } c_{1,z} \geq c_{2,z} \\ 0 & \text{otherwise} \end{cases}, \tag{2}$$

where $\Phi_e^x(N_{e_1}, N_{e_2})$ is a term punishing large deviations in x-coordinates between two landmarks and $\Phi_e^d(N_{e_1}, N_{e_2})$ a term based on the Euclidean distance between candidate locations. The term based on the x-coordinates is defined as

$$\Phi_e^x(N_{e_1}, N_{e_2}) = e^{-\frac{1}{2}(\frac{c_{1,x} - c_{2,x}}{\sigma_x})^2}, \tag{3}$$

where σ_x allows to control the allowed deviation in x, which is set empirically to $2\,\text{mm}$. The model for the Euclidean distance is based on statistics from the training data and defined as

$$\Phi_e^d(N_{e_1}, N_{e_2}) = e^{-\frac{1}{2}(\frac{\|c_1 - c_2\| - \mu_e}{\sigma_e})^2}, \tag{4}$$

where μ_e and σ_e are mean and variance of the Euclidean distance, respectively.

2.3   Intervertebral Disc Segmentation Using Geodesic Active Contours

From the accurate regression forest based landmark localization approach we achieve a very good initialization for segmenting the IVDs using an image processing pipeline that extracts vertebral bodies and restricts the region where the IVDs are expected. This segmentation pipeline, which is shown in Fig. 3, makes heavy use of a convex 3D geodesic active contour segmentation approach based on total variation (TV), which is described next.

Total Variation Segmentation. Our segmentation framework is based on minimizing following continuous non-smooth energy functional $E_{seg}(u)$ which has previously also been used by Reinbacher et al. [12] and Hammerni et al. [13]. It is a minimal surface segmentation approach formulated as

$$\min_u E_{seg}(u) = \min_u \int_\Omega g(x)|\nabla u(x)|\,\mathrm{d}x + \lambda \int_\Omega u(x) \cdot w(x)\,\mathrm{d}x, \tag{5}$$
$$\text{s.t.}\quad u \in C_{box} = \{u : u(x) \in [0,1], \forall\, x \in \Omega\}$$

where Ω denotes the image domain and $u \in C^1 : \Omega \mapsto \mathbb{R}$ is smooth. The first term denotes the g-weighted TV semi-norm which is a reformulation of the geodesic active contour energy [14]. The edge function $g(x)$ is defined as

$$g(x) = e^{-\alpha\|\nabla I(x)\|^\beta}, \ \alpha, \beta > 0, \tag{6}$$

where $\nabla I(x)$ is the gradient of the input image. The second term in (5) is the data term with w describing a weighting map. The values in w have to be chosen negative if u should be foreground and positive if u should be background. If values in w are set to zero, the pure weighted TV energy is minimized seeking for a minimal surface segmentation. The regularization parameter λ defines the trade-off between our data term and the weighted TV semi-norm. The stated convex problem in (5) can be solved for its global optimum efficiently using the primal-dual algorithm [15]. As the segmentation u is continuous the final segmentation is achieved by thresholding u.

Vertebral Body Segmentation. The first step of our segmentation pipeline is to segment the eight vertebral bodies (T11, T12, L1-L5, S1) individually using (5) (see Fig. 1b). The weighting map w is constructed based on the localization results for vertebral bodies and IVDs. We span a cylinder whose normal vector points from the center of the vertebral body to the center of the IVD located above. This cylinder defines the foreground seed ($w = -\infty$) region. A larger, but again cylindrical region around the foreground seed is set to zero in the weighting map w such that the solution u is influenced by the surrounding image edges. Values farther away in the weighting map are set to background $w = \infty$. The edge function $g(x)$ is defined according to (6), where the image $I(x)$ is the input from the preprocessing step with an additionally applied edge-preserving denoising

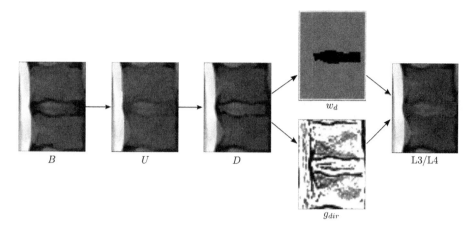

Fig. 3. Exemplary illustration of the segmentation pipeline. The vertebral body segmentation B is used to generate a fused, one-connected structure U containing the IVD. After morphological operations, the difference $D = U - B$ initializes a weighted TV segmentation step using w_d derived from D (black are foreground seeds, white background seeds, grey indicates $w_d = 0$) and g_{dir} as edge indicator function. The final segmentation result shows IVD between L3 and L4.

using the TV-L1 model as explained by Chambolle and Pock [15]. Solving the TV segmentation model in (5) gives us the central part of the vertebral bodies, which is sufficient to constrain the later IVD segmentation.

Fusion of Vertebral Bodies Using the Star Prior Constraint. The second step of our segmentation pipeline is to connect the segmentations of pairs of vertebral bodies to obtain a rough spine segmentation (see Fig. 1c), thus initializing the IVD region. This motivates the use of the star prior constraint introduced by Veksler [16] and extended to multiple star centers by Gulshan et al. [17]. The intention of the star prior is that any ray n sent out from a specified star center is directed in opposite direction of ∇u. This enforces one-connected and star convex objects. The star prior constraint is modeled in terms of a convex set C_{star}

$$C_{star} = \{u : \langle \nabla u(x), n(x) \rangle \leq 0, \forall x \in \Omega\}. \tag{7}$$

This constraint on the segmentation u can be handled easily in our segmentation model (5) by minimizing the energy $E_{seg}(u)$ such that $u \in C_{box} \cap C_{star}$. For more details we refer the interested reader to the work of Hammernik [18].

In our segmentation pipeline we use the star prior to connect the gap between adjacent vertebrae as depicted in Fig. 3. This gap region gives a strong hint of the expected IVD location. For each IVD, we use the two neighboring vertebral bodies as foreground seeds setting their weight $w = -\infty$. The border region of the image domain Ω are background seeds ($w = \infty$) and other regions are set to zero. The edge function is derived from the binary segmentation result $B(x)$

of the two vertebral bodies using the edge inversion function from the original geodesic active contour approach [19], i.e.

$$g(x) = \frac{1}{1 + \gamma \|\nabla B(x)\|^2}, \quad \gamma > 0. \tag{8}$$

We use two star centers defined by the localization results of the respective vertebral bodies. The ray direction $n(x)$ is then defined from the star center which is closest to the position x. After solving the weighted TV model in (5) with the star prior constraint (7), we subtract the vertebral body segmentation $B(x)$ from the segmentation result $U(x)$ and perform morphological opening and erosion operations to achieve one final connected component $D(x)$ that is guaranteed to be located inside the IVD region (see D in Fig. 3).

Intervertebral Disc Segmentation. For the final IVD segmentation we again use the weighted TV model for each IVD as described in (5). The foreground seeds are simply defined by the result of the previous step, defining the region where $(w_d = -\infty)$. The background is defined by the borders of the image domain Ω, all other regions are set to $w_d = 0$. For the edge information we apply a slightly modified variant of the edge function g in (6) to incorporate a small amount of a priori information on the shape of IVDs. As IVDs are prone to have double edges, we only consider those edges which are aligned with rays that are sent out from a specified disc. This disc is defined by a radius r and a normal vector d which points from the located IVD to the next vertebral body. The rays $n(x)$ are calculated for every point x relative to the closest point on the disc. We define the modified edge function g_{dir} considering directed edges as follows:

$$g_{dir} = e^{-\alpha \|\xi \nabla I(x)\|^\beta}, \quad \alpha, \beta > 0 \tag{9}$$

with

$$\xi = \begin{cases} \langle \nabla I(x), n(x) \rangle & \text{if} \quad \langle \nabla I(x), n(x) \rangle > 0 \\ 0 & \text{if} \quad \langle \nabla I(x), n(x) \rangle \leq 0 \end{cases}. \tag{10}$$

3   Experimental Setup

The whole localization and segmentation approach was implemented in C++ and OpenMP, with the exception of the Matlab-based MRF solver. Costly image processing operations were accelerated using Nvidia CUDA to use graphical processing units as parallel numerical co-processors.

Localization. Localization results were obtained using a leave-one-out cross validation on the 15 subjects of the MICCAI–CSI2015 challenge, where centers of the vertebral bodies and IVDs were manually annotated for all subjects by a scientist well experienced in spine image analysis. Hough forests were trained and tested with a voxel size of $1.5 \times 1.5 \times 1.5$ mm. For each HF we trained $K = 64$

trees until a maximum depth $D = 15$ using all voxels in the range $r = 8$ mm around the landmarks. At each node split $F = 10$ candidate feature boxes and $T = 10$ thresholds were generated. The maximum size $s_{f,max}$ and distance $d_{f,max}$ of the feature boxes was set to 20 mm. After non-maxima supression we selected for each landmark the $N = 10$ candidate positions with the highest maxima in the accumulator volume. The MRF made use of a specific statistical model (μ_e, σ_e) computed from the 14 subjects of each cross-validation run and was solved with loopy belief propagation using the publicly available Matlab UGM[1] library.

Segmentation. To provide a realistic, generalizable setup we pooled the individual localization results of each of the 15 leave-one-out cross validation runs to form our input vertebral body and IVD landmarks for segmentation. The further processing pipeline involved a number of parameters. For all edge functions $\alpha = 20$ and $\beta = 0.55$ was selected. We chose a $\lambda = 1.25$ for the edge-preserving TV-L1 smoothing and a radius of 15 mm as well as a height of 7.5 mm to initialize the vertebral body cylinder model. Segmentation of vertebral bodies involved a $\lambda = 0.01$, while the star prior constrained TV segmentation required $\lambda = 1000$ and $\gamma = 0.125$. Finally, IVD segmentation was done using $\lambda = 0.05$ and a radius of 15 mm for the prevention of double edges. All TV segmentation steps were computed until the maximum change of two voxels of subsequent segmentations was below 0.0001 and a threshold of $u = 0.5$ was used to derive a binary result from the convex model in (5).

4   Results and Discussion

Localization. Quantitative results of the individual vertebra/intervertebral discs as well as for the 15 different subjects are shown in Fig. 4. We achieve an overall mean localization error ± standard deviation of 3.9 ± 1.6 mm for all 15 landmarks of the 15 subjects compared to our own manual annotation of the landmark centers. For the vertebrae we achieve an average of 4.0 ± 1.7 mm and for the intervertebral discs 3.8 ± 1.5 mm. These are promising results given the image spacing of the input data of $2 \times 1.25 \times 1.25$ mm, i.e. the mean localization error is on the order of a few pixel and standard deviations are reasonable. Our segmentation results also indicate that this localization performance is sufficient to initialize our image processing pipeline.

For the first test set we achieve a mean localization error of 3.97 ± 1.19 mm, with 2.9 % of landmarks below 2 mm, 42.9 % below 4 mm and 94.3 % below 6 mm of distance. For the on-site test set we achieve 4.37 ± 1.17 mm, with 0.0 % below 2 mm, 37.1 % below 4 mm and 91.4 % below 6 mm of distance.

Segmentation. For quantitative evaluation of the overall segmentation algorithm we used the DSC to compute the overlap of our segmentation result with the provided ground truth segmentation from the CSI challenge data set.

---

[1] Downloaded from http://www.cs.ubc.ca/~schmidtm/Software/UGM.html.

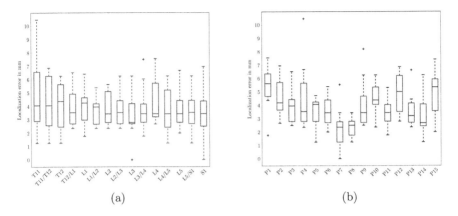

(a)   (b)

Fig. 4. Box-whisker plots of the mean localization error of our proposed method. (a) Location error for vertebrae and IVDs showing individual landmarks (blue for vertebral bodies, green for IVDs). (b) Location error for individual subjects. (Color figure online)

We achieved an average DSC of $89.1 \pm 2.9\%$ over all IVDs from the 15 subjects. Figure 5 shows more details of the performance of our method according to individual IVDs and subjects.

For segmenting the first five test data sets we achieve a DSC of $87.4 \pm 4.8\%$ and a surface distance of 1.47 ± 0.53 mm. Unfortuantely, during the on-site calculation of the segmentation results, in one of the five data sets a severe segmentation error occurred, leading to merged IVDs of T11/T12 and T12/L1, which prevented our method from being compared to the others.

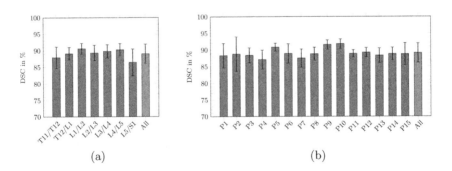

(a)   (b)

Fig. 5. Detailed quantitative Dice similarity coefficients (DSC) results of the IVD segmentation approach (overall: $89.1 \pm 2.9\%$). (a) DSC for individual IVDs. (b) DSC for each of the 15 subjects.

5 Conclusion

In this work, a fully automatic localization and segmentation system for intervertebral disc segmentation from MRI data was shown. It builds upon a regression forest together with a simple global geometric model as well as TV based convex active contour segmentation steps extracting vertebral bodies and IVDs in a geometrically constrained manner. Our results on the data of the MICCAI–CSI2015 challenge are located in the lower third of the nine compared approaches.

Acknowledgements. This work was supported by the province of Styria under the funding scheme "HTI:Tech_for_Med" (ABT08-22-T-7/2013-13) and by the Austrian Science Fund (FWF): P28078-N33.

References

1. Neubert, A., Fripp, J., Engstrom, C., Walker, D., Weber, M., Schwarz, R., Crozier, S.: Three-dimensional morphological and signal intensity features for detection of intervertebral disc degeneration from magnetic resonance images. J. Am. Med. Inform. Assoc. **20**(6), 1082–1090 (2013)
2. Štern, D., Likar, B., Pernuš, F., Vrtovec, T.: Automated detection of spinal centrelines, vertebral bodies and intervertebral discs in CT and MR images of lumbar spine. Phys. Med. Biol. **55**(1), 247–264 (2010)
3. Chen, C., Belavy, D., Yu, W., Chu, C., Armbrecht, G., Bansmann, M., Felsenberg, D., Zheng, G.: Localization and segmentation of 3D intervertebral discs in MR images by data driven estimation. IEEE Trans. Med. Imaging **34**(8), 1719–1729 (2015)
4. Law, M., Tay, K., Leung, A., Garvin, G., Li, S.: Intervertebral disc segmentation in MR images using anisotropic oriented flux. Med. Image Anal. **17**(1), 43–61 (2013)
5. Korez, R., Likar, B., Pernuš, F., Vrtovec, T.: Parametric modeling of the intervertebral disc space in 3D: application to CT images of the lumbar spine. Comput. Med. Imaging Graph. **38**(7), 596–605 (2014)
6. Criminisi, A., Robertson, D., Konukoglu, E., Shotton, J., Pathak, S., White, S., Siddiqui, K.: Regression forests for efficient anatomy detection and localization in computed tomography scans. Med. Image Anal. **17**(8), 1293–1303 (2013)
7. Ebner, T., Stern, D., Donner, R., Bischof, H., Urschler, M.: Towards automatic bone age estimation from MRI: localization of 3D anatomical landmarks. In: Golland, P., Hata, N., Barillot, C., Hornegger, J., Howe, R. (eds.) MICCAI 2014, Part II. LNCS, vol. 8674, pp. 421–428. Springer, Heidelberg (2014)
8. Donner, R., Menze, B., Bischof, H., Langs, G.: Global localization of 3D anatomical structures by pre-filtered Hough forests and discrete optimization. Med. Image Anal. **17**(8), 1304–1314 (2013)
9. Ma, W., Morel, J.M., Osher, S., Chien, A.: An L1-based variational model for Retinex theory and its application to medical images. In: Proceedings of 2011 IEEE Conference on Computer Vision and Pattern Recognition - CVPR 2011, pp. 153–160. IEEE (2011)
10. Nyúl, L., Udupa, J., Zhang, X.: New variants of a method of MRI scale standardization. IEEE Trans. Med. Imaging **19**(2), 143–150 (2000)

11. Gall, J., Yao, A., Razavi, N., van Gool, L., Lempitsky, V.: Hough forests for object detection, tracking, and action recognition. IEEE Trans. Pattern Anal. Mach. Intell. **33**(11), 2188–2201 (2011)

12. Reinbacher, C., Pock, T., Bauer, C., Bischof, H.: Variational segmentation of elongated volumetric structures. In: Proceedings of 2010 IEEE Conference on Computer Vision and Pattern Recognition - CVPR 2010, pp. 3177–3184. IEEE (2010)

13. Hammernik, K., Ebner, T., Stern, D., Urschler, M., Pock, T.: Vertebrae segmentation in 3D CT images based on a variational framework. In: Yao, J., et al. (eds.) CSI 2014. LNCVB, vol. 20, pp. 227–233. Springer, Switzerland (2015)

14. Bresson, X., Esedoḡlu, S., Vandergheynst, P., Thiran, J.P., Osher, S.: Fast global minimization of the active contour/snake model. J. Math. Imaging Vis. **28**(2), 151–167 (2007)

15. Chambolle, A., Pock, T.: A first-order primal-dual algorithm for convex problems with applications to imaging. J. Math. Imaging Vis. **40**(1), 120–145 (2011)

16. Veksler, O.: Star shape prior for graph-cut image segmentation. In: Forsyth, D., Torr, P., Zisserman, A. (eds.) ECCV 2008, Part III. LNCS, vol. 5304, pp. 454–467. Springer, Heidelberg (2008)

17. Gulshan, V., Rother, C., Criminisi, A., Blake, A., Zisserman, A.: Geodesic star convexity for interactive image segmentation. In: Proceedings of 2010 IEEE Conference on Computer Vision and Pattern Recognition - CVPR 2010, pp. 3129–3136. IEEE (2010)

18. Hammernik, K.: Convex framework for 2D & 3D image segmentation using shape constraints. Master's thesis, Graz University of Technology, Austria (2015)

19. Caselles, V., Kimmel, R., Sapiro, G.: Geodesic active contours. Int. J. Comput. Vis. **22**(1), 61–79 (1997)

Localization and Segmentation of 3D Intervertebral Discs from MR Images via a Learning Based Method: A Validation Framework

Chengwen Chu[1], Weimin Yu[1], Shuo Li[2], and Guoyan Zheng[1(✉)]

[1] Institute for Surgical Technology & Biomechanics, University of Bern,
Bern, Switzerland
{chengwen.chu,weimin.yu,guoyan.zheng}@istb.unibe.ch
[2] GE Healthcare & University of Western Ontario, London, Canada
slishuo@gmail.com

Abstract. In this paper, we present the results of evaluating our fully automatic intervertebral disc (IVD) localization and segmentation method using the training data and the test data provided by the localization and segmentation challenge organizers of the 3$^{\rm rd}$ MICCAI Workshop & Challenge on Computational Methods and Clinical Applications for Spine Imaging - MICCAI–CSI2015. We introduce a validation framework consisting of four standard evaluation criteria to evaluate the performance of our method for both localization and segmentation tasks. More specifically, for localization we propose to use the mean localization distance (MLD) with standard deviation (SD) as well as the successful detection rate with three ranges of accuracy. For segmentation, we propose to use the Dice overlap coefficients (DOC) and average absolute distance (AAD) between the automatic segmented disc surfaces and the associated ground truth. Using the proposed metrics, we first validate our previously introduced approach by conducting a comprehensive leave-one-out experiment on the IVD challenge training data which consists of 15 three-dimensional T2-weighted turbo spin echo magnetic resonance (MR) images and the associated ground truth. For localization, we respectively achieved a successful detection rate of 61, 92, and 93 % when the accuracy range is set to 2.0, 4.0, and 6.0 mm, and a mean localization error of 1.8 ± 0.9 mm. For segmentation, we obtained a mean DOC of 88 % and a mean AAD of 1.4 mm. We further evaluated the performance of our approach on the test-1 dataset consisting of five MR images released at the pre-test stage and the test-2 dataset consisting of another five MR images released at the on-site competition stage. The results were obtained with a blind test where the performance evaluations were conducted by the challenge organizers. For localization on the test-1 dataset we achieved a successful detection rate of 91.4, 100.0, and 100.0 % with a MLD $\pm$ SD of 1.0 ± 0.8 mm, and for localization on the test-2 dataset we achieved a successful detection rate of 77.1, 100.0, and 100.0 % with a MLD $\pm$ SD of 1.4 ± 0.7 mm, respectively. For segmentation on the test-1 dataset we obtained a mean DOC of 90 % and a mean AAD of 1.2 mm, and for segmentation on the test-2 dataset we obtained a mean DOC of 92 % and a mean AAD of 1.3 mm, respectively.

© Springer International Publishing Switzerland 2016
T. Vrtovec et al. (Eds.): CSI 2015, LNCS 9402, pp. 141–149, 2016.
DOI: 10.1007/978-3-319-41827-8_14

1   Introduction

Accurate localization and segmentation of intervertebral discs (IVD) on spine magnetic resonance (MR) images is very important for correct diagnosis and treatment planning of spinal disorders in clinical routine. However, automatically identifying and segmenting individual IVDs from MR images is still a challenge tasks due to the repetitive nature of these structures as well as low contrast, noise and intensity inhomogeneity of MR images.

For IVD localization, different methods have been proposed in literature [1–4]. For IVD segmentation, there exist methods based on Hough transform [5], atlas registration [6], AdaBoost and normalized-cut [7], graph cuts with geometric priors from neighboring discs [8], template matching and statistic shape model [9], or anisotropic oriented flux detection [10].

Recently, we presented a data-driven optimization based framework [11] to fully automatically localize and segment three-dimensional (3D) IVDs from MR images. In this approach, the localization of disc centers is tackled by using a data-driven regression method to estimate image displacements. To further exploit the inter-disc relations, we employ dynamic programming to post-process the localization results of each disc to resolve ambiguity caused by the repetitive pattern of IVDs. The output of localization step allows us to defined a region of interest (ROI) for the segmentation step, where we use a similar data-driven classification method as we used for localization to estimate the likelihood of a pixel in the ROI being foreground or background. The estimated likelihood is then combined with the prior probability, which is learned from a set of training data, to get the posterior probability of the pixel. The binary segmentation of the target disc is then derived by a thresholding on the estimated probability. Figure 1 gives an overview of the framework. For more details, we refer to our previous work [11].

In this paper, We presents the results of evaluating our previously introduced approach [11] on the IVD challenge training data and test data of the 3rd MICCAI Workshop &Challenge on Computational Methods and Clinical

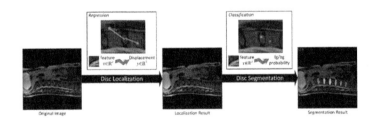

Fig. 1. Overview of our method which consists of the localization step followed by the segmentation step. The localization step is based on estimation of the image displacements of some image patches, while the segmentation step involves the classification of image pixels as foreground (inside disc) or background (outside disc).

Applications for Spine Imaging - MICCAI–CSI2015. We design and present four standard evaluation criteria to evaluate the performance of our method in both localization and segmentation tasks. The details are described as follows.

2   Materials and Methods

2.1   Data Description

Training Data Description. The training data provided by challenge organizers consists of 15 3D T2-weighted turbo spine echo MR images and the associated ground truth segmentation[1]. These 15 3D T2-weighted MR images are acquired from 15 patients in two different studies. Each patient was scanned with 1.5 Tesla MR scanner (Siemens Healthcare, Erlangen, Germany). There are seven IVDs T11-L5 to be localized and segmented from each image. Figure 2 illustrates two T2-weighted MR image and the segmented IVD regions from the image.

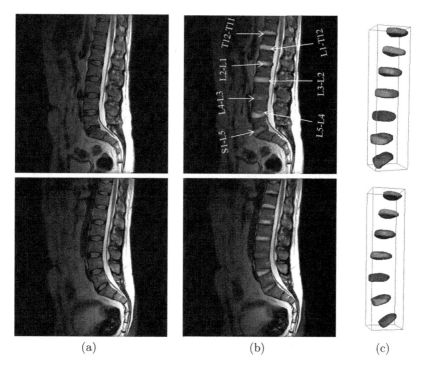

(a)   (b)   (c)

Fig. 2. Manual segmentation of seven IVD regions from a T2-weighted MR image. (a) A sagittal T2 MR image. (b) The seven defined IVDs. (c) Surface models of IVDs.

---

[1] http://ijoint.istb.unibe.ch/challenge/index.html.

Test Data Description. The challenge organizers released two sets of test data while the associated ground truth data were not provided to the participants. At the pre-test stage, five 3D T2-weighted MR images were released as the test-1 dataset and at the on-site competition stage another five 3D T2-weighted MR images were released as the test-2 dataset.

2.2 Experiments

Experiments on the Training Data. We conducted a comprehensive leave-one-out experiment on the 15 training MR images in order to evaluate our previously proposed approach [11]. In each time one patient data out of the 15 data is chosen for test and the remaining 14 data are used for training.

Experiments on the Test Data. Taking the same 15 training MR images as the training data, we further validated our approach on two test datasets with a blind test since the performance evaluations of results obtained from both test datasets were conducted by the challenge organizers. More specifically, we first applied our algorithms to the released test datasets and then sent the obtained localization and segmentation results to the organizers. The organizers then evaluated the performance of our algorithms using the ground truth data that they kept and finally sent back the performance evaluation results to us.

2.3 Evaluation Metrics

We propose a standard evaluation framework which includes both qualitative and quantitative evaluation. For qualitative evaluation, we perform a visual check of the localization results and segmentation results. For quantitative evaluation, we utilize four different metrics and at each step two main criteria are considered for evaluation of our method [11].

For evaluation of the localization performance, we use the following two metrics:

1. **Mean localization distance (MLD) with standard deviation (SD).**
The equation of localization distance R for each disc center is computed by

$$R = \sqrt{(\Delta x)^2 + (\Delta y)^2 + (\Delta z)^2}, \tag{1}$$

where where Δx is the absolute difference between X axis of the identified IVD center and the ground truth IVD center calculated from the ground truth segmentation, Δy is the absolute difference between Y axis of the identified IVD center and the ground truth IVD center, and Δz is the absolute difference between Z axis of the identified IVD center and the ground truth IVD center. The equations of MLD and SD are defined as follows:

$$\text{MLD} = \frac{\sum_{i=1}^{15} \sum_{j=1}^{7} R_{ij}}{n} \quad \text{and} \quad \text{SD} = \sqrt{\frac{\sum_{i=1}^{15} \sum_{j=1}^{7} (R_{ij} - \text{MLD})^2}{n}}, \tag{2}$$

where n is the total number of IVDs.

2. **Successful detection rate with various ranges of accuracy.** If the absolute difference between the localized IVD center and the ground truth center is no greater than t mm, the localization of this IVD is considered as an accurate detection; otherwise, it is considered as a false localization. The equation of the successful localization rate P_t with accuracy of less than t mm is formulated as follows

$$P_t = \frac{\text{number of accurate IVD localization}}{\text{number of IVDs}}. \tag{3}$$

To evaluate the segmentation performance, we use the following two metrics:

1. **Dice overlap coefficient (DOC).** This metric measures the percentage of correctly segmented voxels. DOC [12] is computed by

$$\text{DOC} = \frac{2|A \cap B|}{|A| + |B|} \times 100\,\%, \tag{4}$$

where A is the sets of foreground voxels in the ground-truth data and B is the corresponding sets of foreground voxels in the segmentation result, respectively. Larger DOC metric means better segmentation accuracy.

2. **Average absolute distance (AAD).** This metric measures the AAD from the ground truth disc surface and the segmented surface. To compute the AAD, we first generate a 3D mesh from binary data of seven IVD segmentations. For each vertex on the surface model derived from the automatic segmentation, we found its shortest distance from the surface model derived from the associated ground truth segmentation. The AAD was then computed as the average of all shortest distances. Smaller AAD means better segmentation accuracy.

3 Experimental Results

3.1 Evaluation of Localization Performance

Localization Results on Training Data. Figure 3 shows some qualitative results of disc center localization, where the red crosses are ground truth and the green ones are the detected centers. From the visualization results, we find that our previously proposed method [11] successfully detect all the seven IVDs from 14 data out of the given 15 T2-weighted training MR images. There exists one failure case in which all disc centers are approximately located but the disc identifications are shifted one level up. Our method seems to believe that the real disc L1-T12 is the disc T12-T11. To correct these errors, as proposed in our previous work [11], we manually specify the location of a randomly chosen disc with one mouse click on the middle sagittal image. This simple intervention corrects all mistakes.

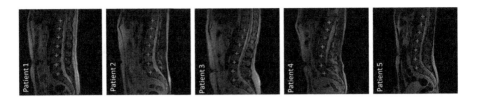

Fig. 3. The qualitative localization result on five images (the mid-sagittal slice).

Table 1 gives the results of successful detection rate with different accuracy range $t = 2.0$, 4.0, and 6.0 mm. Given the specified accuracy range $t = 2.0$ mm, our method successfully detected 61 % IVDs. The successful detection rate is changed to 92 % when t is set to 4.0 mm and this rate is further changed to 93 % when we set t to 6.0 mm. Table 2 gives the results of successful detection rate of our method [11] when one mouse click was used to correct the failed case. When accuracy range t is set to 2.0 mm, the successful detection rate is 67 %. The successful detection rate is changed to 99 % when we set t to 4.0 mm and all the 105 discs are successfully detected when we set accuracy range t to 6.0 mm.

We also compute the MLD with SD on the corrected localization results as describe above. Table 3 (second row) gives the MLD and SD on the given 15 training MR images. We achieved good localization results with an MLD of 1.8 ± 0.9 mm.

Table 1. Successful detection rate with various ranges of accuracy (t). All results are achieved fully-automatically without manual interventions.

	$t = 2.0$ mm	$t = 4.0$ mm	$t = 6.0$ mm
Number of successfully detected discs	64 discs	97 discs	98 discs
Successfully detected rate	61 %	92 %	93 %

Table 2. Successful detection rate with various ranges of accuracy (t) when one mouse click was used to correct the failed case.

	$t = 2.0$ mm	$t = 4.0$ mm	$t = 6.0$ mm
Number of successfully detected discs	70 discs	104 discs	105 discs
Successfully detected rate	67 %	99 %	100 %

Localization Results on Test Data. As announced by the challenge organizers, we respectively achieved a successful detection rate of 91.4, 100.0, and 100.0 % when accuracy range was set to $t = 2.0$, 4.0, and 6.0 mm for the test-1 dataset. Our localization algorithm also achieved a MLD $\pm$ SD of 1.0 ± 0.8 mm on the test-1 dataset. Similarly, for localization on the test-2 dataset, we respectively achieved a successful detection rate of 77.1, 100.0, and 100.0 %, and a MLD $\pm$ SD of 1.4 ± 0.7 mm.

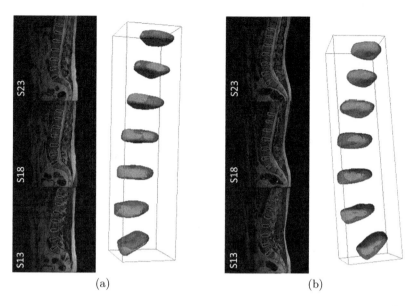

Fig. 4. Segmentation result on two images ((a) and (b)), visualized on the 13th, 18th, 23th sagittal slices and as the 3D surface model of the IVD segmentation (red: ground truth contour, green: our results). (Color figure online)

3.2   Evaluation of Segmentation Performance

Segmentation Results on Training Data. We visually check the segmentation results on randomly selected two training images in Fig. 4. We visualize the results by superimposing the contours of ground truth discs and those of our results on three sagittal slices (slices 13, 18, and 23). The red contours are ground truth and the green ones are our results. We also compare the 3D surface models of the ground truth and the automatic segmentation (Fig. 4). It can be seen that our method [11] gets good automatic segmentation results. For quantitative evaluation on 15 training images, we achieved a mean DOC of $88 \pm 3.7\%$ and a mean AAD of 1.4 ± 0.2 mm as shown in Table 3.

Segmentation Results on Test Data. As announced by the challenge organizers, we successfully segment all the disc regions on both the test-1 dataset

Table 3. Evaluation results for the localization and segmentation performance of the present approach using proposed metrics.

Image #	1	2	3	4	5	6	7	8	9	10	11	12	13	14	15	overall
MLD (mm)	1.9	1.7	2.0	2.4	1.8	1.3	1.9	1.3	1.4	1.6	1.4	1.4	1.8	2.1	2.7	1.8 ± 0.9
DOC (%)	88	88	89	85	87	91	87	89	90	92	86	90	83	86	88	88 ± 3.7
AAD (mm)	1.6	1.4	1.3	1.5	1.3	1.2	1.3	1.2	1.2	1.2	1.5	1.3	1.5	1.5	1.3	1.4 ± 0.2

and the test-2 dataset. For segmentation on the test-1 dataset we obtained a
mean DOC of $90 \pm 2.9\%$ and a mean AAD of 1.2 ± 0.23 mm. Similarly, for segmentation on the test-2 dataset we obtained a mean DOC of $92 \pm 2.4\%$ and a
mean AAD of 1.3 ± 1.54 mm.

4   Conclusions

We present the results of evaluating our fully automatic IVD localization and
segmentation method. We design and present four standard evaluation criteria
to evaluate the performance of both localization and segmentation tasks. Using
the proposed four metrics, we validate our approach on the MICCAI–CSI2015
challenge training data which consists of 15 3D T2-weighted turbo spin echo
MR images and the associated ground truth. For localization, we respectively
achieved a successful detection rate of 61, 92, and 93 % when the accuracy range
is set to 2.0, 4.0, and 6.0 mm, and a mean localization error of 1.8 ± 0.9 mm. For
segmentation, we obtained a mean DOC of 88 % and a mean AAD of 1.4 mm
on the given 15 training data. We further evaluated the performance of our
approach on the test-1 dataset consisting of five MR images released at the pre-
test stage and the test-2 dataset consisting of another five MR images released
at the on-site competition stage. According to the results obtained from the
blind evaluations which was conducted by the challenge organizers, we achieved
for localization on the test-1 dataset a successful detection rate of 91.4, 100.0,
and 100.0 % with MLD $\pm$ SD of 1.0 ± 0.8 mm, and for localization on the test-2
dataset a successful detection rate of 77.1, 100.0, and 100.0 % with MLD $\pm$ SD of
1.4 ± 0.7 mm, respectively. For segmentation on the test-1 dataset we obtained
a mean DOC of 90 % and a mean AAD of 1.2 mm, and for segmentation on the
test-2 dataset we obtained a mean DOC of 92 % and a mean AAD of 1.3 mm,
respectively.

Acknowledgements. This work was partially supported by the Swiss National Science Foundation with Project No. 205321_157207/1.

References

1. Schmidt, S., Kappes, J.H., Bergtholdt, M., Pekar, V., Dries, S.P.M., Bystrov, D., Schnörr, C.: Spine detection and labeling using a parts-based graphical model. In: Karssemeijer, N., Lelieveldt, B. (eds.) IPMI 2007. LNCS, vol. 4584, pp. 122–133. Springer, Heidelberg (2007)
2. Corso, J.J., Alomari, R.S., Chaudhary, V.: Lumbar disc localization and labeling with a probabilistic model on both pixel and object features. In: Metaxas, D., Axel, L., Fichtinger, G., Székely, G. (eds.) MICCAI 2008, Part I. LNCS, vol. 5241, pp. 202–210. Springer, Heidelberg (2008)
3. Glocker, B., Feulner, J., Criminisi, A., Haynor, D.R., Konukoglu, E.: Automatic localization and identification of vertebrae in arbitrary field-of-view CT scans. In: Ayache, N., Delingette, H., Golland, P., Mori, K. (eds.) MICCAI 2012, Part III. LNCS, vol. 7512, pp. 590–598. Springer, Heidelberg (2012)

4. Glocker, B., Zikic, D., Konukoglu, E., Haynor, D.R., Criminisi, A.: Vertebrae localization in pathological spine CT via dense classification from sparse annotations. In: Mori, K., Sakuma, I., Sato, Y., Barillot, C., Navab, N. (eds.) MICCAI 2013, Part II. LNCS, vol. 8150, pp. 262–270. Springer, Heidelberg (2013)
5. Shi, R., Sun, D., Qiu, Z., Weiss, K.: An efficient method for segmentation of MRI spine images. In: Proceedings of IEEE/ICME International Conference on Complex Medical Engineering - CME 2007, pp. 713–717. IEEE (2007)
6. Michopoulou, S., Costaridou, L., Panagiotopoulos, E., Speller, R., Panayiotakis, G., Todd-Pokropek, A.: Atlas-based segmentation of degenerated lumbar intervertebral siscs from MR images of the spine. IEEE Trans. Biomed. Eng. **56**(9), 2225–2231 (2009)
7. Huang, S., Chu, Y., Lai, S., Novak, C.: Learning-based vertebra detection and iterative normalized-cut segmentation for spinal MRI. IEEE Trans. Med. Imaging **28**(10), 1595–1605 (2009)
8. Ben Ayed, I., Punithakumar, K., Garvin, G., Romano, W., Li, S.: Graph cuts with invariant object-interaction priors: application to intervertebral disc segmentation. In: Székely, G., Hahn, H.K. (eds.) IPMI 2011. LNCS, vol. 6801, pp. 221–232. Springer, Heidelberg (2011)
9. Neubert, A., Fripp, J., Shen, K., Salvado, O., Schwarz, R., Lauer, L., Engstrom, C., Crozier, S.: Automatic 3D segmentation of vertebral bodies and intervertebral discs from MRI. In: Proceedings of International Conference on Digital Imaging Computing: Techniques and Applications - DICTA 2011, pp. 9–24 (2011)
10. Law, M., Tay, K., Leung, A., Garvin, G., Li, S.: Intervertebral disc segmentation in MR images using anisotropic oriented flux. Med. Image Anal. **17**(1), 43–61 (2013)
11. Chen, C., Belavy, D., Yu, W., Chu, C., Armbrecht, G., Bansmann, M., Felsenberg, D., Zheng, G.: Localization and segmentation of 3D intervertebral discs in MR images by data driven estimation. IEEE Trans. Med. Imaging **34**(8), 1719–1729 (2015)
12. Dice, L.: Measures of the amount of ecologic association between species. Ecology **26**(3), 297–302 (1945)

Automated Intervertebral Disc Segmentation Using Probabilistic Shape Estimation and Active Shape Models

Aleš Neubert[1,2]([⊠]), Jurgen Fripp[2], Shekhar S. Chandra[1], Craig Engstrom[3], and Stuart Crozier[1]

[1] School of Information Technology and Electrical Engineering,
University of Queensland, Brisbane, Australia
ales.neubert@uqconnect.edu.au, shekhar.chandra@uq.edu.au,
stuart@itee.uq.edu.au
[2] The Australian e-Health Research Centre,
CSIRO Health and Biosecurity, Brisbane, Australia
jurgen.fripp@csiro.au
[3] School of Human Movement Studies,
University of Queensland, Brisbane, Australia
c.engstrom@uq.edu.au

Abstract. Automated segmentation of intervertebral discs (IVDs) from magnetic resonance imaging has the potential to enhance the efficiencies of radiological investigations of large clinical and research imaging datasets. This work presents an automated method for localization and 3D segmentation of IVDs that is applied to magnetic resonance imaging of the thoraco-lumbar spine as part of the segmentation challenge at the 3rd MICCAI Workshop & Challenge on Computational Methods and Clinical Applications for Spine Imaging - MICCAI–CSI2015. Our initialization method involves multi-atlas registration and a hierarchical conditional shape regression for localization of all imaged lumbar and thoracic discs, and active shape model based 3D segmentation. Comparisons between manual (ground truth) and automated segmentation of 105 disc volumes (T11/T12 - L5/S1) revealed a mean Dice score of 0.896 ± 0.024 and mean absolute square distance of 0.642 ± 0.169 mm. Our automated segmentation approach provided accurate segmentation of IVDs from turbo spine echo images which are highly competitive with leading state-of-the-art 3D segmentation techniques.

1 Introduction

Spine-related disorders account for the largest proportion of musculoskeletal complaints in industrialized countries [1,2]. Magnetic resonance imaging (MRI) allows highly detailed, multiplanar investigations of spine pathologies, such as intervertebral disc (IVD) prolapse, herniation and degeneration [3]. Informatic tools offer significant opportunities for improving the efficiency of radiological

T. Vrtovec et al. (Eds.): CSI 2015, LNCS 9402, pp. 150–158, 2016.
DOI: 10.1007/978-3-319-41827-8_15

assessment of the spine by reducing the time- and expertise-intensive encumbrances of tedious tasks as required in three-dimensional (3D) segmentation and measurement of anatomical structures. Precise segmentation of IVDs is a prerequisite for many clinical applications (diagnosis, treatment planning and evaluation), and automated segmentation has the potential to enhance the efficiencies of radiological investigations of large clinical and research imaging datasets.

This work presents a fully automated algorithm for 3D segmentation of lumbar and thoracic IVDs from sagittal T2-weighted MRI scans and evaluates it on a publicly available dataset as part of the challenge on "Automatic IVD localization and segmentation from 3D T2 MRI data" at the 3rd MICCAI Workshop & Challenge on Computational Methods and Clinical Applications for Spine Imaging - MICCAI–CSI2015. The current method extends and fully automates our previous work based on segmentation of lumbar spine IVDs via active shape models (ASMs) [4]. This ASM approach has been applied successfully in a series of studies but requires further development of the pipeline for more generalized application in a clinical framework. Initially, our fully automated approach was developed using 3D sampling perfection with application optimized contrast using different flip angle evolution (SPACE) scans [4], while clinical examinations are routinely performed using two-dimensional (2D) turbo spin echo (TSE) images. In clinical TSE scans, this ASM segmentation scheme was successfully applied to the segmentation of IVDs in the lumbar region although a simple and quick manual initialization step was required in the form of point identification of individual vertebræ [5,6]. The automated initialization on the 3D SPACE scans [4] made use of the detailed high-resolution imaging information in the axial plane that is not available in routine sagittal TSE images. Moreover, the validation of the 3D segmentation algorithm on clinical TSE datasets was performed through a simplified evaluation framework based on 2D manual segmentations in the mid-sagittal slice only. The purpose of the present work is to perform a volumetric validation of our 3D segmentation scheme against the manual segmentation of IVDs acquired from an entire MRI set of TSE sagittal slices, as offered through the MICCAI–CSI2015 segmentation challenge. Notably, two important advances are addressed in this current work: (i) an improved automated IVD localization to provide a fully automated pipeline well-suited to the processing of sagittal MRI scans acquired in routine clinical examinations, and (ii) a larger, external validation of our automated 3D IVD segmentation system on a publicly available MRI dataset having "ground-truth" manual segmentations of the IVDs performed in all sagittal slices in T2-weighted TSE examinations.

2   Methods

The central methodological innovations of this work lie in designing a novel approach for fully automated IVD localization from sagittal TSE images (Fig. 1), which provide a robust basis for subsequent 3D segmentation. The segmentation algorithm is based on a previously presented method of IVD segmentation

Atlases (N=35)   **Case to segment**

L5-S1 3D template

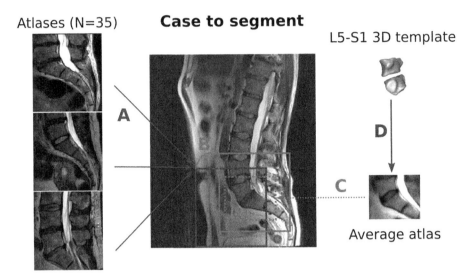

Average atlas

Fig. 1. Summary of the automated sacrum localization method. First, training 2D atlases (A) are rigidly registered to the inferior mid-sagittal, mid-coronal portion of the processed case (B). Second, the best (based on normalized mutual information) result is used to initialize subsequent registration of an average atlas (C). Finally, a 3D deformable template is used to pre-segment the L5 and S1 vertebral bodies (D).

using a 3D ASM-based approach [4]. The initialization pipeline for lumbar spine localization is summarized in Fig. 1 and explained in detail in the next sections.

2.1   Prior Knowledge

The initialization method employs prior knowledge from a training dataset of 2D spine atlases and their segmentations in the following three forms:

2D Atlases. Training atlases were extracted from 35 T2-weighted sagittal TSE examinations (in-plane resolution 0.71×0.71 mm, image matrix 448×448) acquired from a heterogeneous sample of patients (different from the training data provided as part of the MICCAI–CSI2015 challenge). The selection of training atlases focused on including a spectrum of patients with varying anatomy and pathology. This procedure aimed to increase robustness for application to unseen datasets, which would be limited if atlases from the same datasets were used in the leave-one-out fashion. The mid-sagittal sections were individually cropped (to identical dimensions) to include the inferior mid-coronal section of the mid-sagittal training slice. The field-of-view (FoV) differed considerably among the training scans and therefore varying portions of the sacrum and coccyx were visualized in the atlases (see Fig. 1A for some examples). The heterogeneity of the FoV among atlases is important for enabling robustness for varying FoV which may be encountered across the spectrum of cases for segmentation.

Average 2D Atlas. The 2D atlases were also used to create an average atlas of the L5-S1-S2 region (Fig. 1C). The registration during atlas generation was performed using a robust inverse-consistent rigid registration algorithm [7], followed by non-rigid registration based on the method of diffeomorphic deamons [8].

3D Statistical Shape Model of the L5-S1 Vertebral Bodies. Automated segmentations of the 35 original (uncropped) training scans were used to create an ASM of the combined L5 and S1 vertebral bodies (Fig. 1D) [4].

2.2 Spine Localization

The atlases and deformable templates were used to automatically initialize the ASM-based IVD segmentation in the following fashion:

Approximate Sacrum Localization Using Multi-Atlas Registration. For each case to be segmented, all atlases were registered to the mid-sagittal slice using the robust inverse-consistent rigid registration algorithm [7]. The registration was initialized by automatically positioning each atlas to the inferior mid-coronal area of the mid-sagittal slice (Fig. 1A). The registration results were compared using normalized mutual information metric and the best atlas was selected for the subsequent localization step (Fig. 1B).

Refinement of the Sacrum Location by Average Atlas Registration. The position of the selected registered atlas was used to automatically place an average atlas template of the sacral portion of the spinal region (Fig. 1C), which was subsequently registered to the case to be segmented [7]. This step was found to positively complement the multi-atlas selection and increased the accuracy of the localization pipeline. This is likely due to the reduced dimensions of the average atlas that gives space to precisely fit the L5-S1-S2 region, compared to the larger individual atlases (Fig. 1).

Pre-Segmentation of the L5 and S1 Vertebral Bodies Using Deformable Template Registration. The registered 2D average atlas was used to automatically place a 3D deformable template combining the L5 and S1 vertebral bodies (Fig. 1D). The deformable template was 3D, unlike the image atlases that were registered in the mid-sagittal plane to increase the computational efficiency. The deformable template was laterally centered around the mid-sagittal slice and used for approximate segmentation of the S1 and L5 vertebral bodies in 3D. The deformable segmentation was based on an ASM strategy, similar to the one later applied to the IVDs [4].

Localization of the Neighboring Lumbar IVDs Using Conditional Shape Models. Automatic initialization of the ASM segmentation of the IVDs was performed hierarchically using the segmentation of the S1, L5 vertebral bodies and conditional shape models of de Bruijne et al. [9]. The conditional shape models describe relations between neighboring shapes S_1 (shape to be estimated) and S_2 (known shape) using a probability distribution based on Gaussian conditional density $P(S_1|S_2)$. The most likely estimate μ of the shape S_1 can be obtained as:

$$\mu = \mu_1 + \Sigma_{12}(\Sigma_{22} + \gamma I)^{-1}(S_2 - \mu_2), \quad \Sigma = \begin{bmatrix} \Sigma_{11} & \Sigma_{12} \\ \Sigma_{21} & \Sigma_{22} \end{bmatrix}, \quad (1)$$

where μ_1 and μ_2 are the mean shapes of the training data of S_1 and S_2, Σ is the combined covariance matrix, and γ is a ridge regression coefficient to improve numerical stability [9].

Using the conditional probabilities, the shapes of the L5/S1 and L4/L5 IVDs were estimated from the pre-segmented L5 and S1 vertebral bodies. These estimates served as an initialization for the ASM segmentation of these two lumbar IVDs. In the next step, the initial shape of the L3/L4 IVD was estimated from the segmentation of L4/L5 and L5/S1 IVDs. This iterative process continued superiorly until the end of the image FoV was reached.

2.3   Imaging Dataset

Our 3D ASM-based approach for segmentation of lumbar IVDs was validated against the publicly available manually segmented MRI dataset released via the SpineWeb initiative[1]. The datasets consisted of sagittal T2-weighted TSE scans acquired from 25 subjects from a 1.5T MRI scanner (Magnetom Sonata, Siemens Healthcare, Erlangen, Germany). The images (39 slices per case) were acquired with in-plane resolution 1.25×1.25 mm (image matrix 305×305) and slice spacing 3.3 mm [10]. The data was split into three sets: a training dataset (15 cases), a testing dataset (five cases) and a dataset for live segmentation challenge (five cases). Manual "ground-truth" segmentations of seven IVDs (T10/T11 - L5/S1) were provided for 15 cases in the training dataset for quantitative evaluation and parameter tuning.

2.4   Implementation Details

The ASM segmentation in our study was run in two steps. The parameter specifications, enabling progressive refinement of the deformable models, are provided in Table 1 (see Neubert et al. [4] for fuller parameter descriptions).

---

[1] http://spineweb.digitalimaginggroup.ca.

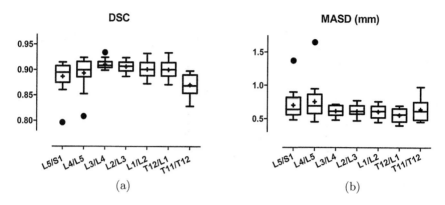

Fig. 2. Quantitative results on the training dataset consisting of 105 IVDs evaluated using (a) Dice score coefficient (DSC) and (b) mean absolute square distance (MASD) similarity metrics.

3   Results

The segmentation results were evaluated using the Dice score coefficient (DSC) and mean absolute square distance (MASD) similarity metrics (Fig. 2).

The testing dataset of 15 cases was segmented with mean DSC value of 0.896 ± 0.024 between our automated and the manual segmentation measures of IVD volumes. The overall mean MASD was 0.642 ± 0.169 mm. The large majority (95 %) of the 105 IVDs were segmented with high accuracy based on having DSC > 0.85, MASD < 1 mm). Two outliers (1.9 %) with lower segmentation accuracy were identified - one L5/S1 IVD (subject 10) and one L4/L5 IVD (subject 4, Fig. 3). The fully automated initialization step worked successfully on 14 out of 15 cases (93 %). Only one case failed and required a simple manual initialization involving one-click identification of a "central" point in the S1 vertebral body in the mid-sagittal slice.

Evaluation on the testing dataset of five cases resulted into mean DSC of 0.828 ± 0.037 and mean MASD of 1.39 ± 0.13 mm. The live segmentation challenge on the remaining five cases was achieved with mean DSC of 0.889 ± 0.033 and mean MASD of 1.22 ± 0.10 mm.

Table 1. Active shape model (ASM) segmentation parameters.

Parameter value	Step 1	Step 2
Iterations	50	50
Profile spacing	0.25 mm	0.25 mm
Points in matching profiles	101	81
Shape constraint	1.5	3
Number of modes	3	90 % of the variation

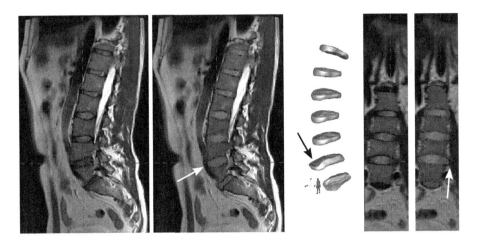

Fig. 3. Qualitative results on an example case (subject 4). The manual segmentation is shown in green, the automated segmentation in red, and the overlap in yellow. The L4/L5 IVD shows lower accuracy (DSC = 0.809, MASD = 1.647 mm) than the remaining IVDs. The automated segmentation extends beyond the IVD region anteriorly and laterally, as indicated by the arrows. (Color figure online)

4   Discussion

The automated initialization performed very well for 14/15 of the training cases providing an excellent basis for our fully automated pipeline. Overall, there was very good agreement between the IVD segmentations from the manual (ground truth) and our automated approaches. In this challenge for segmentation of IVDs from TSE images of the lumbar spine region, our fully automated segmentation approach delivered results highly competitive with leading state-of-the-art 3D segmentation techniques [4,10,11]. Only 2/105 (1 L5/S1, 1 L4/L5 IVD) outliers were identified (Fig. 2) with slightly lower segmentation accuracy (DSC ∼0.80). This was likely due to a combination of factors, such as specific anatomical features (*e.g.* unclear boundaries between an IVD and the hypo-intense closely apposed psoas muscle) as seen in Fig. 3.

To further evaluate our automated scheme, it would be beneficial to validate our approach on larger datasets of heterogeneous clinical populations. Additional work involving an increase in the number of atlases and varying the initial atlas positioning before the rigid registration may further improve our automated approach by increasing the (already high) percentage of cases initialized fully automatically. Importantly, our system offers a quick and simple "fall-back" option for manual initialization in the form of one mouse click, offering a very fast, robust clinical solution. This approach can also be used if fast segmentation of one isolated IVD is required as it overcomes the need for sequential segmentation starting from the S1, L5 vertebral bodies.

A limitation of the presented framework is the reliance on certain features related to the imaging protocol, e.g. sufficient coverage of the sacrum and a good left/right centering of the spine in the FoV. This plainly influences the applicability of our current models to other spinal regions (e.g. the cervical spine), which would involve the future addition of new imaging atlases. However, clinical MRI examinations of the lumbar spine have extremely similar imaging protocols for patients presenting with low back pain. The vast majority of clinical studies that we have encountered would satisfy the FoV requirements for the applicability of our fully automated method.

5   Conclusion

An automated approach for localization and segmentation of IVDs from T2-weighted sagittal TSE scans of the thoraco-lumbar spine was successfully validated on a publicly available dataset with manual "ground-truth" segmentations. The presented method was used in the segmentation challenge at MICCAI-CSI2015.

References

1. Woolf, A., Pfleger, B.: Burden of major musculoskeletal conditions. Bull. World Health Organ. **81**(9), 646–656 (2003)
2. Hoy, D., Brooks, P., Blyth, F., Buchbinder, R.: The Epidemiology of low back pain. Best Pract. Res. Clin. Rheumatol. **24**(6), 769–781 (2010)
3. Haughton, V.: Medical imaging of intervertebral disc degeneration: current status of imaging. Spine **29**(23), 2751–2756 (2004)
4. Neubert, A., Fripp, J., Engstrom, C., Schwarz, R., Lauer, L., Salvado, O., Crozier, S.: Automated detection, 3D segmentation and analysis of high resolution spine MR images using statistical shape models. Phys. Med. Biol. **57**(24), 8357–8376 (2012)
5. Neubert, A., Fripp, J., Engstrom, C., Walker, D., Weber, M., Schwarz, R., Crozier, S.: Three-dimensional morphological and signal intensity features for detection of intervertebral disc degeneration from magnetic resonance images. J. Am. Med. Inform. Assoc. **20**(6), 1082–1090 (2013)
6. Neubert, A., Fripp, J., Engstrom, C., Gal, Y., Crozier, S., Kingsley, M.: Validity and reliability of computerized measurement of intervertebral disc height and volume from magnetic resonance images. Spine J. **14**(11), 2773–2781 (2014)
7. Rivest-Hénault, D., Dowson, N., Greer, P., Fripp, J., Dowling, J.: Robust inverse-consistent affine CT-MR registration in MRI-assisted and MRI-alone prostate radiation therapy. Med. Image Anal. **23**(1), 56–69 (2015)
8. Vercauteren, T., Pennec, X., Perchant, A., Ayache, N.: Diffeomorphic demons: efficient non-parametric image registration. NeuroImage **45**(1 Suppl.), 61–72 (2009)
9. de Bruijne, M., Lund, M., Tankó, L., Pettersen, P., Nielsen, M.: Quantitative vertebral morphometry using neighbour-conditional shape models. Med. Image Anal. **11**(5), 503–512 (2007)

10. Chen, C., Belavy, D., Yu, W., Chu, C., Armbrecht, G., Bansmann, M., Felsenberg, D., Zheng, G.: Localization and segmentation of 3D intervertebral discs in MR images by data driven estimation. IEEE Trans. Med. Imaging **34**(8), 1719–1729 (2015)
11. Law, M., Tay, K., Leung, A., Garvin, G., Li, S.: Intervertebral disc segmentation in MR images using anisotropic oriented flux. Med. Image Anal. **17**(1), 43–61 (2013)

Author Index

Adams, Judith E.   38
Audette, Michel A.   85

Bertelsen, Alvaro   52
Besachio, David A.   85
Borgie, Roderick C.   85
Bromiley, Paul A.   38
Burns, Joseph E.   74

Cates, Joshua   85
Chandra, Shekhar S.   150
Chu, Chengwen   141
Cootes, Timothy F.   38
Cortes, Camilo   52
Crozier, Stuart   150

Ebner, Thomas   130
Echeverría, Rebeca   52
Engelke, Klaus   64
Engstrom, Craig   150
Evans, Linton T.   27
Everson, Richard   125

Fan, Xiaoyao   27
Flórez, Julián   52
Forsberg, Daniel   107
Fripp, Jurgen   150

Gerner, Bastian   64

Hammernik, Kerstin   130
Haq, Rabia   85
Hutt, Hugo   125

Ibragimov, Bulat   117

Jamaludin, Amir   14, 97
Ji, Songbai   27

Kadir, Timor   14, 97
Knez, Dejan   3
Korez, Robert   117

Li, Shuo   141
Likar, Boštjan   3, 117
Lollis, S. Scott   27
Lootus, Meelis   97

Macia, Ivan   52
Meakin, Judith   125
Mirza, Sohail K.   27
Museyko, Oleg   64

Neubert, Aleš   150

Olson, Jonathan D.   27

Paulsen, Keith D.   27
Pernuš, Franjo   3, 117

Roberts, David W.   27
Roth, Holger R.   74
Ruiz, Óscar E.   52

Štern, Darko   130
Summers, Ronald M.   74

Urschler, Martin   130

Vrtovec, Tomaž   3, 117

Wang, Chunliang   107
Wang, Yinong   74

Yao, Jianhua   74
Yu, Weimin   141

Zheng, Guoyan   141
Zisserman, Andrew   14, 97

Printed in the United States
By Bookmasters